ARABS, ISLAM AND THE ARAB CALIPHATE

E. A. Belyaev

arabs, islam and the arab caliphate

in the early middle ages

Translated from the Russian by
Adolphe Gourevitch

PRAEGER · PALL MALL

Published in the United States of America in 1969 by
Frederick A. Praeger Inc., Publishers
111 Fourth Avenue, New York, N.Y. 10003

Published in Great Britain in 1969 by
Pall Mall Press
5, Cromwell Place, London, S.W. 7

Published in Israel by Israel Universities Press, Jerusalem, Israel, 1969

Library of Congress Catalog Number: 77–83393
SBN: 269 025170

This book is a translation of
Araby, islam i arabskii Khalifat
v rannee srednevekov'e
by *E. A. Belyaev*
(Second edition 1966)
Akademiya Nauk SSSR—Institut narodov Azii
Izdatel'stvo "Nauka"
Glavnaya redaktsiya vostochnoi literatury
Moskva

Scientific Consultant—Dr. Emmanuel Sivan
Language Editor—Lesley Hazleton

This book has been composed and printed at the Israel Program for Scientific Translations, Jerusalem, Israel, 1969

CONTENTS

NOTES

Explanatory remarks introduced by the translator and scientific consultant appear in square brackets [ ].

For the sake of legibility, signs of vowel length have been omitted on the maps; there is thus no complete consistency between the maps and the text.

The indexes are not exhaustive but indicate major entries. The index of Arabic and Oriental terms was prepared for this English edition by Prof. A. Gourevitch.

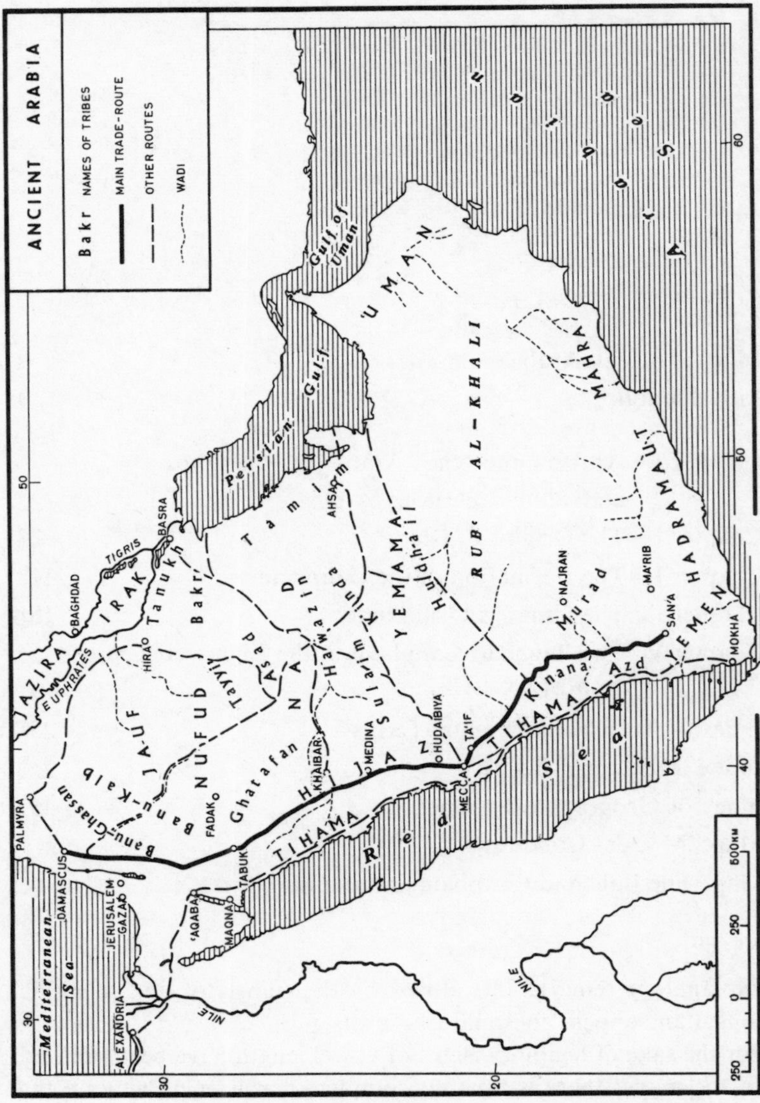
ANCIENT ARABIA
Bakr NAMES OF TRIBES
MAIN TRADE-ROUTE
OTHER ROUTES
WADI
Mediterranean Sea
ALEXANDRIA
NILE
GAZA
JERUSALEM
DAMASCUS
PALMYRA
'AQABA
MAQNA
TABUK
JAZIRA
EUPHRATES
BAGHDAD
TIGRIS
BASRA
IRAK
HIRA
Tanukh
Bakr
Banu-Ghassan
Banu-Kalb
JAUF
NUFUD
FADAK
Ghatafan
Tayyi
Asad
NAJD
Tamim
AHSA
Persian Gulf
Gulf of Uman
'UMAN
KHAIBAR
MEDINA
HIJAZ
TIHAMA
Hawazin
Sulaim
Kinda
YEMAMA
Hudhail
HUDAIBIYA
MECCA
TA'IF
RUB' AL-KHALI
Red Sea
Kinana
Murad
NAJRAN
Azd
MA'RIB
SAN'A
YEMEN
MOKHA
HADRAMAUT
MAHRA
Arabian Sea
30
40
50
60
20
250
0
250
500KM

INTRODUCTION

At the beginning of the Middle Ages, what we now know as the Arab countries were divided between the two major powers of Byzantium and Sassanid Iran.

Constantinople became the capital of the Eastern Roman or Byzantine Empire in 395 A.D., the year which marked the final collapse of the unitary Roman Empire. Of the latter's fourteen "Dioceses," the eight taken over by Byzantium included territories in the Balkan Peninsula and Asia Minor (Anatolia), and the future lands of the Arab East, as well as various holdings in Transcaucasia and what is now the southern Ukraine. Syria, Lebanon and Palestine (today Israel and western Jordan) had been conquered by the Romans in the first century B.C., while Egypt was annexed to the Empire as early as 30 B.C. In the sixth century A.D., Byzantium conquered the eastern parts of that part of North Africa (Tunisia and Algeria) held by the Vandals in the fifth and early sixth centuries.

Soviet specialists in Byzantine history have not yet solved the question of the social and economic structure prevailing in early Byzantium (fifth–seventh centuries). Some believe that by then Byzantine society was already incipiently feudal: that feudal methods of production were becoming preponderant, while the slave economy was dying out. But another view, closer to historical fact, is prevalent today [in the USSR],* namely that Byzantium was actually the focus of a slow process of decay of the slave economy with a concomitant slow formation of feudalism.[1]

* [The wording of the rest of the sentence is more obscure in Russian than it appears to be in our translation: a claim is being put forward about feudalism having its start in the Byzantine East rather than in the Latin, or Latin-Germanic West, a claim which the author does not wish to press too far.]

In the Eastern provinces of the Roman Empire, the crisis of the slave-holding regime was not as acute as in Italy, where violent slave rebellions occurred. Indeed, the Eastern Empire, comprising the lands of ancient Oriental civilization—which had already reached a high level of social production and culture by the Hellenistic period (to say nothing of earliest antiquity)—was richer and economically stronger than the Western Empire.

Moreover, rural freeholders played a marked productive role in early Byzantine economy, though slave production still retained considerable economic importance. This marks one of the main differences between early Byzantium and the Western Empire: in the latter, the crisis of the slave-holding regime, together with the consolidation of the military-political rule of Germanic and other Barbarian conquerors, was paving the way for the development of new, properly feudal relations.

The Eastern Empire, having succeeded in holding the Barbarian onslaught on its Danubian frontier, retained its independence. It also preserved the governmental apparatus created by the reforms of Constantine and Diocletian, an administrative-fiscal system (its main task being to exact taxes and dues from the people) which, together with a numerous army of mercenaries, ensured the rule of an aristocracy of big landowners. The Byzantine Emperor, who was in essence a despot surrounded by this mainly Greek aristocracy, strove with them to preserve the old slave-holding regime and to impede as much as possible the development of feudalism.

Even the Orthodox Church (represented by the Patriarch of Constantinople, as well as by ecumenical councils and local synods) was submitted to the autocracy of the Emperor. Firmly supporting him, it made no opposition to his intervention in affairs of ecclesiastic administration or even in matters of religious doctrine. Indeed, the Church recognized the Emperor as the supreme authority in deciding various controversial points of dogma.

During the transitional period at the beginning of Byzantine history, there arose new systems of management of big landed estates (both lay and ecclesiastical) and of handling primary producers on such estates. In *latifundia* worked by slaves, these new methods aimed at making higher productivity worthwhile for the slaves involved in it; many were actually provided with land and chattels and enabled to retain some of the surplus produce. Some became freedmen, with relative freedom as to their occupation and labor but still bound personally to their former masters.

On the other hand, free tenants or *coloni* became increasingly important in agricultural production. These were legally free farmers, working not only land belonging to a big landowner but also their own small plots, using their own tools. Besides these "free" *coloni* there were also many who were "registered" *(coloni enapographi)* and held no land of their own. Their status hardly differed from that of agricultural slaves or serfs; indeed, they and their descendants were bound to the land, and had no right to leave one proprietor in order to take service with another. The *coloni*, like the agricultural serfs, had to give up part of their harvest, varying from one fifth to a half. They also had to provide unpaid labor, the *corvée*, particularly irksome since it fell due during the busy periods of the year — sowing and harvesting.

The biggest of all the landowners was the Byzantine Emperor himself, who exercized arbitrary control over the vast tracts belonging nominally to the State. The Emperor was surrounded by numerous parasitic court nobles, mainly big landowners, the most greedy and pitiless of whom were undoubtedly the members of the higher Greek Orthodox clergy (in particular the upper echelons of monks), adept at exploiting the lowly and ignorant faith of the common people. Not only did the clergy possess extensive lands of their own, but they knew how to turn to their own profit such objects of ignorant awe and reverence as miracle-working icons, relics and holy places.

The most influential groups among the ruling class practiced a policy aiming at the thraldom of the dependent agricultural population: dues owed by the *coloni* for the land they worked were arbitrarily raised, the *corvée* increased, and various new means of exploitation introduced. Nevertheless, in early Byzantium there were still free communities of peasants who paid their dues to the fisc and were not dependent on any landlords. However, they were legally handicapped in fighting oppression by the landlords, who took advantage of this by despoiling them of their communal land, thus turning them into *coloni* or even into landless tenants who had to pay for working the land that had formerly been their own.

The lot of the working people in the cities was no better. Artisans produced not merely for the ruling class and the richer merchants, but also for the export market: Byzantine products were noted for their workmanship and elegance and were in demand in many countries. Slave labor was still widely used in handicrafts, though free artisans already predominated.

The textile industry was highly developed, not only in Constantinople and other major cities of the Balkan Peninsula, but also in the Asian and African provinces of the Empire. The raw material was chiefly flax, hemp and wool. Silk production, required for the high-grade brocades fashionable among the ruling class and also for sacerdotal vestments, posed a particular problem.

Prior to the sixth century, Byzantium imported raw silk from China and Iran. However, the movements of nomad tribes in Asia and the creation of powerful confederations (the so-called nomadic empires) interfered with the caravan trade on the inland routes to the Far East along the famous "silk road." On the other hand, the maritime trade with India in silk could hardly meet the total requirements of Byzantium. Silk had to be bought from traders coming from Iran, an awkward problem since Byzantium was more often than not in a state of war with the Iranian Empire. Moreover, the Iranian rulers and merchants abused their near-monopoly by raising the price of silk. The Byzantines could not even attempt to produce their own raw silk without silkworms, which the Iranian authorities stubbornly refused to allow to be exported to Byzantium.

According to legend, the situation changed when some pilgrim monks returning from the Orient managed to smuggle silkworm eggs into the Eastern Empire by hiding them inside their staffs. The silkworms were fed on mulberry leaves from Syria, and Syria thus became the first sericultural province of the Empire.[2]

Another important industry was tanning and cordwainery, producing suede and morocco boots embroidered with colored silk, beads and diamonds. Of course, such expensive footwear was not intended for the common people, who were content with coarse sandals (especially so in the Asian and African provinces, where the climate was hot).

The mining and working of metals (copper, iron, lead, zinc and bronze) played a particularly significant role, producing metalware, weapons and agricultural implements. The luxurious way of life of the aristocracy, the urban rich and the princes of the Church established a demand for jewellery and products of other arts and crafts. The artisans reached very high standards, even virtuosity, in making precious ornaments and church vessels; even everyday objects became masterpieces of workmanship.

The artisans of Lebanon and Syria, who preserved the traditions and trade secrets of the ancient Phoenicians, were outstanding in all glass crafts. Egypt was renowned for its papyrus, which was cheaper than parchment for writing material. Since paper was still unknown, Egyptian papyrus was much in demand both in Asia and in western Europe.

The self-employed artisans and the masters of small shops, who often lacked the means to acquire raw materials, had to compete with those well-provided shops belonging to the Emperor's government or to monasteries. Craftsmen could not turn for help and protection to the "demes" (the organs of municipal self-government), for these were dominated by the richer citizens.

Architecture, too, was highly developed, as may be seen from such monuments of Christian art as Saint Sophia, built in Constantinople in the sixth century.

The geographical location of Constantinople and the relatively high level of its economic development favored foreign commerce. Unlike the Western Empire, which was conquered by the Barbarians and reverted to a natural economy by the earliest centuries of the Middle Ages, early Byzantium had a fully developed merchant economy based on monetary exchange. The cities, founded in Hellenistic and pre-Hellenistic time, were growing fast, as the rural population fled their villages in an attempt to escape excessive *corvées* and taxation. These cities were active centers of artisanry and commerce.

The largest city was the capital, Constantinople, "a golden bridge between East and West" (Karl Marx). Economically and culturally, Antioch in Syria and Alexandria in Egypt were hardly less important. Other big cities were significant as ports (Thessalonica [now Salonika], Beirut, and Tripolis in Syria), or as crossroads of caravan routes (Damascus). Jerusalem, the focus of Jewish and Christian legend and tradition, was an object of pilgrimage for all Christendom.

Early Byzantium continued trading with all the lands of the Orient, using the experience and foreign trade connections acquired in the days of the old Roman Empire. However, the overland caravan trade with China ran into obstacles and losses, as the nomadic tribes became stronger and exacted exaggerated fees for free passage, or simply attacked and plundered foreign merchants. As the commerce with China decreased, greater importance accrued to trade with India via the Red Sea. Greek, Syro-Lebanese and Egyptian merchants sailed into the Indian Ocean, ranging with the monsoon winds as far as the coasts of Ceylon. The Byzantine trader was primarily interested in silk, but this was not always obtainable on the Indian Ocean markets. Indeed, merchants from Iran quite often managed to buy up all the available silk and resell it to Byzantium at an inflated price.

South Arabia, which provided Byzantium with incense and other aromatic substances, lay on the same maritime route. An item in relatively high demand was frankincense, required by Christians for ritual purposes. However, South Arabian merchandise was also transported by camel through western Arabia, along the ancient "incense route," since in the Red Sea area, Ethiopia—more exactly, the Axumite Empire—was then the ally of Byzantium's commercial policy, the instrument of this policy being Christianity. The ruling class among Axumite Ethiopians had accepted this religion in the fourth century from Egyptian (Coptic) missionaries. In the same century, the Axumites had started raiding the Yemen, and their raids went hand in hand with Christian propaganda. [The kings and ruling class of Yemen—the Empire of the Himyarites—adopted Judaism as their religion in about the same period, perhaps as a gesture of defiance to Axum and to their Byzantine backers.] Those Yemenites who became converts to Christianity (mainly some citizens of Ṣan'a and most of the inhabitants of the Nejrān oasis) were of course faithful partisans of the Byzantine influence, and, through the agency and help of the Ethiopians, secured the safe passage of Byzantine traders and merchantmen to India.[3]

Byzantine trade in the Mediterranean basin expanded greatly under the Emperor Justinian (527–565), whose policy of re-establishing the Roman Empire met with considerable, if incomplete, success. After prolonged and costly wars with the Goths and victory over the Vandals, the Byzantine army and navy conquered Italy, the islands of the western Mediterranean, a few regions of Spain and some stretches of North Africa (in Tunisia and eastern Algeria). Within these formerly West Roman territories the Emperor and his court attempted to restore a slave-holding regime. As a result, slaves and *coloni* rose *en masse*, and such risings made the acquisition of the new territories precarious. In North Africa, having triumphed easily over the Vandals, the Byzantine army led by Belisarius encountered stubborn resistance from the native Berber population, especially the nomads. Byzantine rule was in fact established only on the coasts and along a belt of inland fortresses, and the only reason why they were not immediately thrown into the sea was the bitter feud between the sedentary (both farmers and city-dwellers) and the nomad Berber.[4]

The wars of conquest, the occupation of conquered lands, and the repression of rebellions among the conquered population led to the exhaustion of the Empire's financial and manpower resources. Also there were frequent mutinies within the army, since the soldiers were not paid for long stretches at a time: the booty, the dues and contributions and the conquered land-holdings all went to the military high command, not to the mercenary rank-and-file. In search of additional means, the Byzantine government tried to exact more taxes and imposts from the people. The situation of the working masses was at times unbearable: in the reign of Justinian, a wave of popular risings swept the Balkan Peninsula as well as the eastern provinces. In addition to the active resistance of slaves and *coloni* in the rural periphery, there were grave troubles among the commoners in the cities, especially among the destitute, the *"Lumpenproletariat."* Like the ancient Roman proletariat, this was a fairly numerous class within the major cities. They had no work nor any permanent means of subsistence, and therefore clamored for "bread and circuses" [*panem et circenses*], which it was the duty of the government and the municipalities to provide. Indeed, this proletariat was fed with free corn received from Egypt, the land of the Nile being at that time the granary of the Byzantine capital.

During the biggest of all the rebellions at Constantinople (the so-called "Nika" riots in 532),* Justinian and his court were in such dire straits that they were on the point of flight to the African provinces by warship when the mercenaries, led by Belisarius, managed to drive the main crowd of rioters into the hippodrome, where some 35,000 were massacred.

The Empire weakened markedly under Justinian's successors, toward the end of the sixth century. Conquered territories in the West were lost again, though Byzantium still retained some degree of predominance in North Africa [and parts of Italy]. Syria, Palestine and Egypt were shaken by major uprisings of slaves, *coloni* and peasants who refused to be made serfs. The Constantinople plebeians rose again, and mutinies occurred in the army of the Danube. The Byzantine Empire was, in effect, in a state of civil war.

The Slavs at that time played a most important role in Byzantine history. In the first half of the sixth century, the advance of Slavic tribes had been held by the Byzantine army on the Danube, but in the last quarter of the century the barrier was broken and the Slavic invasion overwhelmed the Balkan Peninsula. By the mid-seventh century, Slavs had settled nearly everywhere in the peninsula, and some had crossed to Asia Minor. As the Slavs still lived in primitive-communal conditions, ** they had no

* [Called after the watchword used by rioting crowds: *Nika.* "Conquer!"]

** [The author uses the standard Soviet phraseology for sociological description throughout; this dates back to Engels and distinguishes between "primitive-communal," "slave-holding," and "feudal," which are considered as mandatory stages in human development, from "savagery" through "barbarism" to "civilization."]

need for the existing apparatus of class violence and fiscal exploitation, Consequently, in regions conquered and peopled by the Slavs, the situation of the slaves and of those under the poll tax improved considerably, while imperial [State-owned] land and private latifundia were plundered. Thus it was understandable that the working masses should see the Slavs as their allies and deliverers.

The risings of the people and the Slavic colonization resulted in major changes in the socio-economic conditions of Byzantium. Slave production declined and was no longer predominant. Much of the property of the former land- and slave-holding aristocracy now belonged to Slavic agricultural communes and to local farmers, and the free peasant thus became increasingly important in the rural economy. A further significant factor was the presence of first-class soldiers provided by the Slavs in the ranks of the Byzantine army.

The Emperor Heraclius (610–641), who rose to power in this period, was a typical representative of the provincial landed aristocracy, taking no stand against these new, incipiently feudal, relationships. Although the old Greek land-holding noblemen were frightened by the extent of civil wars and incensed at their partial expropriation, they had no choice but to support Heraclius, who wisely recognized the new balance of social forces.

In foreign policy, the major events of the time were connected with the Irano-Byzantine wars. In 611, the Iranian armies of the Sassanid *shahin-shah* ("King of Kings"), Khusro II,* conquered Syria, taking Antioch and Damascus; in 614 they invaded Palestine and stormed Jerusalem. Thereafter the Iranians crossed all of Asia Minor and reached the eastern shore of the Bosporus, where they set up camp at present-day Scutari. Another Iranian army invaded Egypt and captured Alexandria (618–619).

Heraclius, having obtained a heavy subsidy from the Greek Orthodox Church, was able to raise a battle-worthy army. In 622–628, he led it in three successive "Persian campaigns." In 627, this army decisively beat the Iranian forces near the ruins of Nineveh, in the vicinity of present-day Mosul; it then laid

* [The classical Chosrees.]

siege to the Iranian capital of Ctesiphon* and approached Dahesta, the summer residence of the Sassanid kings.

In the peace treaty concluded with Iran, Byzantium regained all her Eastern provinces. Heraclius imposed heavy taxes upon the people of Syria and Palestine, who had already suffered from plunder under Iranian occupation. But the Emperor needed vast sums of money to repay his debt to the Byzantine Church. Moreover, he wanted to punish these provincials for their readiness to accept Iranian overlordship. [Indeed, the Jews, still numerous in the Galilee, had risen at the approach of the Iranian army and taken part in the storming of Jerusalem.]

Heraclius carried on the traditional religious policies of the Byzantine emperors, who were always eager to appear as zealous defenders of Orthodoxy, and who pitilessly persecuted all Christian sectarians and non-Christians. In its turn, the Orthodox Church was always a staunch supporter of Byzantine autocracy, and attempted to justify and sanctify the existing regime of inequality and exploitation. As to the many and various heterodox doctrines and church organizations, these provided an ideological expression of the widespread protest, by the masses, against Byzantine rule: both Nestorianism and Monophysitism became extensive in the Eastern provinces of the Empire.

Claiming to protect the purity of Orthodox dogma, the Byzantine clergy, with the assistance of the lay authorities, persecuted the Nestorians and Monophysites [to say nothing of the still numerous Jews] in Syria, Lebanon and Palestine. Nestorianism had been declared a heresy at the Third Ecumenic Council at Ephesus in 431, but it still had many adepts among Syrian and Mesopotamian Christians. The headquarters of Nestorian propaganda was Edessa,** where the sect had its main school and seminary. At the end of the fifth century, Constantinople ordered the Edessa school to be closed and both teachers and pupils to be driven away. They found refuge, however, within the Iranian

* [Northeast of Baghdad. It was known in Aramaic as *Maḥoza'*, and later in Arabic as *Madā'in*.]

** [Aramaic *Orḥay*, today Urfa within Turkish territory.]

Empire, at Nisibis* in Upper Mesopotamia, where they enjoyed the protection of the *shahin-shah*, who saw in them the irreconcilable foes of Byzantium.

The Monophysitic teaching had arisen in Egypt in the early fifth century, and was declared a heresy at the Fourth Ecumenic Council at Chalcedon in 451. However, the Monophysitic preachers, who condemned the cupidity, the riches and the loose life of the Orthodox upper clergy and castigated the hypocrisy, avarice and shameless behavior of the monks, found many listeners among the masses of the people. But the principal threat of Monophysitism to the ruling circles of Byzantium was as the banner of separatism within the Eastern provinces of the Empire; thus the Monophysitic creed had rallied not merely the plain people in these provinces, but also many among the provincial land-owners and rich burghers who were dissatisfied with Byzantine rule. The struggle of the Byzantine government and the Greek Orthodox clergy against the Monophysites degenerated at times into cruel and bloody mass persecution. In Egypt, for instance, Monophysites were killed in the streets and even in their homes, and the corpses thrown into the Nile. In the eyes of the Greek Orthodox, the Christian sectarians were not merely ideological opponents: they were a direct threat to those in the higher clerical positions and benefices, which the Orthodox reserved of course for themselves, even in the Eastern provinces. Indeed, the Greek clergy tried to dominate the Orient, and were resented for it. The Ecumenical Patriarch of Constantinople was the supreme hierarch of the Orthodox Church, and as such exerted control over the Orthodox patriarchs of Antioch, Jerusalem and Alexandria, who were themselves the highest church dignitaries in the Eastern provinces. All these very profitable positions were usually occupied by Greeks, and so were the positions of archbishop, bishop and abbots of richer monasteries.

Convinced that Monophysitism would not be extinguished by mere violence, some of the Greek Orthodox clergy sought a solution of appeasement and compromise. After the reconquest of the eastern provinces in the "Persian campaigns" of Heraclius,

* [Aramaic *Neṣibin;* today Nuṣaibin, on the Syrian-Turkish border.]

the Emperor decreed such a compromise in the form of a new dogma, to be accepted by both the Orthodox and the Monophysites, namely that Christ had *one will* in spite of the presence of *two natures* in him. This doctrine, known as Monothelitism, should have reconciled the Monophysites (believers in a "single nature" of Christ) with the Orthodox Church, but the attempt proved unsuccessful. The dispute was far more than a mere disagreement on dogma; it was a complex of sociopolitical contradictions, insoluble in the difficult and ominous circumstances of Byzantine tyranny over the peoples of the Near East. The Monothelitic dogma was later accepted only by the Maronite Church,* which has to this day many adherents in Syria and especially in Lebanon.[5]

The Iranian Empire under the Sassanid dynasty was the powerful adversary of Byzantium, competing with it for dominion in Hither Asia and in the Indian Ocean. The Sassanids had overthrown the Parthian dynasty of the Arsacids who, since the first century B.C., had been struggling against the Roman drive to conquer Armenia and Mesopotamia and reach the shores of the Persian Gulf.

The Arsacids put up a particularly stubborn defense against the Romans in Mesopotamia around Ctesiphon, their capital, built on both banks of the River Tigris. Mesopotamia was indeed the most developed and richest province of the Arsacid domains, and also the most densely populated. Its southern part, formerly Babylonia, was a land of very ancient agricultural civilization based on artificial irrigation. Under the Sassanids (224–651), Mesopotamia retained its exceptional economic and strategic importance.

There is a dearth of sufficiently reliable sources on the type of socio-economic regime prevailing in the vast dominions of the Sassanids and on its development. Such sources as are available[6] have still to be thoroughly studied. According to present-day scientific research, two methods of production coexisted in the Parthian Empire of the Arsacids, corresponding to a slave-holding and a primitive-communal state of society. The former existed

* [This statement is controversial.]

principally in the fertile land of Babylonia, where irrigated agriculture had been practiced since antiquity.

Under the Sassanids, slave labor was still widely used in agriculture; Roman prisoners-of-war were put to farming in Babylonia, Khūzistān (ancient Susiana) and Fars [Persis, Persia proper]. When, in 260, the army of Shapur I [Sapor] surrounded the Roman legions commanded by the Emperor Valerian himself, near Edessa, and forced them to capitulate, the captives were driven into the catchment area of the Karun River and inducted into labor on grandiose irrigation projects. Such treatment of Roman prisoners-of-war was the general policy of the Sassanid high command. Certain scholars reason that under the early Sassanids the campaigns of Iranian armies within the Byzantine Empire actually aimed among other things at replenishing the stock of state-owned slaves.[7]

Even in Mesopotamia, however, where slavery had persisted for over four thousand years, the fourth and fifth centuries A.D. saw a decline in its importance as the principal source of labor for agriculture. The principal producers were now peasants who owned their lands communally, though with the breakdown of these farming communes their leaders gradually appropriated the communal land and water, turned the land into private property and rendered the rank-and-file peasants serfs who had to yield their surplus produce and later even some of the main produce to their masters. The owner of an irrigation system made by slave labor now hired out an irrigated plot of land to the peasant against a set proportion of the harvest yield. Thus the feudal rent came into being: the producers became dependent on the owners of the means of production.

With the incipient formation of feudalism in the Sassanid Empire (principally within the more developed regions), a new social category arose—the *"riders"*—, small or sometimes middle-class freeholders who had been granted their land for service in the cavalry.

An important socio-political role was taken by the landed aristocracy, some of whom had even preserved their holdings and power from the days of the Arsacids. They used slaves on their extensive estates, but also dominated the peasant villages and nomad tribes of the district. Some of the aristocratic clans were politically independent within their hereditary domains, and stubbornly resisted the centralizing policies of the Sassanids, which dated from the first "King of Kings" of the dynasty. The Zoroastrian priesthood, with the High Priest, *mobedan-e-mobed,** at their head, were the allies of the aristocracy. This upper crust of the clergy were also big landowners, besides possessing other kinds of real estate; they further derived a vast income in dues from the faithful. Together with the landed aristocracy, this priesthood considerably limited the autocracy of the *shahin-shah*. The principle of the throne supporting the altar and *vice versa* (attributed to the founder of the dynasty) in fact held only against the laboring masses, especially when they dared rise in rebellion. Otherwise there was a continual and often bitter state of strife between the Sassanid autocrats and the aristocracy and higher priesthood that generally went against the former.

The Sassanid rulers therefore sought other, more trustworthy, allies. Shapur I (241–272), the second king of the dynasty, attempted to broaden the society under his rule by introducing an ideological weapon, the new teaching of Manicheism, of which he became the protector. The semi-legendary founder of this religion, a former Zoroastrian priest called Mani, preached a dualistic doctrine which was basically the same as Zoroastrian or Christian dualism: everything that occurs in the Universe and in the history of human society is but a reflection of an unceasing struggle between the two principles of Good and Evil, Light and Dark. In man himself, both principles are combined: the soul derives from Light, the body from Darkness. In order to achieve the triumph of Light, man must conquer the natural needs of his own organism; he must lead a strictly abstemious life (vegetarian, avoiding worldly temptations, refraining from marriage) in order to free his soul from "the prison of the body."

Actually, Manicheism was simply a blend of Zoroastrianism with the Christian ideals of ascetism and zealotry. The popula-

* ["Priest of Priests" in Middle Persian (Pehlevi).]

tion of Irak,* the most advanced of all the provinces of the Sassanid Empire, was basically not Iranian but Aramaic-speaking Semitic. It consisted partly of direct descendants of the ancient Babylonians, Chaldeans and Assyrians, and partly of many Jews, who were either the offspring of those Judeans who had remained in Mesopotamia after the "Babylonian captivity" or were from the Mesopotamian Diaspora.

In permitting Manichean propaganda Shapur I pursued a threefold policy: firstly, Manicheism was made a State religion, with a priesthood dependent upon and faithful to him, so that he acquired a new means of influencing the masses of the people; secondly, he hoped for religious unity among his subjects, including the Christians; thirdly, he expected to deal a crushing blow to the Zoroastrian priesthood and indirectly to the old aristocracy.

However, the aristocracy and the higher priesthood resisted so strenuously that Shapur was ultimately forced to break completely with the Manicheans. Moreover, the Manichean doctrine, now widespread among the lowest classes of the urban population, began to direct its energies against the state as an organ of oppression and against all forms of social and political persecution.

This triumph of the aristocracy and higher priesthood over the King of Kings resulted in a lasting political instability, which merely enhanced the arbitrary power of the upper classes and the exploitation of the working masses. Within thirty years of Shapur's death, the court nobility throned and dethroned no less than six kings. In order to safeguard their stranglehold, the nobility proclaimed Shapur II king in 309, when he was still an infant, or, according to other sources, when he was still unborn.

* [Used here, rather misleadingly, in the quite modern and special sense of Lower Mesopotamia. The term is non-Arabic in origin, and derives from Middle Persian *Erak,* which is itself but a variant of *Iran* — land of the Arians, the original Iranians. The later Arabic form of the name, *'Irāq,* was indeed applied to both Lower Mesopotamia (*'Irāq 'arabī,* i.e., "Arabic-speaking Irak") and to what we now call Iran or Persia ('Irāq 'ajamī, i.e., "non-Arabic, Persian-speaking Irak"). (Cf. G. Levi della Vida, article "Irak" in the great "Enciclopedia Italiana".)]

However, when he reached his majority, this particular king curbed the nobility in the interests of his personal power. This lay mainly in his army, which was proving victorious over the Romans.

After the death of Shapur II in 379, the nobility and the higher priesthood again managed to suppress the autocracy of their Sassanid masters. They removed the famous *shahin-shah* Bahram Gor* from any participation in State affairs, and he contented himself with hunting, music and love affairs. One of his successors, Peroz (459–484),** fell victim to a conspiracy by the nobility, who then enthroned his son after extracting from him a solemn oath to respect their prerogatives (that is, arbitrary dealings) in affairs of government.

The long period in which the nobility guided the administration of the State marked the decay of productive forces in the Iranian Empire. The unlimited opportunities of big landlords to exploit the producers ran against the general interests of the State, and furthermore went hand in hand with the actual plunder of State property. This decline in production was accompanied by manifestations of separatism on the part of the provincial propertied aristocracy, so that entire provinces seceded and civil war raged among the rival provincial claimants.

Even in years of disaster, famine and plague, the workers were still exploited by State fisc officials, avid tax-farmers and the big landlords. Their intolerable sufferings gave birth to the new mass movement of Mazdakism. This movement, which flared up in Mesopotamia in the late fifth and early sixth century, has been grossly misrepresented in the writings of later feudalistic [sic] historians of the Near East. Indeed, Moslem authors of the Middle Ages picture the Mazdakites quite falsely as amoral troublemakers, given merely to plunder and fornication, under the guidance of a leader, Mazdak, who is represented as an impudent fraud, mad with the lust of power. However, Soviet historians

* [Bahram V Gor, or Gur, the "Wild Ass" celebrated in later epics.]

** [Whom Belyaev chooses to mention under the Late Persian form of the name, Firuz.]

have refuted this ideological bias and have revealed the essence of Mazdakism.[8]

The Mazdakite movement started at Ctesiphon, where the number of hungry and dissatisfied people was rapidly increasing due to the influx from rural districts ruined by famine and fiscal oppression. The leadership of the movement (which legend embodies in the figure of Mazdak [originally a Zoroastrian priest] clamored for the private and State-owned granaries to be thrown open to the needs of the populace, threatening to take the food by force if necessary.

The Mazdakite ideology revolutionized the pessimism, decadence and impotence of Manicheism. From the very inception of their movement, the Mazdakites believed that the cause of famine and other evils resided in the unequal distribution of property and other earthly goods, and that thus the happiness of all required simply a redistribution, depriving the rich of their economic and political power. This, they maintained, was only possible by returning to the primeval regime of early agrarian communities, which they pictured as a state of total equality without domination or oppression.

The Mazdakite doctrine reflected the interests and hopes of toilers of the soil reduced to serfdom in the period of incipient feudalism. After increasing suffering under the new social system, the masses of producers sought redemption in a reestablishment of the old communal status. In northern Iran, the Mazdakites formed their own communes on land expropriated from the legal owners. It is remarkable and quite typical that these revolutionaries, while freeing the peasants from social oppression, were not at all in favor of liberating the slaves. In fact, they considered it necessary to preserve slavery in their communes: in addition to communal property in land and means of irrigation, they wanted the slaves to be communally owned, and the commune itself thus became the slave-owner and exploiter.

The spread of the Mazdakite movement and its obvious success prompted King Kavad I (488–531) to join the Mazdakites: unable to fight them, he wanted to make use of them to destroy the aristocracy. According to legend, Kavad appointed Mazdak himself as director of the food depots, with the task of distributing grain and meal to the population. The King sympathized with the setting up of Mazdakite communes, which entailed the expropriation of the noblemen. According to sources hostile to Mazdakism, he even favored Mazdak's proposal to "hold the women in common," and personally participated in this measure. Feudalistic historians of the Orient maintain that this involved an extreme looseness of Mazdakite mores: the normal forms of marriage were allegedly not respected, and "communalization" of wives was considered necessary on a par with communal property in land, water, slaves and stock. Fantastic though this allegation be, Western orientalists have accepted it quite uncritically. In fact, "community of women" meant simply the abolition of those class and caste rules that prevented commoners from marrying women of privileged status. The Mazdakites, profiting by the defeat and confusion of the upper class, married into it.

Now the Mazdakites were acceptable allies to the ruling dynasty only as sworn foes of the aristocracy and higher priesthood. But when this upper crust of society had been sufficiently weakened economically and politically, the Sassanid rulers no longer deemed it necessary to share their rule with the Mazdakite leadership, by which they forfeited part of the State's tax income. As might have been expected, the ensuing reaction saw Mazdakite activists liquidated amid streams of blood.

Kavad's son, Khusro I Anushirvan (531–579), had participated in the suppression of Mazdakism and the destruction of the Mazdakite communes. According to some reports, his mother was the daughter of a small landlord, and Kavad had married her casually and for a short time only.

The Mazdakites suffered extermination at the hands of a new social class, the small and moderately big feudal landlords, to whom Khusro granted their fiefs in return for faithful support. The upper ranks of this class formed the new aristocracy, which was devoted and obedient to the king. A few clans of the old nobility survived, but they had lost their former influence.

A number of measures aimed at strengthening the power of the King of Kings were formulated, known as "the reforms of Khusro I," the most important of which was fiscal reform, which established set rates of taxation. Dues were now exacted not only in produce but also in money (silver). The main income of the exchequer was through a tax on land, the *Kharāg**, the amount of which depended on the crop, the area cultivated and the kind of fruit tree, grain or fodder grown. For instance, one "garib" sown with grain was taxed one silver dirhem [drachma] as against 8 dirhems for the same area planted as vineyard, and 7 dirhems if it was sown with lucerne.

The poll-tax—*gezit***—was levied on every person aged from 20 to 50, except for landlords, soldiers, clergy and state officers or employees. The *gezit* amounted to 4, 6, 8 or 12 dirhems *per capita*, depending on the property status of the individual. A complete land survey was made in the time of Khusro I and all taxable heads were counted, so that a state budget, with items of income and expenditure, became feasible.[10] A fairly complex bureaucracy dealt with taxation, both in produce and money, as well as with customs dues, and thus ensured a measure of centralized government. However, even after the reforms, tax-farming was not abolished with any finality.

Under Khusro I, the Iranian Empire entered its period of early feudalism. Slave labor was still used, however, chiefly in artificial irrigation and in the handicrafts.

Artisanal production in Sassanid Iran was closely connected with the export trade. Due to its geographical location, this vast empire was the center between China and India on the one hand and Byzantium and all the Mediterranean on the other. Silk was the main item in caravan and maritime trade; from raw silk received from China and India, expert Iranian craftsmen manufactured high-grade material which was sold in the Byzantine Empire.

Iran also exported products of flax and cotton, valuable rugs and artistic gold- and silverware produced in workshops attached to the castles of big feudal lords or by free artisans work-

* [A Semitic term meaning "going out." i.e., service in feudal levies owed on land; later on it became the Islamic "land tax," *kharāj* in Arabic. Cf. Richard N. Frye, *The Heritage of Persia,* p. 113. London, 1962.]

** [Corresponding to the later Islamic *jizya*.]

ing in the cities. In such centers as Ctesiphon, Gundeshapur, Hamadhān, Iṣṭakhr, Nishapur and Rayy, there were many craftsmen who worked for both the domestic and the foreign market; these free craftsmen were organized in corporations, which seem to have been incipient forms of professional guilds.

The development of Iran's artisanal production was enhanced by the forced resettlement of townsmen from Mesopotamia and other parts of the Sassanid realm then in the Byzantine Empire. Among those who had left their native cities in order to escape religious persecution were many expert craftsmen. Moreover, the number of artisans increased sharply after each campaign of the Iranian army in Syria. Together with prisoners-of-war, the Iranians brought many craftsmen as captives, who improved and enlarged the scope of their crafts in the Sassanid kingdom.

In foreign policy, the aims of the early-feudal Sassanid Empire, which had grown much stronger economically and militarily under Khusro I and his successors, were to expand its dominion over Transcaucasia and the Asian provinces of Byzantium and to gain a footing on the shores of the Black and the Mediterranean seas. During the sixth century the Sassanids conquered the Yemen and also Lasica [in Transcaucasia], and invaded Syria. In the early seventh century, under Khusro II, the most ambitious plans of conquest seemed, for the time, to have been fulfilled. The Iranian armies by then occupied nearly all the Byzantine domains of the [Asian and African] Near East, and stood at the gates of Constantinople, when the successful counter-offensive of Heraclius regained for Byzantium all the territories she had lost, and more: it posed a direct threat to the Sassanid capital itself.

This long-lasting, bitter conflict between Iran and Byzantium resulted in the utter exhaustion of both empires, so that they were quite unable to resist the onslaught of the new conquerors, the Arabs.

[1] Vsemirnaya istoriya (Universal History, a collective work), t. III, p. 86. Moskva, 1957.

[2] *"Khrestomatiya po istorii srednikh vekov," pod red. prof. N.P. Gratsianskogo i prof. S.D. Skazkina* (Anthology of the History of the Middle Ages, ed. by Gratsianskii and Skazkin), t. I, pp. 174 – 175. Moscow, 1939.

[3] N.V. Pigulevskaya, *Vizantiya na putyakh v Indiyu* (Byzantium on the Routes to India). Moskva-Leningrad, 1951.

[4] Ch.-André Julien, *Histoire de l'Afrique du Nord,* 1st ed. Paris, 1931.

[5] A.A. Vasil'ev, *Lektsii po istorii Vizantii* (Lectures on the History of Byzantium), Chapter 5. Petrograd, 1917.

[6] N.V. Pigulevskaya, *Goroda Irana v rannem srednevekov'e* (The Cities of Iran in the Early Middle Ages). Moscow-Leningrad, 1956.

[7] Pigulevskaya, *Ibid.,* p. 160.

[8] Pigulevskaya, *Ibid.,* pp. 278 – 316; N.V. Pigulevskaya, A.Yu. Yakubovskii, I.P. Petrushevskii, L.V. Stroeva, A.M. Belenitskii, *Istoriya Irana s drevneishikh vremen do kontsa XVIII veka* (History of Iran from Earliest Times to the End of the Eighteenth Century), pp. 56–59, Leningrad.

[9] Ca. 2900 m^2, i.e., ca. $\frac{2}{3}$ acre.

[10] N.V. Pigulevskaya, A.Yu. Yakubovskii, I.P. Petrushevskii, L.V. Stroeva, A.M. Belenitskii, *Istoriya Irana.. (Ibid.),* pp. 60 – 61.

CHAPTER I

ARABIA AND THE ARABS IN THE FIFTH AND SIXTH CENTURIES A.D.

SOURCES

Most of the information on the economic conditions, social regime and mores of the Arabs in the fifth and sixth centuries A.D. comes from ancient Arabic or pre-Islamic poetry, known for its "photographic faithfulness to all phases of Arabian tribal life and its environment."[1] Specialists therefore accept this poetry as the "most important and authoritative source for describing the Arab people and their customs" in this period.

Any study of the geographical environment of Arabia must also take account of the wealth of information from present-day travelers. Nineteenth and twentieth century socio-economic studies, however, may be adduced only in cases of archaic survival or by way of comparison, for although the national environment of Arabia has remained largely unchanged since the fifth century, economic conditions and social relations have been less stable: despite a tendency to stagnation, they did change and develop, especially during the last one hundred years.

It is possible to suppose that the pre-Islamic poetry of the fifth and sixth centuries underwent only relatively minor changes in the hands of collectors and editors of the eighth, ninth and tenth centuries. For any study of this poetry as a historical source—"permeated with life"—the authenticity of the work is especially important. The main problem may be stated as follows: were the pre-Islamic poems genuinely written by fifth- and sixth-century Arabic tribesmen (as asserted by Arabic literary tradition), or were they the work of later poets and learned philologists living in the cultural centers of the days of the Caliphate in the eighth and ninth centuries? This question of authenticity, first raised in West European science in the 1850's–1870's, was disputed time and again either in regard to particular pre-Islamic poets or to entire anthologies. Despite some differences of opinion, most European scholars accepted the authenticity of ancient Arabian poetry. The question was pointedly raised again in the 1920's by the English orientalist [D.] S. Margoliouth and the Egyptian scholar Ṭāhā Ḥusain, both of whom concluded that the entire body of pre-Islamic poetry was a product of later literary activity. However, such extreme views were not shared by the majority, who while they acknowledge that forgeries are found in some of the traditional verses and anthologies, still maintain that the pre-Islamic poetry of the Arabs is authentic in respect to the time and place of its origin: I.Yu. Krachkovskii, for instance, an outstanding specialist in the field, believes in the authenticity of this poetry. Thus, there are not sufficient grounds to discount the pre-Islamic poems as historical source material for the study of the period immediately prior to the rise of Islam.

The voluminous works of the numerous Arabic-speaking medieval historians and geographers are, as a rule, prolix and diversified in their portrayal of political, military and religious life, but lack the richness of the pre-Islamic poetry in reflecting the socio-economic conditions and customs of the Arabs during the fifth and sixth centuries.

As a source for this period, especial regard should be given *Kitāb al-milāl wa-n-nihāl* (The Book of Religions and Sects) by Shahrastāni (died 1153), which contains a chapter on the religious beliefs, rites and customs of pre-Islamic Arabs. Here we find data on anachronistic, vestigial forms of family and marriage, particularly relevant to the present book. The *Muqaddima* [Prolegomena] of ibn-Khaldūn, the most outstanding work of Arabic feudalistic history, is also of special value in the study of the Arabic primitive-communal regime, containing some valuable generalizations and conclusions as well as many interesting data. The author of the *Muqaddima* was very interested in the economy and social structure of Arab tribes, as he saw in these the most typical representatives of the nomadic peoples.

The writings and documents of civilized countries adjacent to Arabia contain only random and not always reliable data on the Arabs of the fifth and sixth centuries, since the writers and their informants had no access at all to the interior of Arabia, which remained *terra incognita*. Only the Syriac chronicles and juridical documents are of interest, in this respect, to the historian.

MODERN RESEARCH

Among the few studies of western orientalists dealing with Arabian society at this time, the monograph by Robertson Smith deserves first mention.[2] This scholar severely criticized the notion then current in west European science that blood ties formed the basic structure of socio-political organization in the primitive-communal Arab society. He showed that such beliefs were based on the spurious conceptions of Arab genealogists, whose "tables" of tribal relations had been composed in the early days of the Caliphate. But although his fundamental ideas were sound, the British scholar tended to be overcritical, so that in the last analysis he underestimated the true value of ties based on blood relationship. Nevertheless, the rich contents of his monograph (in which he also used pre-Islamic poetry as a source, especially the *Kitāb al-aghānī*) give it a lasting scientific value. Another work which still retains considerable scientific importance is Julius Wellhausen's study "Survivals of Arab Paganism."

A third outstanding orientalist specializing in pre-Islamic Arabia was Henri Lammens, an exceptionally erudite scholar of the first part of the twentieth century who was particularly intimately acquainted with Arabic historical and literary works of the feudalistic period, as well as with the relevant European literature. His numerous printed works should be handled with caution, however. An active Jesuit and missionary in the Arab Orient, as well as a professor at the Catholic University of Saint-Joseph in Beirut, his scientific writings and pedagogic activities reveal extreme religious intolerance in regard to Islam, and an obvious overestimation of the historical role of Christian Arabs, so that to the present-day Moslem intelligentsia Lammens seems an odious figure.*

* [A more balanced critical estimate of this great scholar will be found in the paper by K.S. Salibi, *Islam and Syria in the Writings of Henri Lammens,* in "Historians of the Middle East," *op. cit.*, p. 330 ff.]

Nevertheless, as long as a critical approach is retained, his works are highly valuable for their tremendous variety of material (from numerous Arabic sources as well as from European scholarship). His richly documented monograph, *The Cradle of Islam,* deals with the historical geography of western Arabia and the life of its society, using the data of pre-Islamic poetry with a scope and depth unique to Lammens.

Leone Caetani's *Essays in Oriental History*[5] are much less significant from our standpoint. Indeed, the *Essays on Pre-Islamic Arabia* and *The Ancient Arabs* are incomplete and incorrect in their assessment of the geological, climatic and socio-economic conditions in the Arabian Peninsula at this time. These defects are due to the arbitrary "migration theory" [migration, that is, from a prehistoric Arabian cradle] accepted by this scholar.

In view of the small number of studies on Arabia in the fifth and sixth centuries, *The Arabs Before Islam,*[6] by the well known Arabic historian and novelist Jirjī Zaydān, should also be mentioned as a fairly typical product of bourgeois scientific vulgarization resulting in mere superficiality. Published at the very beginning of the twentieth century, this book has already been outdated by archaeological discoveries in Irak, Syria and Arabia.

Still more outdated is Caussin de Perceval's work on the pre-Islamic history of the Arabs, published in 1847.[7] Although it contains many legends and anecdotes, there is very little attempt at a sociological analysis of historical phenomena.

Among recent publications, *Ancient Bedouin Society,* a collection of papers published in 1959 by the University of Rome and edited by Prof. F. Gabrieli,[8] demands especial attention. The various papers deal with the social regime, the literature and the religion of the pre-Islamic Bedouin.

The general histories of the Arabs published in Europe during the nineteenth and twentieth centuries follow a set pattern of chapters, a geographical description of the Arabian Peninsula usually being followed by a chapter on "ways and manners" and on the pre-Islamic clan and tribal system of the population. The best among such works, which still deserve serious attention, are those of Clément Huart and Philip K. Hitti.[9]

The chapter "Before Muhammed" in A. Müller's *History of*

Islam is of no interest to us, since it makes no attempt at sociological analysis; much the same applies to the corresponding chapter in A.E. Krymskii's *Istoriya arabov i arabskoi literatury* (History of the Arabs and of Arabic Literature), published in Moscow in 1911.

Although Soviet scientific literature has paid little attention so far to the history of Arabia during this period – no Soviet Arabists have specialized in it – the essence of the historical process taking place in Arabia in the fifth and sixth centuries has been covered in Volume III of *Vsemirnaya istoriya* (Universal History).

Finally, since survivals of socio-economic relationships in Arabia may date to a very remote past, indeed to a past antedating even the class division, the historian cannot neglect such books as the well-documented *Khozyaistvo i obshchestvenno-politicheskii stroi Severnoi Aravii v XIX—pervoi treti XX v.* (The Economy and the Socio-Political Regime of Northern Arabia in the Nineteenth and the First Third of the Twentieth Century), by A.I. Pershits. This monograph, published in Moscow in 1961, includes a wealth of information from west European travelers, and also gives due attention to those "considerable features of patriarchal-clannish and patriarchal slave-holding regimes" still surviving. It is this analysis of "strong survivals from a pre-feudal state" which makes Pershits' work particularly valuable, especially in view of the fact that non-Soviet and many Soviet scholars tend to underestimate the significance of such survivals.

GEOGRAPHICAL ENVIRONMENT

One cannot imagine Arabia without the Arabs; historical sources from remote antiquity within the period of slave societies already mention the Arabs as the indigenous inhabitants of the Arabian Peninsula.

Arabia is an enormous peninsula, 3 million km^2 in size. The Arabs themselves call it *Jazīrat al-ʻArab,* "the Island of the Arabs," since, as later Arabic writers say, it is surrounded on all sides by seas and rivers. However, the northern limits of

Arabia were never well defined: the celebrated medieval Arabic* geographer Yāqūt al-Rūmi (1179–1229) states that there are many opinions as to this northern frontier,[10] while another Arabic geographer, (ibn-al-Hā'ik) al-Hamdāni (died in 945), who dealt especially with the geography of the Arabian Peninsula, considered the northeastern border as that marked by the lower course of the Euphrates while the northwestern border coincided with the Palestinian shores of the Mediterranean Sea.[11] Except of course for the inclusion of Palestine, this description is quite acceptable. There is no doubt that the Syrian desert *(Bādiyat ash-Sha'm)* was at that time part of the Arabian Peninsula; indeed, the political borders of the Byzantine and the Iranian empires in the fifth and sixth centuries were drawn in such a way as to leave the entire area of the Syrian desert in full possession of the local population, the Arabs.

The Arabian Peninsula has a seacoast more than 5,500 km long, with very few indentations, resembling in this respect the shores of the adjacent continent of Africa.

The subdivision of Arabia into regions (by physicogeographical and economic criteria) has always been rather vague, in fact often groundless and inconsistent. Al-Hamdāni and Yāqūt propose a division into five parts: Tihāma, al-Ḥijāz, an-Najd, al-'Arūḍ and al-Yaman.[12]

The territory of each of these principal regions of Arabia was never determined very precisely, so that nearly every Arabic geographer expressed his own opinions as to regional borders. Abū-l-Fidā' (1273–1331) [a member of the Ayyūbid Kurdish dynasty], relying on the writings of his predecessors, defines each of the regions in the following way: "Tihāma is the southern part of Ḥijāz; Najd is the country between Ḥijāz and 'Irāq (Irak). As to the Ḥijāz itself, it consists of the mountainous land stretching from the Yemen to Syria; Medina and 'Ammān are within its bounds; and 'Arūḍ is simply the Yamāma, that is, the territory [on the southern outskirts of Najd] stretching toward Baḥrein."[13]

Whoever wishes to study the past of Arabia – a past which goes back almost 1,500 years – must decide on the question of

* [Actually a Greek by heritage, born within the Byzantine Empire.]

whether or not the geographical conditions, in particular the climate, of Arabia have changed over the last 1,500–2,000 years. Modern geographical science has proved not, so that there has quite definitely been no decrease in precipitation, nor any desiccation, in Arabia during these two millennia.[14]

The problem has been discussed by Lammens[15] who, on the basis of abundant data drawn personally from Arabic sources, criticized the historical conceptions of Winckler and Caetani and their belief that Arabia had been subjected to continuous desiccation due to a progressive increase in mean annual atmospheric temperatures and decrease in atmospheric precipitation; this would have reduced the size of pasturage and arable land, which were also under constant threat from the advance of drift sand.

In fact, there have been no considerable changes in the geographic conditions of Arabia (climate, hydrography, soil makeup), and the study of the geographical environment in fifth–sixth-century Arabia should thus make use of both Medieval literature and the detailed descriptions of nineteenth- and twentieth-century travelers.

A complete geographical survey of Arabia was not made until the period between World Wars I and II; even by the end of the nineteenth century, Europeans knew less about the interior of this vast peninsula than they knew about the visible face of the moon.

In the eighteenth century, Edward Gibbon, with a naïveté in regard to Arabia that is typical of Europeans of his period, wrote: "In the dreary waste of Arabia a boundless level of sand is intersected by sharp and naked mountains; and the face of the desert, without shade or shelter, is scorched by the direct and intense rays of a tropical sun. Instead of refreshing breezes, the winds, particularly from the southwest, diffuse a noxious and even deadly vapor; the hillocks of sand which they alternately raise and scatter are compared to the billow of the ocean... The common benefits of water are an object of desire and contest..."[16] As late as the beginning of the present century, Caetani could still say: "Arabia is a rocky and sandy desert, only occasionally covered with sparse vegetation... A forbidding, inhospitable country, without rivers, without meadows, without trees; it is awful to look at, and quite terrible to have to dwell in; it seems that the very soil is burning from a twofold fire, as the heat of the torrid skies is reflected by the blinding sands and rocks."[17]

Such superficial notions about Arabia might have been considered old-fashioned even in the latter half of the eighteenth century. The Danish scholar and traveler Carsten Niebuhr, who had journeyed to the southwestern part of the peninsula, wrote: "Traversed by sand deserts and wide ranges of mountains, Arabia is on the one hand the very image of the barren desert at its worst, but on the other it is adorned with all the beauties of the most fertile lands."[18]

The least attractive districts of the Arabian Peninsula are its shores, barren sandy lowlands in the west and east, and no less barren abrupt cliffs in the south. European knowledge of the entire peninsula was for centuries derived mainly from the impressions of seafarers viewing Arabia from the Red Sea and the Persian Gulf, and it is largely for this reason that Arabian soil and climate were held in such disrepute.

From the early Middle Ages onward, the best studied and best known part of Arabia was the mountain-desert region adjacent to the Red Sea. The particularly unfavorable soil and climate peculiarities of this region, the center each year for hundreds of thousands of Muslim pilgrims from many countries, were quite erroneously taken to be characteristic of the whole peninsula. Information about central Arabia was based almost exclusively upon the reports of Palgrave, who had journeyed to Arabia in 1862–1863 along a diagonal line starting at the Dead Sea and ending at the Persian Gulf. However, as finally established in the 1920's, Palgrave's reports were incorrect and dishonest in respect to certain districts of the interior of Arabia: he may not even have visited them at all.[19]

Only in the twentieth century are central and southern Arabia finally being surveyed and misconceptions connected with these regions dispelled. This, the last chapter in the scientific exploration of Arabia, was initiated by the Englishmen Philby and Bertram Thomas.

In relief, Arabia is a vast and massive plateau or tableland, rising abruptly beyond the coastal districts of the Red Sea and falling off very gradually to the east in a continuous slope toward Irak and the Persian Gulf. The high mountains along the coast of the Red Sea merge imperceptibly with the hills overlooking the Persian Gulf. The slope from the west and southwest toward the east and northeast is interrupted by only three exceptional features: 1) the granite mountains of Jabal Akhḍar in the extreme east, in 'Omān ['Umān], reaching a height of 3,020 m to the west of Muscat (Musqāṭ); 2) the mountain range of Jabal Shammar in the north, up to 1,400 m above sea level; 3) the range of Jabal Tuwaiq which curves round the central Arabian plateau from the east.

The mountain range running parallel to the Red Sea in western Arabia begins in the north, in the mountainous region of Madyan [the Biblical Midian], reaching a height of 1,600–1,700 m between Ma'ān and 'Aqaba. In the Gulf of 'Aqaba the mountains border the sea, but further south they run more to the east, giving way to a low sandy seashore which widens to the south. The distance between the coast and the western foothills seldom exceeds 20 km, and is sometimes only 8, 6 or even 2 km.

To the south of the Gulf of 'Aqaba, as far as the vicinity of the town of Ṭā'if, stretch the Ḥijāz mountains. These do not form a continuous range, but are traversed latitudinally by deep valleys narrowing to canyons, the gates of the routes from the coastland to central Arabia. In the Ṭā'if district the range is known as the Sarāt, the average elevation of which is below 2,000 m, the highest peak being about 3,000 m. The Arabs often call the entire mountain range of western Arabia Sarāt; inasmuch as this Sarāt (in its widest sense) separates the central Arabian plateau of Najd from the maritime lowland of the Tihāma (or Ghaur [Ghōr]), they also call this range the Ḥijāz, which means "obstacle" or "barrier."

The town of Ṭā'if, about 1,500 m above sea level, was considered one of the most attractive localities in Arabia, due particularly to the striking contrast between the humidity and luxuriant vegetation of this picturesque area and the sand and rock surrounding it. In the vicinity of Ṭā'if, fertile and well-irrigated valleys alternated with green slopes, and fields of grain grew side by side with fruit orchards and groves of date palms, while the nearby mountains were renowned for their pastures.[20] Ṭā'if was further celebrated throughout Arabia for the beauty of its gardens, which spread at the foot of the mountains surrounding the sandy plain on which the town was situated.[21] The grandeur of the Sarāt range, between Ṭā'if and Mecca [*Makka*], has been enthusiastically described by European travelers: from Jabal Qura the landscape is like a "yellow ocean of stone."[22]

Southwestern Arabia, separated from Africa by the straits of Bāb-el-Mandeb ("The Gate of Tears"), is known as Al-Yaman the Yemen. It is a mountainous and very fertile country, renowned in antiquity for its high level of culture. It is usual to identify the Yemen with *Arabia Felix*, the "Happy Arabia" of classical authors, which is actually a mere play on words. The Arabic [and common Semitic] root y-m-n means "to be to the right, on the right side"; to the primitive mind, the right hand was lucky, thus happy, as against the left hand which was unlucky. The ancient Arabs, like all peoples who worshipped the Sun, found their bearings by turning to the sunrise, the east, so that the south was to the right and the north to the left. This is reflected in the geographical nomenclature, where the southern land became known as the "Right" land, *al-Yaman*, and the northern as the "Left" one, *ash-Sha'm* (Syria).*

Yemen's mountain system is the terminal part of the main west Arabian range and is its highest section, formed at the intersection of two giant rifts. The highest point is Jabal Ḥaḍur (about 3,000 m above sea level), to the west of the city of Ṣan'a, itself at a height of 2,250 m. The mountain slopes are overgrown with luxuriant and varied vegetation: hence a second name for the Yemen is *al-Khaḏrā'*, "The Green One." Up to the early Middle Ages, the Yemen also included the district of 'Asīr, which consisted of a practically inaccessible massif of granite.

The Yemen was subdivided into two principal zones: 1) the Tihāma, a plain 40–70 km wide, and 2) the mountain zone, with higher altitudes to the south.

* [Here we may be dealing with a comparatively late pun: Arabic *sha'm* in the sense of "left" seems of doubtful authenticity. Moreover, *al-Yaman* covered a territory far larger than the present Yemen and comprised most of the peninsula.]

Western Arabia thus comprises two vast regions: the Yemen to the south and the Ḥijāz to the north. The latter can be subdivided topographically into three parts: 1) the maritime zone of Tihāma, a completely desert sandy lowland (not counting some sparse scrub of acacia and mimosa); 2) the mountain zone with steep and often sheer slopes, where the rocks are bare and the canyons very deep; 3) an undulating desert surface, sloping to the east, which is a transitional zone between the mountain range and the central Arabian plateau. The width of the Hijāz (west-east) varies from 100 to 200 km, while its length (north-south) is about 1,000 km.

By "Tihāma" the Arabs mean any low-lying area with a hot and unhealthy climate, so that taken in its wider sense the term applies to all the low shorelands on the west, south and east of the Arabian Peninsula, though the Arabs distinguish between the Hijāz and Yemenite Tihāma. The western shores of the Persian Gulf and the southern coasts of the peninsula are also known as Tihāma (though only adjectivally).

The central tableland of Arabia, the Najd (meaning precisely "plateau" or "tableland"), consists chiefly of limestone formations, though granites are also found. Its whole surface is dissected by valleys which diverge in various directions. To the north, the Najd (600–900 m above sea level) is limited by the granitic mountain range of Jabal Shammar (about 1,400 m above sea level), to the east by the sands of Dahnā' or Lesser Nefud [Nafūdh], and to the south by the Great Desert. The Arabs oppose the Najd as a "highland" to the maritime lowland or Tihāma. The northern Najd is a rather rugged and barren land, stony and occasionally sandy; the southern Najd is less sandy and comparatively better watered, with spots of luxuriant vegetation.

The zone of sand which stretches to the east of the Najd separates the latter from the low seashore of the Persian Gulf. This is a maritime region with sandy soil near the coast and a hilly surface toward the west; it is known as al-Ḥasā or al-Aḥsā'.

Most of al-Ḥasā is barren desert, with the exception of a few oases. From the very shores of the Gulf extends an undulating sea of sand, the depressing monotony of which is broken only by a few stunted palm trees, whose dates are so small and dry that only famished nomads would eat them. However, a relatively abundant vegetation, with various species of desert grasses predominating, may appear on the slopes of sandy ridges and in the intervening troughs.[23]

The sand is simply a mantle covering the limestone; occasionally, the bare rock crops out to form barren islands in the sea of sand. The western part of al-Ḥasā is mostly an infertile limestone plateau, with a few spots of thorny scrub.

To the east of the Yemen, stretching from the sea in the south to the Great Desert in the north, is the extensive land of Ḥaḍramaut, the eastern part of which, adjacent to 'Omān, is known as Mahra. The Ḥaḍramaut may be subdivided topographically into three zones, running more or less parallel to the seacoast, namely 1) the coastland or *sāḥil*, 2) the mountains or *jibāl* and 3) the inland valleys. In the western part of the *sāḥil* the mountains border the seashore, leaving only a narrow and uneven sandy tract of *tihāma.* The slopes toward the coast are cliff-like and quite bare. The *sāḥil* widens considerably in eastern Ḥaḍramaut, in the region of Dhufar. In the opinion of one modern traveler: "If there be any region in Arabia entitled to the epithet 'Happy,' other than the Yemen, whose glories were well known to the ancients, it is this province of Dhufar, an Arcadia of luxuriant forests that clothe steep mountains overlooking the sea, of perennial streams and sunny meadows, of wide vistas and verdant glades."[24]

'Omān (*'Umān),* a massive plateau sloping rather steeply to the northeast, forms the southwestern part of the Arabian Peninsula. The mountain slopes toward the sea are somber and barren, without any vegetation, in contrast to the meadows and relatively dense forests of the slopes of the inland valleys, which are thus known as the "Green Mountains" [*Jabal Akhḍār*]. The seacoast is a plain up to 30 km wide. The plateau of 'Omān is surrounded by a belt of oases in an almost uninterrupted line at the foot of the mountains, both on the coastal plain and along the margin of the Great Desert.

The topography of Arabia is characterized by numerous large and small wadis, which dissect the peninsula in various directions. In most cases, a wadi is the dry bed of a torrent at the bottom of a valley. On both sides of the valley are mountains or hills varying in height and shape.

Among the better-known and more important wadis stretching in a northeasterly direction are *Wadi-r-Rumma* and *Wadi Dawāsir*. The former starts at the heights to the east and northeast of Medina, near the Tropic of Cancer,* proceeding without any considerable deviation toward the northeast to the vicinity of Baṣra (in Irak), altogether some 950 km in length. In some places, it takes the Arabs a whole day to cross the wadi. In years of exceptional rainfall, *Wadi-r-Rumma* turns into a real river for a short time, though this happens only two or three times in a century. The wadi is usually dry, but is rich in subsoil water, which sometimes wells up to the surface.

Wadi Dawāsir has two valleys at its headwaters, with many smaller ramifications. One of these valleys begins at the eastern slopes of the Sarāt, to the south of Mecca, the other originates in the northern Yemen. Somewhat to the south of the Tropic of Cancer, the two valleys join into one wide valley which crosses the Tropic and continues in a northeasterly direction toward the Persian Gulf.

Wadi-l-Hums, with its many ramifications, crosses northern Arabia, winding through the heights of the Medinese plateau in a general northward direction until it turns to the west, toward the Red Sea. Two major wadis cross the Syrian Desert from west to east, toward the Euphrates: *Wadi Sirḥān* which crosses the oasis of Jauf, and *Wadi Haurān.*

In addition to these major wadis, each region of Arabia possesses tens or even hundreds of smaller and very small dry streams of this kind. Each system of heights gives rise to several wadis, dissecting the slopes and fanning out from the foot of the highland. The Arabs have described such wadis, picturesquely, as "tails of canyons."

* [In fact, several degrees north of it.]

In a remote geological past, the present-day wadis were permanent rivers and streams, feeding a lush vegetation. In our own day, however, the beds of most wadis are quite bare of any plant cover, as the stony or sandy ground provides insufficient nutrients for plants; according to one pre-Islamic poet, many wadis are "naked like the belly of an ass."[25] Quite often, the barren bed of a wadi is enclosed on both sides by cliff-like, sometimes quite sheer banks, so that the wadi looks like a sinister canyon to the traveler following its bed.

Through most of the year, the wadis served as caravan routes, and camels enlivened these wild solitudes somewhat! The wadi is the Arab's security against losing his way in the desert, a security greater than reliance merely on the stars. In the rainy season, the wadis "come alive" as swift torrents of water roll along their beds. By no means are all wadis infertile and dead: wherever the subsoil water comes close to the surface, one finds a rich and fairly varied vegetation, including groves of date palms.

The accounts of European travelers in western and central Arabia show that many of the wadis were centers of agriculture, with a considerable sedentary population. Thus Burckhardt, describing his itinerary from Mecca to Medina, speaks of cultivated fields, gardens and groves of palm trees on the slopes of diverse wadis. Doughty reports that Wadi Dawāsir provided the nomads who dwelt to its south with dates; plantations of date palms in this wadi stretched practically unbroken over a distance which a fast camel would take three days to cover, so that Wadi Dawāsir, with the neighboring wadis, fed a good many villages.[26] Philby states that in the wadis of southeastern Najd there are fields of wheat and barley, as well as groves of date palms.[27]

Other wadis, however, impressed travelers as being completely barren and uninhabited. In *Wadi Fāṭima* there were stretches where one would meet with no wayfarer; the wild sandy soil was overgrown only with species of desert flora, and the only tracks found were those of small lizards. As Doughty's Arab guide commented, "in this wadi there is nothing but snakes."[28] T. E. Lawrence writes: "We were very weary of

(Wadi) Sirhan. The landscape was of a hopelessness and sadness deeper than all the open deserts we had crossed. . . There was something sinister, something actively evil in this snake-devoted Sirhan, proliferant of salt water, barren palms, and bushes which served neither for grazing nor for firewood."[29]

THE DESERTS

Only ignorance or misunderstanding can represent Arabia as a continuous sandy-stony desert, deprived of water and vegetation and therefore uninhabited. In fact, a considerable part of those territories which on school maps are still colored as desert is really steppe or semi-desert, the semi-deserts becoming steppes when there is sufficient water (in periods of rain and for some time thereafter). The geographical areas of Arabia known as "deserts" may be subdivided into three types, namely 1) *dahnā',* 2) *nufūdh* and 3) *ḥarra.*

The *dahnā'*, meaning "red" or "purple," covers a tremendous area, about one million square kilometers, as it stretches from the Najd to the Ḥaḍramaut and Mahra and from the Yemen to Oman. This vast sea of sand is known as *al-Rub' al-Khālī,* "the Empty Quarter," and the local Arabs call it *al-Rimāl,* simply "the Sands." Its western part is sometimes singled out as *al-Aḥqāf* ("the dunes") or *al-Baḥr aṣ-ṣāfi* (the "white" or "shiny" sea of sand.)

The Rub' al-Khālī, or great southern desert of Arabia, was until lately represented as a peculiarly terrifying and mysterious region. One imagined that the quicksands and drifts would necessarily bury any rash traveler who dared penetrate these boundless, waterless solitudes. As late as the nineteenth century, some Arabs (relying on the credulity of foreigners) told tales about entire caravans being swallowed up by the drifting sands of the Aḥqāf.

The German traveler von Wrede, who began the scientific exploration of Ḥaḍramaut more than a hundred years ago, reported treacherous abysses in the sands of the Baḥr aṣ-Ṣafi; with a sounding lead and a 12 m long line he went close to one of the white spots which stood out against the sandy surface: "With the greatest caution I approached the border to examine the sand, which I found almost an impalpable powder, and I threw the plumb-line as far as possible; it sank instantly, the velocity diminishing, and in five minutes the end of the cord had disappeared in the all-devouring tomb."[30] Yet it is known that Arab nomads crossed this terrible Rub' al-Khālī as early as the thirteenth century (perhaps by following the outskirts of the desert) to carry merchandise from Irak to the coastal towns of Mahra.

The first European explorer of the Rub' al-Khālī was the Englishman Bertram Thomas, who crossed the desert on camel from south to north, Dhufar to Qaṭar, in 58 days (winter 1930–1931) with a small party of Arabs. The second explorer of the South Arabian "ocean of sand" was Philby, who also rode with Arab camel-riders, but from north to south and from east to west (January-March, 1932).

The topography of the Rub' al-Khālī is quite varied. The desert is formed by sandy hills and dunes, whose shape reminded Thomas of mosques with a thousand cupolas, or on the other hand of enormous amphitheaters, or again of the shapely breasts of a young girl. With the wind blowing through the dry sand, lifting grains of sand into the air, it sometimes seemed to him as if smoke were coming from the crests of the dunes: the upper layer of sand is in constant motion, so that the tracks of men and animals are soon erased, and even experienced pathfinders are unable to "read the sands" here; when there is a high wind, clouds of sand are lifted amid shrieks and whistles, blinding the traveler, clogging his nose and ears, and permeating all his baggage.

The flora and fauna of the Great Desert are extremely poor: due to the extreme paucity of moisture, only the most xerophylic herbs and shrubs can survive here. The slightest rain, however, will cause this seemingly dead desert to blossom, though rainless periods may last as long as seven or eight years, in which circumstance, writes Philby, "drought and famine march through the land with a naked sword of fire."[31]

The quicksands of the Rub' al-Khālī are quite impassable for horses, and even a camel may founder in them down to his belly, but the greatest obstacle is the absence of fresh water. Even brackish water cannot always be found in the very few available wells, or, if found, may be such as even the most tolerant camel would refuse to drink. The fear of dying of thirst, which transforms "men into women,"[32] can be overcome, and the sandy wastes of the Great Desert rendered superable, however, by the acquisition of a milch-camel, since camel milk can be drunk instead of water.

The imagination of the Arabs has peopled this almost inaccessible desert with fantastic jinns, whose voices disturb the prevailing silence from time to time. Bertram Thomas heard such a "voice of the desert," and compared it to the siren of a steamer.

However, the Rub' al-Khālī is far from being quite as lifeless and forbidding as had been generally imagined. European travelers have found quite a few different species of plants and animals there, especially in the southern and eastern parts which turn to steppe after rainfall. Even in the most infertile central districts of the Rub' al-Khālī, an occasional fox, hare, wolf, wildcat or sand rat can be seen. Indeed during the short rainy season, the outskirts of the Great Desert are invaded by Arab nomads who graze their herds of camels there. Thus, after having crossed the length and the width of the Empty Quarter, Philby reached the following conclusion: "The Empty Quarter would seem to be far from justifying the lurid colours in which it has been painted by some European travelers and in which it is always painted by the Arabs of settled tracts who have never been within view of it."[33]

To the north of the Rub' al-Khālī stretches the *dahnā'* (properly called), sometimes known as the Lesser Nefud. This Dahnā' (or Dahana) begins to the northeast of Jabal Shammar, skirts the foot of Jabal Tuwaiq to the east like a wide river of sand, and at 23°N joins the sand sea of the Rub' al-Khālī. The Dahnā' has a fair amount of grass and low scrub growing between the sandy ridges or on sandy hills, providing the favorite pastures of the local nomads, who quite often cross it on foot without having to take any food or water with them.[34] Indeed the Dahnā' impressed Ameen Rihanī as the most hospitable of all the deserts in which he had ever traveled.

The Dahnā' has good pastures even in summer; there are spots of green in the tall grass even before the rains, and thorny scrub, which provides fodder for the camels, grows abundantly. Of course this desert also has many areas which are unfit as grazing land and lack any water, where the traveler feels hard soil underfoot, and sees a flaming sky above him.[35]

The Great Nefud, usually called just *nafudh,* is situated to the north of the mountain region of Jabal Shammar. A chaotic ensemble of sandy hills, hillocks and ranges, occasionally 100 m high or more, this desert is much poorer in vegetation and wildlife than the Dahnā'. It is a vast region of dunes, formed as a result of the depositional activity of an entire network of wadis rising from the Jabal Shammar and the mountains of Ḥijāz and going down into the depression of northern Arabia. The masses of sand brought down by freshets after each rain were reshaped as high hilly dunes by the action of westerly and easterly winds. The ceaseless activity of these winds had given rise to the so-called *fulj* formation, which is typical of the Nefud landscape. A *fulj* (or more properly a *ka'r*, a hole or a hollow) is a deep funnel through the entire thickness of the sand stratum down to the hard (rocky or clayey) bed, and is shaped like a giant horseshoe. In fact, on looking down from the crest of any such *fulj* or *ka'r* onto the surrounding sea of sand of the Nefud, it really seems as if some herd of giant horses has been galloping here from east to west. The bigger *fulj* formations may reach 450–500 m in width, sometimes even 2 km, and vary from 30 to 70–80 m in depth.[36]

The sandy Nefud desert is covered in shrubs and even trees; after rains it provides rich green pastures for camels and sheep, so that a rainy winter turns the Nefud into "a paradise for pastoralists," who particularly favor the grassy depressions between the dunes.[37]

To the north of the Nefud extends the Syrian desert *(Bād-iyat ash-Sha'm),* which is a vast sloping surface inclining gradually to the northeast. The western, higher part is sometimes called *al-Ḥamād,* while the eastern half is known as "the Land of the Wadis" *(al-Wadyān)* because of the numerous wadis that dissect it in a northeasterly direction toward the banks of the Euphrates. In winter, the Syrian desert turns into a real steppe, but even in the hot and rainless summer months some vegetation persists within the wadis in the eastern part. For a few weeks after the winter rains, water is found at the surface nearly everywhere; subsoil water is available at a shallow depth throughout the year.

The third type of Arabian desert is represented by the areas known as *ḥarra.* According to medieval Arabic scholars "*ḥarra* is a land with black, cracked stones, looking as if it had been scorched by fire." It is "covered with black stones; if it includes a stony height, it consists of cliff-like rocks; if something stands out above the land, it is the crest of a mountain range."[38]

The name of such stony areas derives from the Arabic [and common Semitic] root *ḥ-r-r,* "to burn" or "to be hot," since the Arabs consider the *ḥarra* areas as districts of fire or heat, a *ḥarra* having been formed as a result of eruptive phenomena belonging to a distant past when there were active volcanos in western and northwestern Arabia.

However, in the period under consideration, nearly all the volcanos of Arabia had already become extinct. Some none too explicit verses of old poems concerning fires in the *ḥarra* do not provide us with sufficient evidence of volcanic eruptions. The last such eruption mentioned in Arabic historical literature occurred in 1256 in the vicinity of Medina. It lasted four days; flows of incandescent lava reached the outskirts of the city, and the bright light of the crater made the moonless night as bright as day.[39]

The *ḥarra* areas are scattered fields and spots of lava on the territory stretching from southeastern Ḥauran to Mecca. On each field of *ḥarra* rise peculiar hills, usually in the shape of truncated cones or polyhedra narrowing toward the top. The abundance of stones makes it extremely tiring, and even dangerous, to negotiate a *ḥarra;* moreover, the summer sun heats the stones to a point at which they feel like hot coals; only a camel born and bred locally can cross a ḥarra district without risk of injury to his hoofs. The sand from neighboring steppes, continuously blown by the wind over the surface of the *ḥarra,* polishes it so that it sometimes shines blindingly in the sun.

The *ḥarra* impressed Doughty as an "iron desert"[40]; another European who crossed a district of *ḥarra* to the east of the Ḥauran defined it as a bleak, terrifying stony desert, a sea of lava among whose undulations water and vegetation are extremely scarce.[41]

The *ḥarra* is not absolutely barren, however; its hollows and ravines accumulate some moisture, so that a number of species of desert flora occur there, including acacia trees and leafless shrubs, which look like brooms stuck in the ground. In the cracks and crevasses of the lava mantle there are nearly always (especially in rainy periods) some handfuls of grass to be plucked as fodder for the camels or a few twigs to be broken off as brushwood. In those quite exceptional cases of a spring gushing out on the *ḥarra* surface, considerable greenery is also found in the area; also wherever a patch of soil is watered by rains or subsoil waters, the sight of grass and flowers, which not even the July sun can burn off, comes as a pleasant surprise.

However poor the *ḥarra* resources, they prove sufficient to feed the camels and sheep or goats of various tribes who spend a considerable part of the year in such areas.

THE CLIMATE

Arabia is located in the torrid zone, that is, the zone between the north and south isotherms of +20°C. However, if one accepts the division of the Earth into five thermal zones, then nearly all Arabia will fall within the boundaries of the subtropical zone, in which the monthly mean temperature drops below +20° for a period varying from one to four months. There is a quite definite contrast between seasons; only the southernmost part of Arabia—the coastland of the Indian Ocean—is situated within the tropical zone, where there are very high temperatures with little oscillation during the year, and the temperature is never below +20°.

In a hydrological scheme of climatic classification, Arabia should be referred to the group of dry climates, where evaporation absorbs all the precipitation. The dry climates are subdivided principally into steppe and desert climates. Most of Arabia belongs to the former, though the Rub‘ al-Khālī, part of the Dahnā' and to a lesser extent the Nefud belong to the latter, where the average annual precipitation is up to 250 mm, the dry, rainless period lasting at least eight months.

The "thermal equator" which crosses Africa goes through

Ethiopia and Somalia and issues in the Indian Ocean. Due to the heat given off by the sands of the great Arabian desert, the Rub' al-Khālī, this "thermal equator" is deflected northward and follows the southern coasts of the Arabian Peninsula.

Thus the climate of Arabia is characterized chiefly by high annual temperatures. Other factors of importance are the vicinity of the sea, the land area and the wind direction.

In western Arabia, in the Tihāma, on the eastern shores of the Red Sea, the heat is heavy, occasionally tempered by the wind; this heat lasts through most of the year. Temperatures often exceed +45° and seldom fall below +15°. The Red Sea itself is a narrow hot corridor with extremely high evaporability; the European, even in October, feels as if he is in a steam bath, and may even be unable to speak because of the intense heat.

European sailors describe the harbors of western Arabia as hell. The hot and motionless air is extremely humid; for instance in Jidda the humidity is so high that in September, on a hot day and under a completely cloudless sky, a cloth left outside a house will be soaking wet after only two hours.

On the coast of 'Omān the terrible heat, made worse by the way in which the dark surface of the sheer mountain slopes reflects the sun like a mirror, is catastrophic for foreigners. In Musqāṭ, the thermometer shows 87° in the sun, and even at night does not drop below 42°. A Dutch skipper, Streiss (an adventurer and profiteer, in command of a sailing ship), wrote in 1673 that in Musqāṭ "In August and September, the heat is simply incredible... In the evening, such a wind blows from the shore that you feel as if boiling water was being poured over you."[42] These temperatures also gave rise to such obvious exaggerations as this mid-fifteenth-century Persian report: "The heat was such as to burn the marrow in the bones; a sword became soft as wax in its scabbard; the precious stones adorning the hilt of a dagger turned into coals. On the plains, hunting was an easy sport: indeed, the desert was full of roasted gazelles."[43]

The hot and humid climate of al-Ḥasā is similar to that of the Tihāma on the Red Sea, but it is easier to bear. Generally speaking, in climate as in topography, the coastlands of Arabia are the most forbidding parts of the entire peninsula. In the eastern half of the Ḥijāz, protected by its mountain range from the humidity of the evaporation from the Red Sea, the climate is already considerably drier: a scorching heat prevails for most of the year, but without the intolerable humidity of the coastlands.

Temperature in Arabia is liable to very abrupt oscillations, not so much in the course of a year as in the course of the 24-hour cycle of day and night. European travelers in Arabia generally complain of the cold at night rather than of the heat during the day. Eldon Retter, for instance, mentions with distaste the severe cold which he suffered one December morning, before sunrise in the mountains of the Sarat not far from Ṭa'if. Even in April, nights are rather cool in the vicinity of Medina, and there is quite often a mild, fresh wind from the northwest. In the torrid Rub' al-Khālī, the nightly cold (at least in December and January) is a regular phenomenon, and the native nomads suffer very much from it when fuel is not available. Nightly temperatures as low as $+8°$ may persist here for an entire week.

In northwestern Arabia (especially to the southeast and east of the Dead Sea), the temperature may be below freezing throughout December and January. There may be snow (with some interruptions) for several days, alternating with cold rain, and mud, the upper crust of which may freeze altogether, impedes traveling. Sometimes there is a heavy mist, and the stones become gray with hoarfrost. The snow may settle on the land for hours at a stretch, persisting on the roofs of houses, thus giving the impression of a northern landscape. Such weather is highly unpleasant, especially when the bare plains are swept by northerly or easterly winds. Winter weather of this kind usually brings the Arabs to a state of complete despondency: if they cannot find shelter under a roof or light a fire, they try to fight the numbing cold by pressing against their camel, horse or donkey.

Generally speaking, the Arabs (especially the nomads) are very sensitive to cold. Even during the warm evenings and nights of August, the local nomads sit together in a tight ring around the camp fire. Pre-Islamic Arabic poetry sings of a hero who throws his bow and arrows into a fire which is dying for lack of fuel: he would rather remain defenseless, without his weapons, than suffer from the night cold. Only exceptional heroes, strong in body and mind, such as the fearless, untiring and unconquerable Shanfarā, were able to boast:

> "During many a night, when he who has a bow and arrow burns them for fire,
> I went on, in the dark, under the rain,
> with cold, hunger, and fear as my companions."[44]

In the harshest winters, the snow forms a thin white carpet for some time over the areas of *ḥarra* above 1000 m. In the mountainous district two days' travel southeast from Ma'ān [in northern Ḥijāz], the snow persists for a considerable time nearly every winter, but in central Arabia snow is a much more exceptional phenomenon: the native inhabitants assert that it falls every 40 years, although once fallen, it may persist for three days.

Throughout the rest of Arabia, frost and snow are extremely rare. Arabian geographers know of only two places where water will freeze: a mountain near Ṭa'if, and the city of Ṣan'ā in Yemen. A mountain is also recorded in the Yemen where snow falls nearly every winter. According to rumor, there is even a spot in the otherwise torrid 'Omān—a spot remote from the sea—where the earth is sometimes covered with a thin blanket of snow.

Important factors governing the changes of temperature are the winds, cloudiness and rainfall. The Arabs named the winds according to the cardinal points of the compass. Those who dwelt in the Syrian desert and in the Ḥijāz considered the north wind to be the worst. This cold winter wind caused a sharp drop in temperature over northern and western Arabia; in Ḥijāz it prevented the inflow of warm air from Erytrea and the Indian Ocean. This sharp and bone-chilling *shimāl* or "northerly"* caused great suffering. Arabian poetry has preserved for us a vivid picture of the evils that the people of Ḥijāz had to endure from these cold spells: a crowd of children and widows besieged the tent of the tribal leader, asking for help, crying from hunger and shivering from cold. The north wind (even when it was warm after the winter) was considered noxious by the Arabs, both

* [*Shimāl* means literally "left," "north" to those who turn to the sunrise in order to find their bearings.]

to men and animals. The west wind, which usually blew in summer, had no such bad reputation, but the Arabs considered the south wind the best, with its supposed beneficial effect on the soil, enhancing the growth of grass.[45] A terrible and destructive wind in Arabia, however, was the burning easterly, known as *samūm* [hot and "poisonous"], the very breath of the Arabian desert. In the *samūm,* water-skins dried out completely by immediate evaporation of the liquid; those who were overtaken by this cyclone [sic] would often perish of thirst.

Except for the *samūm,* which would bring destruction to men and animals, the winds of Arabia also played an important beneficial role, carrying rain into a country continually suffering from drought. In the absence of perennial rivers or freshwater lakes (except in the Yemen), the amount of precipitation (rainfall and dew) was particularly important; it was highly irregular, however, and a yearly norm of rainfall could really be established only for the mountainous parts of the Yemen.

In the Najd, rain might fall in both summer and winter; August and September rains would turn the parched steppe into bountiful pastures. Sometimes there were strong showers accompanied by thunderstorms; such showers, though rather exceptional in central Arabia, were exceedingly destructive, causing abundant, torrentially flowing freshets capable of washing away and silting up extensive areas of cultivated land.

In western and central Arabia, rain is brought by winds blowing from the north and northwest, from the Mediterranean and Black seas. In Ḥijāz, the rain usually falls in winter or early spring in irregular amounts. Showers occur at considerable intervals, between which shepherds would wait patiently for signs heralding the coming of "the water from the sky," the start of the rainy season. Sometimes they wandered around, looking for land moistened by rain. Some years no rain at all would fall, and when the drought lasted for three or four consecutive years, the plight of the population grew desperate. The Arabs describe such years as "gray," since then the Arabian steppes, deprived of moisture, turn gray in color.

Rains in Arabia fall in very heavy showers, as is typical of rainfall in the subtropical zone. In the period of history under consideration, showers were indeed characteristic of the Arabian climate. The Arabs would describe such cloudbursts as literally a bursting of the clouds ("like some worn-out fabric"), and the strong jets of rain were likened to the milk issuing from the udders of a well-fed she-camel. The bare rocky slopes, without soil or plants, could neither absorb nor hold back the abundance of rainwater. Powerful, swift-flowing streams formed; flooding the plains, the torrents rapidly filled in all the hollows, making temporary pools as large as lakes. The water rushed noisily through the dry wadis and sped along valleys and canyons, carrying away and shattering everything in its path. When the rain was particularly heavy and long-lasting, the wider and deeper wadis were transformed for a short time into rivers comparable to the Nile and the Euphrates.[46]

Sometimes an irresistible flow, carrying stones and large fragments of lava rock, as well as tree trunks, destroyed entire encampments of nomads: men, animals, tents and all. In the *Mu'allaqat* poem of Imru'-l-Qais (fifth century), we find a description of the devastating power of such a freshet. In the morning it had uprooted tall trees and left them upside down; not a single stump of palm was left standing, nor a single building except those built of stone; and in the evening the corpses of wild animals which drowned could be found far away from their lairs.[47]

If the torrent overtook an encampment at night, when everybody was asleep, all perished. It was not always possible to foresee and escape such disaster: a freshet caused by sudden showers might travel with amazing speed for distances of tens of kilometers, spreading ruin and death in places where no cloud had been sighted nor any rain sensed. The noise of the rushing torrent, like a continuous rolling of thunder, warned men and animals, but too late. Two days' march to the east of Medina there is a place which had an evil repute in the eleventh century because "in a certain year many pilgrims congregated there; suddenly, a mountain torrent struck, and all perished."[48]

The Arabian flora, however, flourished in the rains. Toward the end of the rainy season, the steppes carried a variegated carpet of grasses and flowers. The shrubs came alive with foliage, and put out new shoots; wild trees were provided with a new reserve of moisture and many edible plants appeared. While feeding the vegetation, the rains also cleaned the topsoil: the onrush of water would wash away the mineral particles (including salts) still covering the soil after the rapid evaporation of the previous year's rainwater.

Temporary pools and lakes formed in depressions, the largest of which, large enough to swim and dive in, were called *ghudar* or *ghudur** by the Arabs. One such *ghadīr* known was 15 km long. However, the water rapidly evaporated in the dry air, under the cloudless sky, so that the smaller pools were completely dry within a few weeks. Only the largest *ghudur* were able to conserve a constantly decreasing amount of moisture over periods as long as three months.

Not all these natural reservoirs held water fit for drinking. Some had such a high content of salt and other mineral particles (brought by freshets from the adjacent terrain) that their water was not only unpleasant but also unfit for drinking

On a hard terrain baked by the sun, and especially on a stony slope, the water would run off immediately, but in sandy areas it would seep into the soil to form abundant groundwaters. The sandy mantle served as an excellent filter and also prevented evaporation, so that once filtrated down to the hard ground, the water persisted there for a fairly long time. These subsoil reserves of water were sometimes so near the surface that they could be reached simply by shoveling the sand away with one's bare hands. At least at the start of the summer, after the end of the rainy period, the sand cover over the groundwater was no deeper than the length of a spear or a staff. A large part of the groundwater ran along subterranean channels: in the steppes of the Ḥijāz, we can assume the existence of a ramified network of underground streams feeding the numerous wells. Both the taste and composition of the filtrated groundwater were of high quality, which is why the Arabs preferred to drink from wells rather than from open reservoirs.

* [Plural of *ghadīr*.]

ECONOMY AND SOCIETY

NOMADIC ANIMAL HUSBANDRY

In the pre-Islamic period, the great majority of Arabia's population consisted of nomads. They peopled Arabia's vast steppes and semideserts, known under the general name of *badw*. Hence in Arabic *badawi,* "Bedouin." the appellation of Arabian nomads (which European languages have received in its plural form, *badawiyyūn*). This term is not a synonym of "Arab" or "Arabian,"* but corresponds to the Russian *stepnyak* ("man of the steppe"), applying only to those who dwelt in the steppes and semideserts, and not to agriculturalists or townsmen.

The bedouin's livelihood was animal husbandry, chiefly camel raising. Horses and sheep were, on the whole, of secondary importance, while goat herding was on a very limited scale. The peculiar climatic conditions of the desert-steppe of Arabia (in particular the precipitation), as well as the specificity of its flora, were reflected in the varieties of Arabian animal husbandry.

The bedouin were entirely dependent upon their natural environment. After the winter rains came the spring, *rabī',* the season of abundance and prosperity for the bedouin and their herds. Milk and buttermilk "flowed like a river," men and animals grew fat and this fat would serve as a store of energy for the lean and harsh seasons to come. The brief spring over, the bedouin had to suffer the inferno of the Arabian summer. The tropical sun quickly burnt out the green carpet of spring, by which time the surface moisture had evaporated and the wells run dry with the subsidence of the water table. The bedouin would have to seek new pastures, as the underfed she-camels could no longer yield milk. Toward the end of summer, they would make more and more frequent use of such measures against hunger as tying flat stones to their shrunken bellies.

* [This statement is somewhat misleading. "Arab" in fact has no meaning as a common name in Arabic, as the word is not of Arabic but of ancient Semitic origin: *aribu* in Assyrian, *'arabhi* in Hebrew, from *'arabha,* "steppe." But in ancient Semitic it meant precisely the same as *bedu* in Arabic: "man of the steppe."]

With the onset of winter, the bedouin began to search the horizon in the hope of discovering a sign of approaching rain. They enquired ever more frequently about the skies from every traveler coming from the north, and once favorable information had been received, or even on the strength of rumors, they broke camp rapidly, drove their herds northward and sought new pastures where the rains had fallen. They sometimes covered tremendous distances in this way, coming up to the Syrian desert from the very heart of the peninsula, reaching deep into the nafudh and wandering along the outskirts of the "Empty Quarter," the Rubʿ al-Khālī. If the rains were late, after a hot summer, the bedouin literally raced around steppes and deserts in search of water and fodder.

Owing to the geographical environment then, and especially to the precipitation and vegetation, which depended on a number of meteorological factors, the people of the Arabian steppes and semideserts could subsist only by animal husbandry, and that only in a nomadic form. For the great majority of the population, this was necessarily the main occupation and branch of production.

The same geographical environment placed the bedouin in a position of complete dependence on the camel. It is quite justified to say that Arabia* would have remained uninhabited if there were no camels there. Alois Sprenger[49] called the bedouin "a parasite of the camel," for this animal is perfectly adapted to life in the hot and nearly waterless steppes of Arabia. Ibn-Khaldūn in his *Muqaddimāt* reports that the strongest, most beautiful and most alert camels were to be found among those born in the very heart of the sun-scorched sandy deserts of Arabia. The camel can do without water for five days in summer, twenty in winter. When provided with relatively succulent fodder on spring pastures, it can live without water for several weeks. It will drink the salty and bitter water of the desert, and even the stinking liquid mud from the bottom of a dry well. Summer and winter, during the long spells of wandering from one encampment to

* [Not Arabia, but only its desert areas; it is quite certain that Yemen was inhabited prior to any domestication of the camel.]

another and the trying marches over deep sands, with a heavy load on its back, the camel will be content to feed on the hard, bitter, thorny plants of the desert.

In districts rich in dates, camels were fed on ground stones of this fruit; on the shores of southern Arabia, they were fed on sardines and locusts.

While requiring very little attention, the camel gave a great deal in return to the bedouin, serving and feeding him in the severe conditions of the desert, providing food, clothing, footwear, shelter, fuel and many other things besides, things which the inhabitants of the Arabian desert-steppe could obtain only from their camels. Camel milk and dates were the principal and sometimes the only foods of the Arabian nomad, for whom bread and other farinaceous foods were expensive and therefore very seldom consumed. On pastures remote from wells, camel milk was the only liquid that could quench thirst.

Camel flesh, however, was never the usual meat of the Arabian nomad. The rank-and-file bedouin possessed only a few camels, and since this animal multiplies rather slowly—a she-camel produces not more than one young in two years—a young camel was eaten only on exceptional occasions: to honor guests or on feast days.

The bedouin dressed in fabrics woven from camel wool, the same material which served as the felting of their tents, their only dwellings. Thus, they were known as the "people of felt" as against the "people of clay," the settled population living in mud-brick or wattle-and-daub cottages.

Camel leather was used for the simple footwear of the bedouin, their saddles and their harness. Strips of camel hide were often used for strapping the merchandise transported in bulk by caravans. Camel droppings provided fuel, and camel urine was an ingredient in cosmetics and medicine. The women also used camel urine—in the absence of water—to wash their babies; it was a well-tried deterrent of parasites, and the women therefore preferred this liquid to water when dressing their hair, which seemed quite elegant both to them and to their lovers. According to Arabian folk-medicine, camel urine is the best remedy against fever; it is also used as a tonic. The juices of the stomach of a young camel were considered prophylactic in case of stomach illness.

Even today, only one species of camel is to be found in Arabia, namely the dromedary *(Camelus dromedarius)*. The two-humped Bactrian camel never occurred in the Arabian Peninsula.

Zoologists do not consider the camel to be a very intelligent beast: it is thought of as phlegmatic, stupid and cowardly. The Arabs, however, and especially the bedouin, have always thought very highly of it, considering it to be not only the most useful but also the best-looking animal. In Arabia's pre-Islamic poetry, it is quite usual to compare the bodily charms of a beautiful girl whom the poet loves to various parts of the she-camel's anatomy. In the set form of composition known as the *qaṣīda,* the Arab poet pictures himself riding in the desert on his camel and proceeds to describe his mount. Krachkovskii writes: "Sometimes the poet employs such detail that one must be a connoisseur in order to appreciate the merits of this noble animal."[50] The camel, together with the horse, provided the Arabian poet with an inexhaustible store of epithets.

Arabians have always distinguished between the riding camel (the dromedary in the narrow sense of the term) and the pack animal, the latter being the more common. The ordinary camel caravan traveled for six hours a day at a speed of 5.5 km per hour, whereas a good dromedary could run as much as 130 km in twenty-four hours. The usual load carried by a pack camel did not exceed 270 kg, though the strongest animals might carry more than 450 kg. The Arabs discovered a long time ago that the camel had an unexpected liking for music: it transpires that, like the cavalry horse, the camel is sensitive to rhythm, and on this basis there arose a "camel" theory of Arabic poetry. Some orientalists consider that Arabic prosody was formed in direct relationship to the rhythmic motions of the camel, when the rider attuned his song to the even pace of the mount. On the other hand, the song itself helped to control the pace of the musically receptive camel.[51]

However, in his use of the camel the bedouin never shows the care and tenderness with which he deals with the horse. A good horse is always the object of pride and glory, not only for its owner but for the entire clan or tribe. Fast mares were particularly valuable, and their gallop was compared with the wind. An Arab poet sings of his horse as follows: "She is lean and hot, and when heated her snorting is like the boiling of a kettle. She has the croup of a gazelle, the shanks of an ostrich; her running is like that of a wolf, her jumping—of a young fox!"[52]

Every owner of a good horse took boundless pride in the purity of his horse's blood and memorized its entire pedigree. The mutual attachment and devotion of an Arab and his horse is well known, even from European school anthologies.

In west European literature and painting, even recently, there was a tendency to depict the Arabs as inseparable from their horses, as if they were practically some breed of centaurs. In fact the vast majority of bedouin are camel riders; horses were relatively few in Arabia, and only a small number of Arabs had the opportunity to ride and fight on horseback. The areas in which horses could be reared were restricted principally by natural conditions. Unlike the frugal camel, a horse must drink pure, fresh water two or three times a day. The main horse fodder in Arabia is barley, and the barley-growing districts are also quite restricted. Oats seldom grow in Arabia and are not considered suitable for fodder (in the Arabian climate they have a heating effect). Horse breeders had only limited possibilities of foraging in central and eastern Arabia, and therefore used date meal mixed with dry clover for fodder. In the Najd, horses were trained to eat meat, either raw or boiled; incredible as it may sound to us, this considerably increased the stamina of the horse. According to one Syrian, his horse, which had been fed for some time on roast pork, became so excited that even an experienced rider could not tame it. In some places horses were given locusts to eat, in the belief that this strengthened their muscles; in Ḥaḍramaut, even dried fish was used as fodder. Because of the scarcity of water, the horses drank chiefly camel milk. The more prosperous horse owners would "attach" a milch camel to their horse so that it would be the only consumer of the camel's milk. A rank-and-file bedoui, if he possessed a horse, would often "water" it with camel milk to the deprivation of his own family. Generally speaking, it was a difficult and thankless task to raise and keep horses in the Arabian desert-steppe. There was a saying among the Arabs: "He who has a wife and a horse has not a moment of rest."

The horse was never of any economic importance in Arabia, its role being restricted to raiding and sporting.

AGRICULTURE

As compared with the bedouin or nomads, the sedentary population of Arabia in the fifth and sixth centuries was smaller, though still quite substantial, although it is of course impossible to compile any statistical information, even approximate, on the ratio of settled to nomadic people in this period.

The sedentary population of Arabia lived chiefly by agriculture, tending grain, date palms and vines. In most parts of the peninsula, crops could be raised only under irrigation.

The Yemen was agriculturally the most developed part of Arabia, with a long tradition of sedentary life. By the last millennium B.C., when slave-owning civilizations flourished in Hither Asia and northeast Africa, southern Arabia was also a prosperous civilized country. A high level of agriculture was ensured by a complex system of irrigation; moreover, artisanal production and commerce were fully developed in the towns.

The people of ancient Yemen, who spoke a particular tongue of the Semitic group, had created their own culture, including an alphabetic script [borrowed from the Canaanite or so-called "Phoenician"]. The literary monuments of this people have been preserved to this day in inscriptions on stone and metal. Besides these epigraphic monuments, we have other witnesses to the civilization of ancient Yemen, namely the ruins of splendid palaces and temples and the remains of large-scale irrigation facilities such as dams and reservoirs. As Engels wrote, as early as 1853: "Wherever the Arabs [sic]* lived sedentary lives, they seem to have been just as civilized as the Egyptians, Assyrians, and so on; this is proved by their architectural achievements."[53]

* [As just stated by the author, these were not Arabs, not even Arabic speaking.]

For a number of reasons still not fully understood, the material as well as the spiritual culture of the Yemen suffered a decline in the pre-Islamic period under the rule of the "second" (late) empire of the Himyarites (the Homerites of Greek authors), which flourished from about 300 to 525 A.D. [and whose rulers were followers of Judaism]. This empire included not only the Yemen but also Ḥaḍramaut. The principal events contributing to the decline of the Himyarite kingdom were probably a migration of nomadic tribes from the Yemen northward* and invasion by the Ethiopians from the [Christian] kingdom of Axum. The Ethiopian inroads into southern Arabia, begun in the second century A.D., in places resulted in the establishment of Axumite rule over some parts of the Himyarite territory. By the second quarter of the sixth century, the dynasty of the Himyarite kings (under the title of *tubba'*) had come to an end. The Yemen was now ruled by a viceroy of the Ethiopian Negus; a combined fleet and army of the Sassanid *shahin-shah* Khusro I put in on the shores of southern Arabia, and in the decade following 570 the overlordship of Sassanid Iran became established in the Yemen.

In the fifth and sixth centuries, the Yemen, having lost its former economic importance and ultimately also its political independence, still remained a land of agriculture. Dry farming was combined with artificial irrigation. The periodical rainfall yielded sufficient moisture for sown crops and orchards, while the system of dams and reservoirs ensured the conservation of rainwater and its gradual distribution throughout the year by way of irrigation ditches. The biggest reservoir in the mountains of Yemen was held by the celebrated dam at Ma'rib, which collapsed in the sixth century, causing great damage to Yemenite agriculture. However, the Ethiopian viceroy was able to mobilize the local population to repair the dam. Apparently the size of the irrigation system became more restricted after this catastrophe, and the irrigation technique was also impaired. Yemenite farmers were forced to increase the area under drought-resist-

* [The reverse is more likely: the northward migration was a consequence of Yemen's decline.]

ant crops such as durra (sorghum), which came into wider use side by side with wheat.

Terrace cultivation has been practiced in the Yemen from remote antiquity to the present. The crops are sown on fertile mountain slopes, one terrace above the other, and are irrigated by reserves of rainwater collected in reservoirs and gradually distributed onto the fields by a network of small ditches. At present, many such terraces are coffee plantations, the coffee bush having been imported from Ethiopia in the fourteenth century. Coffee was thus quite unknown in Arabia earlier than this. On the other hand, the date palm and the vine have been cultivated in the Yemen since antiquity. Vegetal dye stuffs for the textile artisanal industry were an important industrial crop.

In addition to textiles, Yemenite craftsmen specialized in tanning and leather work. Yemenite leather was renowned throughout Arabia for its high quality. An Arab poet compares his she-camel's lips to "something worked in Yemenite leather that never wrinkles."[54] Yemenite weapons—especially swords and body armor—were also highly valued. Another pre-Islamic poet, Ta'abbata Sharran, describing an imaginary encounter in the desert with a spook, an evil witch which was about to jump him, explains: "But here, in the darkness of the night, there flashed above her my Yemenite blade!"[55]

Ḥaḍramaut, the region adjacent to Yemen, was also known to classical European writers as a country producing frankincense. Medieval Arabic geographers have little to say about Ḥadramaut: it was situated at the periphery of the Caliphate, away from its main economic and cultural centers, and was of no particular interest for Arabic authors, but one may safely assume that in the period under consideration the Ḥaḍramaut, like the Yemen, was a land of irrigation agriculture, which persisted there until the nineteenth century. The learned traveler von Wrede, who opened up the country to Europeans, was amazed and charmed by the agricultural development and lush vegetation of inland Ḥadramaut. In the ramified network of wadis terminating in the large valley crossing this region from west to east, and in the valley itself, von Wrede admired the well-tilled and irrigated fields with crops of wheat and durra, and with palms, *arei* (a kind of poplar) and other trees intertwined with lianas. On the meadows he saw a great many domestic animals. On the slopes of the wadis "there rise, as in an amphitheater, the towns and villages, between which one may see the scattered farmsteads and tombs of the saints." The local farmers inherited their technique of irrigating fields and plantations from their forefathers: quite often they used the very facilities which had been built by generations long since forgotten. These reports by von Wrede were received in Europe with diffidence and even sarcasm, but later European travelers in Ḥaḍramaut finally dispelled those notions about the country as "an abode of death."[56] *

To the east of Ḥaḍramaut lies Mahra, a poverty-stricken region without palms or sown fields, but renowned since olden times for its fast riding-camels, known as *mehari* [that is, from Mahra], which were readily purchased in countries inside and outside Arabia. The sellers accounted for the swiftness and stormy temper of these dromedaries by relating that jinns were wont to copulate with the she-camels, who then produced such fleet offspring. Some orientalists, however, assume that the sires in question were simply he-camels who had become feral in the sandy solitudes.

In 'Omān, agriculture was developed on the fertile seashore known as *al-Baṭīna* ("lowland" or "plain"), where, in addition to date palms, various grain crops (including wheat) and vegetables once grew. Most of 'Oman, however, is mountainous and desert and quite unsuitable for cultivation, although even there one could find oases where fields of crops and vegetable gardens grew under the date palms. The rich nature and the high agricultural level of 'Oman justified its comparison by medieval Arabs with "a garden." Agriculture, especially in the oases, was feasible because of the abundant groundwater in a water table that was often near the surface.[57] According to reports by medieval Arabic geographers, 'Omān was a land with many palm trees and various fruits (bananas, pomegranates, and so on).

An important agricultural region of Arabia in the fifth and

* [Ḥaḍramaut, the Biblical *Ḥaṣamawet,* can indeed be interpreted, literally, as meaning "Abode of Death" in Hebrew.]

sixth centuries was *Jaw-al-Yamāma*, "the Yamāma Valley." Although we cannot establish the territory and the limits of this region exactly, it possibly extended along the slopes of Arid and along Wadi Ird in the southeastern part of Najd, with its eastern boundary at the Dahnā' desert. It was certainly a very extensive area, as the Arabic geographers of the ninth and tenth centuries gave a long list of settlements in the Yamāma,* and indicated that its population yielded very high taxes (510,000 dinars). Some authors (including Philby) assume that parts of this flourishing agricultural district were destroyed in the Middle Ages by floods due to disastrously heavy rainfall.

In Yamāma, agriculture (mainly wheat cultivation) was based on artificial irrigation. The wadi which crossed this region held abundant groundwater in a water table near the surface. Jacut describes the Yamāma as an agricultural territory where entire districts were covered by cultivated fields. Philby speaks of an extensive oasis at Dilem, the whole of which was planted with wheat and barley. The area cultivated in Yamāma has more recently been severely reduced by the advance of drift sands from the neighboring desert.[58] In the early seventh century the Yamāma was inhabited by the banū-Ḥanīfa tribe, which became renowned in the days of the rise of Islam because of the activity of the local prophet Musailima. This representative and ideologist** of the Yamāma farmers, addressing the members of his tribe, used to say: "By sowing the field, reaping the harvest, winnowing the wheat, milling the flour, baking the bread and slicing it and eating it with fat and melted butter, you are better than the 'people of felt' and not worse than the 'people of clay,' so you must stand in defense of your fields, giving shelter to those that seek mercy and driving away those who dare attack you!"[59] Thus the Arabian agriculturalists presumably considered themselves superior to the nomads and no worse than the city dwellers.

The role of the oases in the economy of Arabia went side by

* [The Russian original has here "Yemen" instead of Yamāma, but this is certainly a typographical error.]

** [A somewhat different appraisal of this personage is put forward by W. Montgomery Watt, *Mohamhed at Medina,* Oxford 1956. pp. 135–136.]

side with that of the more extensive farming areas. An oasis, however, does not consist of a mere plot of land irrigated by a spring and feeding a few palm trees. Such insignificant islands of greenery could not subsist in the immense sea of sand, as they would soon be buried in the sand drifts. The three palms of the poem by that name by [the Russian poet] Lermontov are a product of an artistic imagination which hardly corresponds to reality.

An oasis is a substantially large area where cultivated fields, gardens and palm groves are abundantly watered from perennial wells. The sedentary population of an oasis dwelt in large villages with bazaars, a resting place for caravans and a temple of the local deities; some of these townships even grew into cities. The size and importance of such oases may be gauged by agricultural districts such as Kāsim and the Jauf.

In Ḥijāz the largest oasis was Yathrib, which even prior to Islam became known as "the City," *al-Madīna* (Medina).* This oasis, bounded by barren areas of *ḥarra*, contained a number of scattered village settlements or *diyār* (sing. *dār*) consisting of the common dwellings owned by some clan, but one also found single houses. These settlements and homes were separated from each other by palm groves, orchards and fields of wheat and barley

Another important settlement was the town of Ṭā'if, renowned for its gardens and sometimes known as the "garden-city." Its experienced gardeners and orchardists provided fruit and vegetables to the citizens of Mecca. There was a group of oases in northwestern Arabia, not far from the southern borders of the Syrian desert, each of which was like Medina, though smaller.

A study of the economy of Arabia in this period must also take into account the activity of a half-settled half-nomadic population. No doubt the slow process of nomads settling on the land took place over the millennia. These settlers included tribes which dwelt in the neighborhood of major oases and agricultural districts and came to cultivate and sow a few plots of fertile soil. Most of the tribe would then wander away with its herds into the

* [*Medina* is an Aramaic term, introduced apparently by the local Jews.]

steppe, leaving only a few families to guard the maturing crops, and would return in time for the harvest. Sometimes the tribe remained by its fields for the entire winter, and in spring, after sowing, reverted to its nomadic life. Other tribes possessed merely palm groves, and visited them only to harvest the dates.

Thus the Arabia of the fifth and sixth centuries consisted of nomads and agriculturalists side by side. This has already been noted by Karl Marx: "With all Oriental tribes, since the very beginning of history, there is a *general* relationship between the sedentary way of life of part of the population and the continued nomadism of another part."[60]

THE CLAN AND TRIBE ORGANIZATION OF THE ARABS

During this period, the great majority of the Arabs, except for the sedentary population of the Yemen, were at the stage of primitive-communal relationships. In this pre-class society, the state and its institutions had not yet arisen. The Arabs lived under a clan* and tribe regime, where the only organization was based on blood relationships, on groups of kindred people. The entire population of Arabia, either nomadic or settled, was subdivided into tribes, and each tribe in turn comprised a greater or smaller number of sibs and clans (depending on its numbers and the size of its territory).

According to Arab "specialists in genealogy" of the seventh and eighth centuries, all Arabs originated from the Biblical Abraham (*Ibrāhīm* in Arabic). The forefather of the northern Arabs was considered to be Ishmael (Arabic Ismā'īl), a son of the patriarch Abraham. The southern Arabs were thought of as descendants of [the Hebrew] *Yoqṭān* identified [arbitrarily] with the Arabic *Qaḥṭān*. The second of these two major groups of Arabic tribes was considered as "truly Arab," *al-'Ariba*, whereas the first group consisted of "arabized Arabs," *muta'arriba* or *musta'*-

* [The Russian term *rod* is the equivalent of Greek *genos*, Latin *gens*, and is best rendered in modern west European languages by the Scots "clan" or the Germanic "sib."]

*riba.** Each of the main groupings comprised many tribes, and each tribe bore its own name, but the larger tribes, spreading over the Arabian peninsula or outside its boundaries, broke up in turn into further autonomous tribes, each with a new name. The scattering of the tribes, which started in the latter half of the last pre-Christian millennium, proceeded from south to north, and some also spread to the steppe and semidesert regions of the neighboring countries of Mesopotamia, Syria and Egypt. Neither folk traditions nor written sources indicate any movement of Arab tribes in the opposite direction.**

The earlier conception of the clan, the component of the tribe, as merely a naturally overgrown family has by now been definitely disproved. W. Robertson Smith has demonstrated that the notions or "theory" of Arab genealogists, elaborated in the first century of the *hijra* [or *hegira,* the Moslem era of the seventh and eighth centuries, A.D.], do not correspond to historical reality as reflected by pre-Islamic poetry. Robertson Smith believed that the Arab clan was not a unit of kith and kin, but rather a group of people forbidden to fight each other or to shed each other's blood. Every adult male in this group, which bore its own name, was obliged to participate in blood feuds: he had to avenge the murder of any fellow clansman and to defend a murderer belonging to his own clan. The recognition of brotherhood among members of the clan (who called each other by the title of "brother") cannot be held as proof of actual blood relationship. Indeed,

* [The assertions in this paragraph are highly misleading, and show disregard for or lack of knowledge of Arabic genealogical traditions and Biblical text. Not *all* Arabs are descended from Abraham, but only the northwestern "Arabized" tribes, children of Ishmael, to whom Muhammed, among others, belonged. *Yoqtān,* alias Qaḥṭan, is *not* a descendant of Abraham but an older Hebrew patriarch. The identification of the two names, from roots that are obviously different (q. ṭ. and q.ḥ.ṭ.), is late and secondary. The "true," that is, aboriginal Arabs or *'Ariba* were definitely *not* the children of *Yoqtān*, but largely pre-Semitic tribes, "sons of *Hām*." The Yoqṭanites (or Qaḥṭanites), and they alone, were termed *muta-'arriba,* "Arabians" by residence, and only the Ishmaelites were *musta'riba,* "unauthentic, Arabized Arabs."]

** [The entire genealogical lore of Arabic historians quite definitely implies an earlier north—south movement of the forefathers of both Yoqṭanites and Ishmaelites.]

in the Semitic languages "brotherhood" is a rather indefinite notion. Among the Arabs, two men might become "brothers" by mutual consent, without any natural kinship at all. Moreover, many tribes did not bear the name of their common forefather, not even of a legendary one. Most of the tribes were called after totemic animals, after toponymics, or after deities, yet the genealogists have turned these names into a catalogue of imaginary "forebears" of clans.

Although his critical analysis is of great scientific importance, Robertson Smith overstressed his point by attributing a universal character to his criticism, for one cannot deny the fact that kinship was a powerful social force. However, it is very true that a clan did not consist solely of blood relations, but also comprised people who had "acquired" kinship in some manner, for instance by the rite of fraternization, in which a member of some other tribe, or even a stranger from another country, could become the adopted "brother" of a clansman by means of certain sacramental acts. Herodotus, in the fifth century B.C., already knew of the ritual of fraternization among Arabs.[61] The protection which a clan accorded to a man from another tribe, or even to a foreigner, also included the right of kinship.

Usually, not all the clans of a tribe were related by blood. Sometimes the tribe included a clan or a group of people who were formerly of another tribe but who had acquired their new tribal affiliation by a sworn agreement. The tribe was thus not only an alliance of kith and kin but also a political federation.

An Arab clan lived in their camp *(ḥayy)*, either in tents or in huts *(bait)*, each of which sheltered a separate family. Usually a camp numbered 100–150 tents, but sometimes their number reached as much as 500.[62] The bedouin of a definite camp wandered together. Sedentary Arabs lived in mud-brick or wattle-and-daub houses, grouped in villages or in town quarters. All members of such territorial and kinship organizations constituted an *ahl* (kith and kin group) or *qaum*. Tribes consisted of clans, the numerical importance of whose membership determined the power and the inter-tribal influence of the tribe.

A tribe was headed by its leader, the *sayyīd* ("senior," "sir"), who in later days came to be called *sheikh* ("elder"). Each clan and separate group of nomads also had its *sayyid.* In peacetime the *sayyid* supervised the migration from pasture to pasture, selected the proper spot for camping, represented the tribe in any negotiations with other tribes, heard the plaints and settled the disputes of his fellow tribesmen (if the tribe had no proper judge) and sometimes, though very seldom, acted as a priest of the tribal cult. During raids or in warfare the *sayyid* was in command of the armed men of the tribe, and was then known as a *ra'īs* ("chieftain" or "captain").

The *sayyid* presided over the assembly *(majlis* or *nadwa)* at which the richest, noblest or otherwise influential members of the tribe decided all current affairs. The *sayyid* was further obliged to receive guests and to treat his own entire tribe to feasts and entertainment. He incurred still greater expense in redeeming fellow tribesmen who had been taken prisoner by other tribes and in paying blood money (wergild—*diyya*) to the kinsmen of a murdered man of another tribe. The *sayyid* usually had a poet attached to him, a *shā'ir* (which at that time actually meant "warlock" or "medicine man" in Arabic). The *shā'ir* either lived with the tribe or enjoyed their hospitality only in visits; the Arabs of those days regarded his verses not only as laudatory but also as having a magical effect: indeed, the warlock was thought to be in communication with jinns. If the tribe had an idol, the *sayyid* always had a *kāhin,* a priest, in attendance.

Each tribe (or even, at times, any major clan) was a completely independent organization, answerable to no external authority. The security of its members and the inviolability of their property depended on constant mutual aid and support between tribesmen (or clansmen). Any inhabitant of Arabia without tribal affiliation was in the position of outlaw and could be killed without retribution and his property plundered. An Arab who had been chased out of his clan or tribe or who had fled from it (after committing a crime, perhaps) therefore had to seek the protection of another tribe. He became the *mawla* or "client" of some *sayyid* or other influential member of the new tribe, and was then known as a *dakhīl* (literally one who "creeps in, comes in seeking protection"). The same circumstances account for the preservation of the ancient institution of adopted brotherhood, and for similar reasons freedmen, that is, freed slaves, would prefer to remain with the tribe in the capacity of *mawālī* (plural of *mawla*) rather than be left quite defenseless outside the tribe.

If a tribesman had been murdered or injured in some manner, all members of the tribe were duty bound to avenge him. Revenge could be exacted not merely from the guilty party but from all members of his clan or tribe. This indeed was the strongest manifestation of clannish and tribal solidarity and mutual help: each member of the group considered himself responsible for the behavior of all other members. As the poet Duraid Ibn-as-Simma wrote: "I am one of the tribe of Jaziyya; if it blunders I blunder with it; if it goes straight I go straight with it."[63] The blood feud, the vendetta (*(tha'r)* between single tribes, could last for several decades and cause great loss of life and property. In the pre-Islamic period, then, the Arabs began to recourse to blood money *(diyya)*, at the rate of as many as 100 camels for one human life.

Clan and tribe solidarity was expressed in the *'aṣabiyya* (family spirit, patriotism), which Ibn-Khaldūn defines as the feeling of community based on kinship.[64] "Be loyal to thy tribe," said another Arab writer, "its claim upon its members is strong enough to make a husband give up his wife."[65]

Each clan comprised a greater or lesser number of families. The family dwelt in a separate tent, the master of which was the head of the family. A grown son, after marrying, left the tent of his father and put up his own tent beside it, in which he now became the master. The Arab family was patriarchal. Division of labor between the sexes having already been accomplished, all the weight of domestic work fell on the shoulders of the wife and daughter, provided they had no female slaves. Bedouin women, however, still possessed freedom and relative independence; they were certainly not yet objects of private property.

The earlier forms of marriage and family were preserved only as fast-disappearing archaic survivals. There remained no trace of promiscuity in the way of life, and neither had polyandry been preserved in any pure form: to the Arabs of this period the report by Strabo about a princess of Yemen married simultaneously to fifteen brothers[66] was simply a memory from the past.

Vestiges of a matriarchal society remained, however. There were frequent cases of matrilocal residence of the husband: after the wedding, the wife remained in her clan with her parents, while the husband came to visit her occasionally. The children born of such wedlock also remained in their mother's clan, and were named after her (son or daughter of a given woman, not of a man). The preservation of this type of marriage is due to the frequent and prolonged absences of men accompanying the camel caravans. A similar form of marriage was that of a woman who had her own tent and remained mistress of the tent. She had the initiative of divorce, having only to turn her tent so that it opened in the opposite direction to manifest her decision that the marriage had become invalid; she could also hand over a tent and a spear to a man, thus signifying that their marriage was at an end and that the former husband must now live and hunt separately.

The survival of polyandry was in the form of a marriage wherein a woman, the mistress of a tent, married several men, each of whom dwelt in the tent for the time between two consecutive monthly "cleanings." During menstruation, the woman hung a red rag on the tent and none of her husbands was allowed to enter. When she bore a child, she herself indicated who was the father.

These vestiges of polyandry had practically died out by the seventh century. However, fairly widespread polygamy was preserved even after the spread of Islam, and continued within Moslem society. Not every Arab, of course, could afford to be polygamous, since it was largely a means of ensuring numerous male offspring. Another form of polygamy consisted in a married man taking slave concubines. The sons born of such wedlock had full rights, provided the father recognized them as his own children.

A further type of polygamy was temporary marriage for a stated period of several months, days or even hours. This form of marriage was widespread due to the needs of the many men in the caravan trade, who provided themselves with temporary wives in the settlements where their caravan had to stay, sometimes for prolonged periods of time. Lammens asserts that the rich caravan traders from Mecca had whole harems at their disposal in some of these towns. Temporary marriage was later made legal in shi'ite Islam, under the designation of *muta*.

In the fifth and sixth centuries, the Arabs admitted both exogamous and endogamous marriage. On the whole, they perhaps preferred the former, having observed that healthier and stronger offspring were produced by girls and widows from alien tribes. Moreover, marriage with a woman from one's own tribe resulted in parents and close relations of the wife interfering in one's married life, with all the attendant strife and misunderstanding. Thus the custom of abduction of a bride became widespread (of course with the bride's consent).

Shahrastāni recorded that when a woman married a stranger to the tribe her relations sent her off with expressions of malevolence such as: "You shall not be delivered easily! Nor bear a boy! For you will bring strangers close to us, and produce enemies!"[67] To the bedouin the birth of a son was as much an occasion for rejoicing as that of a pedigree colt (provided that it was from a noble mare), but the birth of a daughter was a misfortune or even a shame, especially if the father was a poor man. Pre-Islamic poetry quite often pictures the lamentations of the father and the unenviable position of the daughter. There were cases, though not frequent, of the baby girl being buried alive in years of famine, but such desperate cruelties disappeared after the spread of Islam. By the nineteenth century, the bedouin considered reports of infanticide to be inventions by European travelers.

DECAY OF THE PRIMITIVE-COMMUNAL REGIME

Idyllic notions about the equality, freedom and independence prevailing in bedouin society lack any historical foundations whatsoever. The Arabic pre-Islamic poetry reflects quite a different reality.

Firstly, the results of unequal distribution of property among Arabs in this period (either nomadic or sedentary) were quite obvious. Each tribe and clan had its élite, based on aristocracy of birth, which owned many head of cattle and claimed paramount right to use of the tribal pastures and watering points. It is well known that cattle became private property earlier than did land. A distinction should be made here between personal and private property. Each inhabitant of Arabia had some personal property (his dwelling, clothing, utensils, animals and weapons, and also—if he happened to be an agriculturalist—his livestock and implements).

Private property, however, gives rise to profits, the proprietor gaining surplus produce. The tribal aristocracy, consisting of wealthy cattle-owners, could not of course consume all the meat and dairy produce of their herds. They sold camels and horses not only within Arabia but also in neighboring lands, and such sales yielded both money and merchandise.

Slave labor was of prime importance in animal husbandry as well as in irrigated agriculture. Slaves were recruited chiefly among foreigners, since raids by one tribe upon another could not yield a sufficient number of slaves, and a tribe considered itself bound to redeem any tribesman taken prisoner in war or to exchange him against a captive of theirs. Raids against the adjacent Byzantine and Iranian regions were infrequent and none too successful, since the frontiers of the two empires were well protected. True, there were in Arabia some *'ajami* [alien, or more specifically Iranian] slaves taken in Irak, but most of the slaves were African and were known as *aḥābish* (Abyssinians). In those days, caravans of African slaves traveled through Arabia, where some slaves settled, having been either bought or captured in raids on the caravans.

A typical figure in pre-Islamic poetry is the poet 'Antara, whose father was a well-known *sayyid,* while his mother was a black slave girl. In his position as a slave, due to his mother, he refused to participate in defending the camp against a raiding enemy tribe, saying: "A slave does not understand how to fight; his work is to milk the camels and bind their udders."[68]

Rich Arabian cattle-owners exploited the slaves in grazing and tending the herds. The use of slave labor enabled the tribal aristocracy to increase the number of cattle they owned, thus increasing their profit. Cattle (especially camels and horses) came to be in great demand.

This increasing inequality in property within the tribes gave rise to the class of the *ṣa'lūk,* which comprised bedouin possessing no means of production (in particular, no cattle). In the eyes of the tribal aristocracy, these were a highly dangerous class. Having no she-camels, the *ṣa'lūks* found subsistence in hunting the beasts of the steppe, or went in search of occasional employment in the merchant towns, where they worked in unloading the camel caravans. They were reminiscent of the forerunners of classical proletarians, but nobody gave them bread or entertainment. Hungry, and hating the rich, the *ṣa'lūks* stole their property and sometimes killed or otherwise offended their own tribesmen, as well as attacking members of alien tribes. The tribe (or more precisely its élite) therefore expelled them and deprived them of its protection. Thus arose the *ṭarīd*, the outcast, who, with no clan or tribe to turn to, sometimes hid in the desert, whence they fell upon the encampments, singly or in groups, in order to rustle cattle and gain some other booty.

The poet Shanfarā was himself a *ṣa'lūk*. Wandering in the desert, he declared haughtily: "To me now, in your default, are comrades a wolf untired; A sleek leopard, and a fell hyena with shaggy mane."[69] In the poem "The Song of the Desert," Shanfarā derided the dwellers of bedouin encampments, the dandies who courted women and were cowards, and who were terrorized by the sudden raids of the robber.[70] Another outstanding *ṭarīd* was the poet Ta'abbata Sharran, whose very name struck his contemporaries with panic and fear. "Solitude his chosen comrade, on he fares while overhead; By the Mother of the mazy constellations he is led," the Mother being the Pole Star.[71]

European specialists in Arabic literature describe such outcasts as extreme individualists whose excessive vanity made it impossible for them to live with their tribesmen or to respect the accepted norms and usages. But in fact the *ṣa'lūk* and the *ṭarīd* were outstanding figures whose characteristic social nature has not yet been fully clarified. There is no doubt, however, that they arose as a result of the decay of socio-economic relationships within bedouin society, and that they rebelled against inequality.

The material advantages of the tribal aristocracy (especially of the *sayyids* and *ra'īses*) enabled them to achieve a way of life whose standards differed sharply from those of the rank-and-file bedouin. The tent of a *sayyid* was the most spacious in the camp; it was raised on higher ground, at a distance from the tents of the ordinary nomads. Inside were spread rugs and carpets; exquisite harnesses and expensive weapons were hung, and metal and glassware displayed. All this had been bought from traveling merchants from neighboring civilized countries. A *sayyid* was supposed to be endowed with generosity and had to practice the most lavish hospitality. This was by no means a manifestation of a generous personal disposition or of personal vanity, but had important social implications, since it had to make some show at least of attenuating the economic inequality which was a source of public discontent. The festive meals which a *sayyid* and his relatives offered from time to time, as well as the help which he gave to widows and orphans, were not considered by the bedouin as a free gift but as a leader's obligation. The *sayyid* himself, understanding very well the socio-political meaning of his own generosity, tended to self-glorification without restraint, for which purpose he employed the potent tool of poetry. Many bedouin were actually connoisseurs of poetical works. The *shā'ir* (court poet), well paid by his *sayyid,* was not afraid to use the most inflated hyperboles. In his poems of praise he sang fantastic songs of lavish abundance and open-handedness: behind the *sayyid's* tent, there were always roasting fires like volcanos; while the kettles in which the meat was boiling were as big as Solomon's pools...

Thus, in the "pre-class" society of the bedouin, there was a continuous process of decay of socio-economic relationships. The *sayyids* and their relatives, who played the part of the elders of the clan, based their power not merely on custom, authority and respect, but also on their own economic strength, which came to be felt more and more keenly by their tribesmen. Grazing land and water resources remained tribal or clan property, but the tribal aristocracy owned a disproportionate number of cattle and naturally made the widest use of tribal pasture and watering holes.

An interesting but as yet insufficiently studied phenomenon was the *ḥimā*. In most cases the term designated a small oasis with an idol or a sanctuary revered by some tribe, so that it became an object of pilgrimage for members of the tribe. A *ḥimā* was considered a holy place, under the special protection of some deity, or even as his property. The regular gathering of pilgrims led to the development of a market where the nomads exchanged their goods against those of the sedentary population. The religious ceremonial of pilgrimage in Arabia was always connected with commerce in this way.

The tribal aristocracy derived certain benefits from the *himās* (though exactly which we still do not know), and therefore ensured peace and order in them and encouraged pilgrimage. We learn that in some *himās* horses were bred by rich owners; the oases perhaps served as "stud farms" for improving the breed.

The widespread institution of the *ukhuwwa* ("fraternity") was also profitable to the *sayyids* and their entourage, and became a form of overlordship and protection. Usually, some tribe which was not numerous (and therefore not influential and impoverished) sent out one or several members to a neighboring stronger tribe. These representatives of the feeble group sought by every means to become the adopted brothers of a tribesman of the powerful tribe. If they succeeded in this, the weaker tribe acquired a powerful ally and protector, for if two men from two different tribes had become "brethren" their two tribes were then also considered as related, with all the ensuing rights and obligations.

Ukhuwwa was of particular importance—indeed essential—for agricultural tribes and clans living on the border of nomad territory. Years of drought forced the bedouin, in their hunger, to pillage their sedentary neighbors who did not suffer from the drought, since they practiced irrigation in cultivation. In this situation, the settled people preferred to forego a part of their produce in order to gain the protection of the nomads, and for this purpose entered into an *ukhuwwa* relationship with the latter, giving the *sayyid* a stated proportion of their crops, from fields gardens or date groves. In return, the tribe of the *sayyid* protected the agriculturalists against depredation by other nomadic tribes. There is no reason to interpret such *ukhuwwa* as an incipiently feudal relationship. Indeed, it contains none of the basic traits of feudalism, neither a personal dependence of the farmer on the *sayyid* nor any feudal rent.

THE CULTURAL CONDITION OF ARABIA

If we accept Engels' definition of "pre-class" society in *The Origins of the Family, Private Property and the State,* the level of production and culture of the Arabs in the fifth and sixth centuries (except for the sedentary population of the Yemen) corresponds to the highest stage of "barbarism." This stage "begins from the working of iron ore and turns into civilization as a result of the invention of alphabetic writing."[72]

In Arabic-Moslem literature, the pre-Islamic period in Arabia is known as the *jāhiliyya,*[73] which means "ignorance" or "barbarism." The Moslems gave this term a specific meaning: lack of knowledge of the "true faith" of Islam. The term is used historically to designate the period immediately preceding the rise of Islam.

Prior to the *jāhiliyya* period, at the "middle stage of barbarism," the Arabs had already completed the earliest major social division of labor, namely, separation between animal husbandry and farming. In the *jāhiliyya* period a second process was completed: separation of artisanal production from agriculture. By this time the Arabs had not only fully mastered ceramic and textile craftsmanship, but had reached mastery in working hot metals. In western Arabia iron ore was found on the territory of the Sulaim tribe [to the east of Medina], and the Sulaim were indeed known as the "tribe of smiths" *(quyūn)* and were renowned as smelters of iron ore. Silver and placer gold were procured in Arabia as raw material for jewellers, among whom the so-called "Medina Jews" were some of the most celebrated.

In agriculture, fairly varied iron tools were in use, including a plow with an iron share. In artificial irrigation of fields, date groves and vineyards, camels were used for traction, working irrigational devices drawing water from wells. At Medina and elsewhere, the palm tree was artificially pollinated at the time of flowering, and this considerably increased the yield of dates.

The development of the various branches of the economy resulted in more active commerce, with the added produce becoming a further object of merchandise. As animal husbandry was predominant, its main product, camels, were used as "live money." The caravan trade of the Arabs grew in scope, and they became middlemen in international commerce, on the one hand, between India and China, on the other the Mediterranean countries. This enhanced foreign cultural influences in Arabia; not merely merchandise, but also knowledge, customs and ideas for improving production arrived from neighboring civilized lands. In Mecca, for instance, Iranian culture made itself felt for a considerable length of time.[74]

The Arabs of the fifth and sixth centuries were in fact at a transitional stage between barbarism and civilization. They even had walled cities such as Ṭa'if, which was able to stand a stubborn siege against the army of Mohammed in 630.

Among the Arabs of the *jahiliyya* period there were expert sailors who crossed the Red Sea in various directions, and who perhaps even sailed into the Indian Ocean. The idea seems to be established in the literature that the pre-Islamic Arabs feared to risk their lives on the high seas, and that only their remote descendants, two or three centuries after the rise of Islam, very gradually learned the art of navigation. This, however, does not agree with our information* on the constant relations between western Arabia and Africa across the Red Sea. One may assume that the inhabitants of the coastlands of 'Omān and those of the Yemenite Tihāma had already learned to follow the maritime coast route to India and Ceylon in antiquity; the captains from Musqāṭ followed a seaway which had already been explored by the fleet of Nearchus [Alexander's admiral] in the sixth century B.C. The Koran serves as further proof of the pre-Islamic Arabs' knowledge of the sea.[75] Arab seafarers used light sailing ships built in local shipyards. They did not use metal nails in the construction, but bound the planks with ropes made of palm fiber.

* [It would seem that the Arabs proper were seldom sailors, and that navigation was mainly in the hands of non-Arab or pre-Arab peoples such as the ancient Yemenites, who were geographically "Arabians" but not Arabic-speakers.]

An important achievement of Arab culture in this period of the *jahiliyya* is undoubtedly the ancient Arabic, or pre-Islamic, poetry, remarkable for the variety of its genres and styles; its works can be placed on the same level as the poetic creations of the Mediterranean peoples of antiquity. The vehicle of this poetry was the Arabic language, in a form which was later accepted as classical, on a par with the language of the Koran itself.

Krachkovskii writes: "Prior to Mohammed, this poetry, which proved so vital and powerful, had already reached its highest point of perfection, both in language and metrical form and in variety of themes and maturity of composition . . . Some linguists, not without reason, consider it as the climax of Semitic linguistic creativity. One is immediately impressed by the immense vocabulary, the elaboration of forms and the flexibility of syntax."[76]

In the *jāhiliyya* period, the perfected poetical language became common to most of the inhabitants of the Arabian Peninsula (except in the Yemen, Ḥaḍramaut and Mahra), as well as to those Arabs scattered in Syria and Mesopotamia. Peculiarities of local dialect of various Arab tribes are rare in pre-Islamic poetry. Such linguistic unity in a time of primitive-communal relationships, and also the very high level of linguistic culture as expressed in this poetry, have indeed caused doubts in the minds of several Arabists concerning its authenticity.

For two or three centuries, the poems were memorized by the *rāwūn* (or *ruwāt*, sing. *rāwī*, "memorizer" or "narrator"), the bards of Arabia who transmitted their poetry only orally, and were not committed to paper until the eighth century.

Alphabetic writing, the invention of which* marks the transition from barbarism to civilization, appeared among the northern Arabs in the fourth century A.D. We refer here to inscriptions found in Syria and Jordan in the so-called Nabatean script,** which soon ousted the (older) south Arabian (Sabean) alphabet in Arabia itself, and which served as a basis for the development of medieval Arabic writing.

* [In the Middle Bronze Age, first half of the second millennium B.C., among the Canaanite ("Phoenician") speaking Semites.]

** [A variety of Aramaic script; the earlier Nabateans, though they were ethnically Arabs already, used Aramaic as their official written language.]

RELIGIOUS BELIEFS OF THE ARABS IN THE JAHILIYYA PERIOD

In this period, the Arabs (in particular the nomads) did not yet possess any developed religious concepts, and those that did exist were not united in any ideological system; religious fantasy was not at all productive, a characteristic feature of "pre-class" society. A pantheon of deities had been formed only by the sedentary and civilized inhabitants of the Yemen, where there existed temples and a developed religious cult. The religious beliefs of the rest of the population of the Arabian Peninsula consisted of a rather disordered mixture of fetishism, totemism and animism. One may assume that fetishism was the most ancient form of Arab belief and cult, expressed in the reverence of stones of meteoritic and volcanic origin. The cult of the "baetyls"* was widespread, and it survived in Islam as the reverence accorded to the "Black Stone" (the *Ka'ba* of Mecca). The classical Greek authors reported at this time that the Arabs were worshippers of stones. Totemic beliefs seem to have been less conspicuous, but obvious traces have survived in the names of many tribes, such as *Asad*—Lion, *Kalb*—Dog, *Bakr*—Young Camel, *Tha'lab*—Fox, *Thawr*—Bull, *Dubb*—Bear and *Dhi'b*—Wolf. Taboos on killing totemic animals and eating them were rare in a country of frequent famine. Indeed it became a widespread custom for all the members of a clan to feast together on a camel or on the flesh of some other strong beast, in the superstitious belief that they would acquire the strength of the devoured animal. This (and not merely hunger) would also account for the custom of "eating the idol," made out of dough. These cases should be interpreted as manifestations of the rite of "eating the god" in order to introduce into the human organism the divine force hidden in the idol.

Notions about the soul, about the condition of the body after death and about afterlife were all very vague, being rather similar to such notions among pre-classical Greeks. Some bedouin, who imagined existence beyond the grave as the continuation of life on earth, killed a camel on the tomb of a man who had just died

* [The Greek term derives from Hebrew-Canaanite *bet-el,* "dwelling of a god."]

to make things easier for him in the afterlife. Because of the absence of any very definite conceptions concerning the state of the departed, no cult of ancestors developed.

The belief in jinns, imagined as reasonable beings consisting of smokeless fire and of air, covered nearly all of Arabia. These creatures, like humans, were dimorphic and possessed not only reason but also passions. This is why they often left the wilderness in which the Arabs supposed them to live and had intercourse with men and women. Sometimes offspring with outstanding physical and mental qualities were born from such intercourse.

Idol worship became widespread in this period, entailing sacrifices and a fairly simple ritual. The fullest catalogue of tribal idol-deities is to be found in a work by Ibn-al-Kalbī, *Kitāb al-aṣnām* (The Book of Idols),[77] and Shahrastāni also discusses some idols. From these authors it appears that the pre-Islamic Arabs had not created any system of mythology, but possessed myths only in the most embryonic form.

Shahrastāni states that there were many sceptics among the Arabs; their mood was expressed by a poet who said: "Life, death, then resurrection—all this is hearsay and fable!"[78]

Religions from the neighboring lands of civilization, mainly Christianity and Judaism, now gained converts among the Arabs. Christianity (in the forms of Monophysitism and Nestorianism) was widespread among Arab tribes in Mesopotamia (The *Jezīra* between the Upper Tigris and the Middle Euphrates), in Irak (proper, lower Mesopotamia), in Syria and in Palestine. But Christians were also found among the tribes of northern and western Arabia. Pre-Islamic poetry has preserved the figure of the Christian anchorite *(rāhib)*, the light of whose lamp, streaming from his hut in the desert, attracted the wayfarer.[79]

Judaism spread as a rival to Christianity in Yathrib (Medina, the "City" *par excellence*), and in some other cases of northwestern Arabia. In the Yemen, Judaism was proclaimed as the state religion at the start of the sixth century.*

* [Actually not later than the fifth century: the last of a series of Ḥimyarite kings who were followers of Judaism perished in a war against the Christian Ethiopians as early as ca. 525 A.D. (*Yūsūf Dhū-Nuwās*).]

Partly under the influence of these monotheistic religions, but mainly due to the aspirations of some Arab tribes toward political unification, there also arose in Arabia an autonomous form of monotheism known as "Hanīfism."

[1] I. Yu. Krachkovskii, *Ash-Shanfarā. Pesn' pustyni* (The Poetry of the Desert). t. II, p. 238, Moskva-Leningrad, 1956.

[2] E. Robertson Smith, *Kinship and Marriage in Early Arabia,* Cambridge, 1885.

[3] *Reste arabischen Heidentums,* gesammelt und erlaütert von J. Wellhausen. 2 Ausg. [2nd ed.]. Berlin-Leipzig, 1927.

[4] H. Lammens, *Le berceau de l'Islam.* Rome, 1914.

[5] L. Caetani, Studi di storia orientale, Vol. I. Milano, 1911.

[6] Jirjī Zaydān, *Al-'Arab qabla-l-Islām.* Cairo, 1922.

[7] A.P. Caussin de Perceval, *Essai sur l'histoire des Arabes avant l'islamisme, pendant l'époque de Mahomet et jusqu'à la réduction de toutes les tribus sous la loi musulmane,* tome I, 1847.

[8] *L'antica societa beduina,* Studi. . raccolti da F. Gabrieli. Roma, 1959.

[9] Cl. Huart, *Histoire des Arabes,* t. I – II. Paris, 1912 – 1913; Ph. Hitti, *A History of the Arabs,* London, 1953. 5th edition.

[10] *Jacut's geographisches Wörterbuch*. . herausgegeben von F. Wustenfeld, Vol. II, p. 76. Leipzig, 1866. (Designated henceforward as *"Jacut."*)

[11] *Al-Hāmdāni's Geographie der arabischen Halbinsel*. . herausgegeben von D.H. Müller, Vol. I, p. 47. Leiden, 1884. (Henceforward *"Hamdani."*)

[12] *Hamdani,* Vol. I, p. 47; *Jacut,* Vol. II, pp. 76 – 78.

[13] *Géographie d'Aboulféda,* traduite. . par Reinaud, t. II, partie I, p. 99. Paris, 1848. (Henceforward–*"Aboulféda."*)

[14] A.A. Kruber, *Obshchee zemlevedenie (Fizicheskaya geografiya)* (General Geognosy–Physical Geography), pp. 320–321. Moskva-Leningrad, 1938.

[15] H. Lammens. op. cit., pp. 113 – 121, 154 – 182.

[16] E. Gibbon, *The Decline and Fall of the Roman Empire,* Vol. III, pp. 57 – 58. New York.

[17] L. Caetani, *Studi di storia orientale,* Vol. I, p. 53. [Retranslated from the Russian. The same applies to most of the quotations in this book.]

[18] C. Niebuhr, *Description de l'Arabie d'après les observations et recherches faites dans le pays meme,* Copenhagen, 1773.

[19] Cf. V.V. Bartol'd, *Istoriya izucheniya Vostoka v Evrope i Rossii* (History of the Study of the Orient in Europe and Russia), p. 22. Leningrad, 1925.

[20] H. Lammens, *La cité arabe de Taif à la veille de l'hégire,* p. 22. Beirut, 1922.

[21] J.L. Burckhardt, *Voyages en Arabie,* t. I, pp. 111–112. Paris, 1835.

[22] E. Rutter, *The Holy Cities of Arabia,* p. 354. London, 1930.

[23] H.St.-J.B. Philby, *The Heart of Arabia,* pp. 13–14, Vol. I. London, 1922.

[24] Bertram Thomas, *Arabia Felix: Across the Empty Quarter of Arabia,* p. XXIII. London, 1932.

[25] The *"Mu'allaqat Poem of Imru-'l-Qais,"* in "Divans," ed, by W. Ahlwardt. London, 1870.

[26] Charles M. Doughty, *Travels in Arabia deserta,* Vol. II, pp. 38, 324. London, 1924.

[27] H.St.–J.B. Philby, *The Heart of Arabia,* Vol. II, p. 43.

[28] cf. C.M. Doughty, *Travels in Arabia deserta,* Vol. II, pp. 532 – 533.

[29] T.E. Lawrence, *The Seven Pillars of Wisdom,* pp. 278 – 279. London, 1946.

[30] Cf. B. Thomas, *Arabia Felix: Across the Empty Quarter of Arabia,* p. 184.

[31] H.St.–J.B. Philby, *The Empty Quarter; being a description of the Great South Desert of Arabia, known as Rub'al-Khāli.* London, 1933.

[32] *Ibidem.*

[33] *Ibidem.*

[34] H.St.–J.B. Philby, *The Heart of Arabia,* Vol. I, pp. 41, 46.

[35] A. Rihani, *Ibn Sa'oud of Arabia. His People and his Land,* pp. 107, 110. London, 1928.

[36] Anne Blunt, *A Pilgrimage to Nejd,* pp. 158–160. Vol. I. London, 1881; J. Euting, *Tagebuch einer Reise in Inner-Arabien,* t. I, pp. 142 – 143. Leiden, 1896.

[37] H. Lammens, *Le berceau de l'islam,* p. 57.

[38] *Jacut,* Vol. II, p. 247.

[39] R.F. Burton, *Personal Narrative of a Pilgrimage to al-Madinah and Meccah,* Vol. II, pp. 60 – 61. London, 1907.

[40] Cf. C.M. Doughty, *Travels in Arabia deserta,* Vol. I, p. 379.

[41] M. Oppenheim, *Vom Mittelmeer zum Persischen Golf..*, Bd. I, pp. 89, 204. Berlin, 1899.

[42] J.J. Streiss, *Three Voyages* (in Russian transl. *Tri puteshestviya*), p. 341. Moscow, 1935.

[43] S.M. Zwemer, Arabia: *the Cradle of Islam.* p. 80. London, 1900.

[44] I.Yu. Krachkovskii, *Ash-Shanfarā. Pesn' pustyni* (The Poetry of the Desert). Izbrannye sochineniya, t. II, p. 243.

[45] J.L. Burckhardt, *Notes on the Bedouins and Wahâbys, Collected During his Travels in the East.* London, 1830.

[46] H. Lammens, *Le berceau de l'islam,* pp. 23 – 24.

[47] *The Mu'allaqat Poem of Imru-'l-Qais,* in "Divans," ed. by W. Ahlwardt. London, 1870.

[48] Nasir-i Khusrau, *Safar-namé* ("Book of Travels") [from the Persian], p. 135. Moscow-Leningrad, 1933.

[49] "Zeitschrift der Deutschen Morgenländischen Gesellschaft," Bd XIV, p. 361. Leipzig, 1891.

[50] I.Yu. Krachkovskii, *Arabskaya poeziya* (Arabic Poetry). - *Izbrannye sochineniya* (Selected Works), t. II, p. 251.

[51] Carl Brockelmann, *Geschichte der Arabischen Litteratur,* Bd. I, p. 14. Weimar.

[52] *The Mu'allaqat Poem of Imru-'l-Qais.*

[53] Letter from Engels to Marx, ca. 26 May 1853.

[54] A. Krymskii, *Arabskaya literatura v ocherkakh i obraztsakh* (Arabic Literature, Essays and Specimens), p. 184. Moscow, 1911 (lithography).

[55] S.P. Olfer'ev, *Iz oblasti drevnearabskoi liricheskoi poezii* (Essay on Ancient Arabic Lyric Poetry). –"Yubileinyi sbornik v chest' V.F. Millera," p. 269. Moscow, 1900.

[56] V.A. Krachkovskaya, *K stoletiyu izucheniya Khadramauta* (A Hundred Years of Studies in the Hadramaut).—"Izvestiya Vsesoyuznogo geograficheskogo obshchestva" (Bulletin of the All-Union Geographical Society), t. 75, vyp. 4, pp. 31–45. Moscow-Leningrad, 1943.

[57] J.R. Wellsted, *Travels in Arabia,* Vol. I. London, 1838.

[58] V.V. Bartol'd, *Museilima* (Musailima).—"Izvestiya AN SSSR" (Bulletin of the Academy of Sciences of the USSR), No. 12–15, pp. 486–489. 1925.

[59] *Ibidem,* p. 502.

[60] Letter from Marx to Engels, June 2, 1853.

[61] Herodotus, *The Histories,* p. 176, (Book III). London, 1954.

[62] J. Henninger, *La société bédouine ancienne.*—"L'antica società beduina," p. 81. Rome, 1959.

[63] F. Gabrieli, *La letteratura beduina preislamica.* – Ibid., p. 102.

[64] *"Prolégomènes d'Ebn-Khaldoun,"* texte arabe, publié par M. Quatremère, t. I, p. 235. Paris, 1858. [Quoted henceforward as ibn-Khaldūn, Muqaddimāt.]

[65] Al-Mubarrad, *al-Kāmil,* ed. W. Wright, p. 229. Leipzig, 1864.

[66] Strabo, *Geography,* XVI, 4.

[67] Cf. *"Proiskhozhdenie islama." Khrestomatiya* (The Origin of Islam. An Anthology), sost. Evg. Belyaev (ed. E. Belyaev), p. 87. Moscow-Leningrad, 1931.

[68] R.A. Nicholson, *A Literary History of the Arabs,* p. 115. London, 1928.

[69] I.Yu. Krachkovskii, *Ash-Shanfarā. Pesn' pustyni* (The Poetry of the Desert). – *Izbrannye sochineniya,* t. II, p. 240.

[70] *Ibidem,* p. 241.

[71] R.A. Nicholson, *A Literary History of the Arabs,* p. 82.

[72] Friedrich Engels, *The Origins of the Family, Private Property and the State,* in Russian, *Proiskhozhdenie sem'i, chastnoi sobstvennosti i gosudarstva,* in K. Marks i F. Engel's, *Sochineniya* (Collected works), 2nd ed., t. 21, p. 32.

[73] Ignaz Goldziher, *The Cult of Saints in Islam.*

[74] [A quotation from Engels, *ibidem,* p. 33, is omitted in this translation.]

[75] Cf. V.V. Bartol'd, *Koran i more* (The Koran and the Sea), in the book: "Aziatskii muzei Rossiiskoi Akademii nauk. Zapiski kollegii vostokovedov" (Asiatic Museum of the Russian Academy of Sciences. Essays by a body of Orientalists), t. I, pp. 106–110. Leningrad, 1925.

[76] I.Yu. Krachkovskii, *Arabskaya poeziya* (Arabic Poetry), *Izbrannye sochineniya* (selected works), t. II, pp. 247–248.

[77] *"Ibn al-Kalbî, Kitâb al-Asnâm.* Das Götsenbuch." Übersetzt mit Einleitung und Kommentar von Rosa Klinke-Rosenberger. Leipzig, 1941.

[78] *"Proiskhozhdenie islama"* (The Origins of Islam), sost. Evg. Belyaev (ed. E. Belyaev) pp. 84 – 88.

[79] V.V. Bartol'd, *Islam* (Islam), p. 10. Petrograd, 1918.

CHAPTER II

THE ORIGINS OF ISLAM

SOURCES

Our main source of information on incipient Islam, the period when this religion arose, is the Koran (al-Qur'ān). This very complex product of Arabic literature took shape principally in the seventh century. The oldest manuscripts of the book, written in Kufic script, probably date back to the early eighth century. According to Moslem tradition, the Koran as we know it was composed and edited during the reign of the Caliph 'Uthmān (644–656), and was therefore known as the 'Uthmān Koran, or the Koran as edited by this Caliph. However, besides this, the canonical edition, other editions exist which have reached us only in small fragments. According to a tradition of medieval Arabic historians, the leading representatives of the first generation of Moslems still had their own texts of the Koran, which were used to edit the 'Uthmān Koran, but it is obvious that not all such texts were used for the purpose. Indeed, divergent editions of the Koran were in circulation as late as the tenth century.

The problem of the authenticity of the 'Uthmān Koran is rendered more complicated, since nearly all European Arabists and specialists in Islam consider the entire Koran *a priori* the work of the prophet Mohammed, whom they consider "the founder of Islam," and thus cannot perceive the serious discrepancies arising from any theory which assumes the sole authorship of Mohammed. The various styles in the book (even in translation) are immediately noticeable, and could not belong to a single author. The traditional explanation of this diversity points to the peculiar traits in Mohammed's character and to the vicissitudes in his career, but such arguments are neither justified nor convincing. Furthermore there are eyewitness descriptions in the

Koran of places which Mohammed (according to his traditional biography) never visited. Dating the Koran is an even more difficult task due to the lack of any chronological references in it or any clear mention of otherwise authenticated events or historical figures. Lastly, the subject matter of the Koran is not merely diverse, but is arranged as a rule according to a purely external criterion, the length of the verse, into 114 component "chapters" or *sūrāt (suwar,* singular *sūra).* With few exceptions, these *sūrāt* are so disposed that the longer ones are at the beginning of the Koran and the shorter ones at the end.

Until specialists succeed in determining the exact date of the Koran and in establishing the sources of its various parts, we are forced to consider it for the time being as a literary monument of the period in which Islam arose and as a historical source for that period.

There are many good nineteenth- and twentieth-century translations of the Koran into west European languages, the most recent of which is that by Régis Blachère.[1]

The Koran was translated several times into Russian during the eighteenth and nineteenth centuries, though not from the original but from west European versions. The first Russian translation from the Arabic was by G. S. Sablukov, published in Kazan in 1878. The translation by Krachkovskii published in 1963, provided as it is with valuable philological comments, suffers from certain stylistic defects, because it was not thoroughly edited after the death of the translator.

Another basic source for the period under consideration is *Sīrat rasūl Allah* (The Life of God's Messenger), written in the latter half of the eighth century by the Medinese ibn-Isḥāq, which has come down to us in the edition by the outstanding philologist of the ninth century, Ibn-Hishām. An important supplement to this work consists of passages from the "History" by Ṭabari, who used ibn-Isḥāq's work in its original edition, only a few fragments of which written on papyrus reached us.

The *Sīra* of ibn-Isḥāq was written in Baghdad at the request of the 'Abbāsid Caliph Manṣūr (754–775), and thus reflects the political claims of the 'Abbāsids, founded on their origin from 'Abbās, the uncle of Mohammed. In the *Sīra,* this "kinsman of the prophet" is given an important historical role. Mohammed himself is represented not merely as an Arabian but as a universal prophet, a concept which reflects the polemics between Moslems and Christians or proponents of other monotheistic religions. In using the *Sīra* as a historical source, the legends contained in it should be rejected, as they are apt to be obscure and to deform the true historical figure of Mohammed.[2]

As a supplement to the *Sīra* one may use the *Kitāb al-maghāzi* (Book of Warlike Campaigns) by Wāqidi (747 – 823), also a tendentious work full of religious legends and myths.

These works of Arabic literature serve as the basic source material for the study of the origins of Islam; although not quite satisfactory, they represent the best first-hand material available.

Later Moslem authors of biographies of Mohammed—in whose person they accounted for the whole complex process of the rise of Islam—all used these same sources, only adding to and complicating them by introducing fanciful elaborations of later days.

LITERATURE ON ISLAM

The first Europeans to write about Islam and its "founder" were the Byzantines, who waged long-lasting and bitter wars against Moslem states and people during the Middle Ages, while still maintaining economic and cultural relations with them. The authors of Greek Byzantine historical and theological writings, inspired by official orthodoxy, could view Mohammed only as a false prophet and the sole culprit for the rise of Islam: their attitude was one of uncompromising hostility, so that the picture of Islam in Byzantine literature is completely distorted by religious intolerance.

In western Europe, the earliest knowledge of Islam (also inauthentic and extremely tendentious) came at the time of the Crusades, and was spread by Catholic missionaries, who were of course ideologically opposed to Islam. In the twelfth century, after the first Crusade, the Catholic monk Robertus Cetenensis (Robert le Moine, Robert the Englishman), who lived in Spain and knew Arabic, translated the Koran into Latin. The translation was made on the initiative of the abbot of Cluny, Pierre le Vénérable, for the purpose of "refuting" Islam, so that the translator gave an incomplete and at times purposely deformed version of the contents of the Koran. This first translation was published only in 1543 in Basel, Switzerland.[3]

From the Renaissance on, a number of works appeared in western Europe concerned especially with Islam. These were due not only to the widening intellectual interests of Europeans, but also to the policies of conquest practiced by the Ottoman Empire, the most powerful of all Moslem states.

In the remarkable productions of west European "bourgeois" writers of the Enlightenment (especially Frenchmen of the eighteenth century), Islam was viewed as some exotic phenomenon arising out of man's stupidity and ignorance and of the swindles practiced by the clergy. Voltaire's drama *Mohammed or Fanaticism* bears no relation to the Orient beyond a few garbled Arabic names. Voltaire was in fact attacking not Islam but the Catholic church and its head, the Pope.

At the dawn of west European orientalism, when France, the most advanced country in Europe, was on the eve of the great bourgeois revolution, concepts about Islam were typified by this excerpt from the *Bibliotheque Orientale* of d'Herbelot: "Mohammed, a well-known fraud, founder and initiator of a heresy which was named the Mohammedan religion ... a false prophet."

In the great French *Encyclopédie,* edited by Diderot and d'Alembert, was the following: "Contradictions, absurdities and anachronisms abound in this book (the Koran); crass ignorance is particularly visible in regard to the simplest and best-known natural phenomena." However, the *Encyclopédie* was generally sympathetic towards Islam and Mohammed. Its enlightened authors were merely protesting against the rank ignorance which is the hallmark of any religious literature.

Not until the nineteenth century was any more objective study of Islam made, when the current attitude of European Oriental historians toward the rise of Islam was as a manifestation of Mohammed's personal activity.

The author of the first European biography of Mohammed was an Austrian physician and orientalist, Alois Sprenger (1813–1893), whose work *The Life and Teaching of Mohammed* is by now out-dated and worthless as a biography.[5] Sprenger started from the unfounded premises that "Islam is the only universal religion that arose in full daylight" and that "we can trace Islam step by step." These impressions he gained by naively accepting the tales which he found in historical sources of Islam, in particular the *Sīra* and the *hadīth* collections[6] (traditional "narratives" about the Prophet). The complete groundlessness of Sprenger's thesis became evident by the nineteenth century with the publication of the researches of Ignaz Goldziher, who demonstrated the unreliability of the *ḥadīths* as a source for the study of incipient Islam.

Another well-known European biography of Mohammed, which appeared just before Sprenger's, is that by the Englishman William Muir.[7] Unlike Sprenger, Muir (1819–1905) was grossly tendentious in the manner of a Christian missionary in the colonies. He explained the rise of Islam by saying that Mohammed was tempted by the devil: this sort of work, written in the spirit of medieval obscurantism, can have no scientific significance.

The German Arabist Hubert Grimme (1864–1942)[8] was the first to attempt an explanation of the origins of Islam by social causes. But his concept of incipient Islam in the Meccan period of Mohammed's activity not as a religion but as a "socialistic" movement and doctrine is invalid, though the concrete data in his book deserve serious attention.

Two important twentieth-century European biographies of Mohammed are those by the Danish orientalist Franz Buhl and the Englishman Montgomery Watt. Buhl's "Life of Mohammed,"[9] the second edition of which was published in 1955, contains abundant and well-selected data, thoroughly and scientifically analyzed, even if from the standpoint of historical idealism.* The introduction gives a description of Arabia in the period prior to the rise of Islam, while the actual biography is set against a broad historical background.

Montgomery Watt's biography consists of two books, published in Oxford in 1953 and 1956,[10] richer in factual material

* [In contradistinction to historical materialism, the official doctrine of the USSR.]

than Buhl's work, and presented not merely in chronological order but systematized according to subject (such as "Muhammed and the Jews," "The Character of the Moslem State," "The Reform of Society"). Unfortunately the worth of these books is undermined by the author's confident attitude toward Moslem tradition, as well as his uncritical acceptance of traditional concepts of Arabic Moslem historians. The same applies to the author of the latest French biography of Mohammed, Gaudefroy-Demombynes.[11]

By the beginning of the twentieth century, the work of Ignaz Goldziher had seriously questioned the reliability of Moslem tradition (the *ḥadīths*) as historical sources of incipient Islam. Many European orientalists began to treat the *Sīra* more critically as well. Caetani, for instance, suspected all the data of the *Sīra* on Mohammed's activities prior to the *hijra* (hegira—the exodus from Mecca) to be merely legends.[12]

In 1925, Bartol'd wrote: "Although there exists a vast literature concerning the first decades in the life of the Moslem community, nearly all questions pertaining to the history of that period require re-examination."[13] However, the excessively critical attitude toward the *Sīra* was no longer fashionable by the mid-twentieth century.

Present-day Arabic authors of biographies of Mohammed display complete confidence in the *Sīra* of ibn-Isḥaq, and it is clear that for them the Koran itself is sacrosanct, "the Word of God," and beyond any kind of criticism. In this respect we must mention the scandal which arose in Egypt in the 1920's on the appearance of a book by Ṭāhā Ḥusain on Arabic pre-Islamic poetry. This Egyptian scholar used the Koran as source material and, following the example of European orientalists, handled it critically, upon which he was censured, persecuted and slandered, and his book was taken out of circulation.[14]

The abundance of modern popular Arabic literature concerning Mohammed, actually Moslem religious propaganda written for the faithful, is absolutely worthless for any serious study. Biographies by Arabic Moslem historians are simply more or less detailed paraphrases of the Koranic "revelation" and of the *Sīra* of ibn-Isḥāq, with no attempt at objective evaluation; among these, however, the most detailed and best written is the *Life of Mohammed* by Muḥammed Ḥusain Haikal, which appeared in Cairo: *Ḥayāt Muḥammad*, Al-Qāhira, 1947.

Haikal's book gives clear expression to the (bourgeois) ideology prevalent today in many Moslem countries. Quoting the Koran, he refutes the much-advertised fatalism of Islam and attempts to show it as favoring private initiative and competition. In accordance with the notions propagated by present-day Moslem ideologists, Haikal contrasts "Islamic civilization" with "western civilization," asserting that the first has a "spiritual basis" whereas the second is founded on "economics." A further ideological difference, in his opinion, was that in the west there was a permanent struggle between Church and State, whereas in the Moslem world the two institutions were organically interconnected. Such concepts, assiduously entertained by the bourgeois ideologists and propagandists of Islam are completely at varience with the regular processes of development of human society. There are no special laws of history valid only in the East or in the West; religions and churches have been bulwarks of social inequality and enhanced class oppression of the faithful in all human societies. Lastly, Haikal discusses the socialistic nature of Islam—a characteristic element of the official ideology—although it is well known that scientific socialism and religion are totally incompatible.

The best-known Russian biography of Mohammed is a short book by the idealist philosopher and religious specialist Vladimir Solov'ev *"Magomet"* (Mohammed), in the biographical series of Pavlenkov. This work, though free of any religious intolerance, is so entirely inspired by religiosity and mysticism that it had no scientific importance at the time of publication and by now has no significance whatsoever. A more interesting work is that of M. N. Petrov, *Magomet, Proiskhozhdenie islama* (Mohammed, The Origins of Islam), though it is merely a compilation from the books of Sprenger and William Muir.[15]

A. E. Krymskii was seriously interested in the life of Mohammed and started on his valuable "Sources of the History of Mohammed" *(Istochniki dlya istorii Mokhammeda)*, also writing on Islam in his "History of the Islamic Religion" *(Istoriya musul'-*

manstva) and "History of the Arabs" *(Istoriya arabov)*. The book by Washington Irving, *The Life of Mohammed,* is noteworthy only for the review of its Russian version *(Zhizn' Magometa)* by N. A. Dobrolyubov, since it is more of a historical novel in form and content and is by now completely out of date.

Considerable attention, both academic and popular, was given in Russia to the problem of the origins of Islam. Several theories were put forward. The first, the so-called "merchant-capitalistic" theory, was that of M. A. Reisner, inspired no doubt by the early historical conceptions of M. N. Pokrovskii. This theory—clearly at variance with the fundamental tenets of Marxism-Leninism—was current in the late 1920's and early 1930's. Two other theories, the "nomadic" and the "agricultural," also proved groundless. The nomadic theory saw incipient Islam as reflecting the interests of the bedouin masses of Arabia and constituting their ideology, while the agricultural theory vastly overestimated the importance of agriculturalists in the economy of pre-Islamic Arabia and viewed incipient Islam as the ideology of "the landless peasantry."[16]

S. P. Tolstov's conception of Islam was more justified, giving serious attention to slave-holding conditions in Arabia in the sixth and seventh centuries.[17] The author's extreme and subjective views on certain details aside, his examination of the social roots of incipient Islam seems historically convincing.

The concept of incipient Islam as an ideology of early feudal society arose in the 1930's, when it was claimed that the Arabs had entered this stage of early feudalism by the seventh century. Smirnov was the first to publish this theory in his "Summary Program of Islamic Studies" *(Programma-konspekt po islamu,* Moscow, 1931*)*, but nearly all later authors of anti-religious books, pamphlets and papers touching upon the question of the social roots of Islam sustained this theory without any foundation, as if it were a self-evident dogma, even proclaiming the few "companions" of Mohammed whose names happened to be known to be prominent feudalists.

The same theory is taught in many university courses on medieval history, having found literary expression in a textbook published by Moscow University: "History of the Lands of the non-

Russian Orient in the Middle Ages" (*Istoriya stran zarubezhnogo Vostoka v srednie veka,* MGU, Moscow, 1957). Chapter VII of this book ("The Rise of Feudal Relationships in Arabia and the Formation of the Arabian State") contains many data which could actually be used to demonstrate that feudalism did not exist at all in the Arabia of the sixth and seventh centuries.

Shortly after the book was published, L. I. Nadiradze (one of the authors of the seventh chapter) attempted to prove this "feudal" theory of the origins of Islam, but his paper "The Question of Slavery in Arabia in the Seventh Century" (*K voprosu o rabstve v Aravii v VII v.*) only unwittingly demonstrates that Arabia was then a country with a slave-holding regime and by no means a country of feudal relationships.[18]

Professors A.Yu. Yakubovskii and I.P. Petrushevskii, two outstanding Soviet orientalists who studied this problem from the original oriental sources, oppose the "feudal" theory and concentrate instead on the birth and development of slavery in Arabia.

In the absence of any Marxist writing on the origins of Islam, the most well-grounded and convincing study is that included in the extensive collective work of Soviet historians, the "Universal History" (*Vsemirnaya istoriya,* t. III).

Some futile attempts were made, chiefly by N. A. Morozov, L. I. Klimovich and S. P. Tolstov, to refute the historical existence of Mohammed and thus turn him into a mythical figure. Morozov put forward his views in a voluminous, chaotic, anti-historical work called "Christ" (*Khristos,* t. V), in which his general conceptions are quite unscientific, while his chapters on Islam are utterly worthless, his information stemming from casual and erratic reading (of second-hand sources) complemented by his own boundless fantasy.

Klimovich wrote somewhat later,[19] but used some of the same material, in particular the antiquated work of Sprenger, while neglecting the writings of Arabic historians. Adamantly refusing to take any account of the source material or of scientific research, Klimovich failed to produce any proof as to the birth and development of the alleged myth of Mohammed.

Islam arose in Mecca at the time when it was the biggest township in Ḥijāz. The area around Mecca was quite barren and desert-like: the sparse grass cover and poor scrub fed only small herds of camels and puny flocks of sheep, while wells were few and far apart and the water table far from the surface, so that water was often found only at the very bottom. The inhabitants of Mecca thus relied neither on animal husbandry nor on agriculture for their living. We can assume that Mecca originated as a station on the ancient frankincense route near the spring of Zemzem, though it is impossible to make even an approximate determination of the time of the first settlers near this spring. Some historians believe that the town of Makaraba mentioned by Herodotus (fifth century B.C.) ["Macoraba" of Ptolemy] might well be the early Mecca.*

The religious significance of this town, which was to become an important city (by Arabian standards), had been growing since antiquity. The waters of Zemzem became holy water, perhaps due to purgative properties. Near the spring stood the age-old temple of Ka'ba, which now became an object of pilgrimage for the bedouin tribes of Ḥijāz. The Meccans and the bedouin had probably had commercial relations during the pilgrimage season since ancient days. According to Moslem tradition (historically quite worthless), the Ka'ba had been built by the Biblical Abraham (Ibrāhīm) and his son Ishmael (Ismā'īl), the mythical ancestors of the northern Arabs.

Mecca is situated in a trough, "in a valley lacking any grass" (Koran, XIV, 40), surrounded by high naked hills called "mountains" *(jībal)* by the Meccans, which are separated by "canyons" *(shi'āb)*. When rain fell, a sudden freshet would storm through the valley. Several times, Mecca was subjected to such severe

* [*Makka* is a name having no meaning in Arabic; *Makaraba* seems to be a south Semitic though non-Arabic toponym, signifying "place of sacrifice" (from the root k. r. b., "to perform a ritual, a sacrifice"). The later Arabs would have treated this to them incomprehensible name as a compound, and dropped its second half.]

flooding that the walls of the Ka'ba—built of rough local stones—threatened to collapse.

The city was built around this ancient sanctuary, known as the "House of Allah" even prior to the rise of Islam; the Meccans thus took pride in their title of "neighbors of Allah." The Dutch orientalist Snouck Hurgronje wrote: "Allah did not grant his 'neighbors' anything but the bitter Zemzem water, stones and sand, and unbearable heat."[20]

The significance of Mecca as a religious center for the pagan tribes of Ḥijāz and the western Najd was actively linked with its role as an important commercial station. Besides trading with the Ḥijāzi bedouin, Meccans participated in the international transit trade, for which Mecca, at a crossroads of caravan traffic on routes from Yemen to Syria, Palestine, Irak and Egypt, was well situated, with further connections with East Africa by the Red Sea. Yemen exported not only local produce but merchandise which came by sea from India, China and Africa, for merchant shipping had become more active in Hellenistic times, both in the Indian Ocean and in the Red Sea. In summer, profiting from the southwest monsoon, the merchantmen reached India, sailing back in winter when the northeasterlies took over. This development of a direct sea trade between India and the Red Sea harbors of Egypt did not interfere with the caravan traffic along the ancient "frankincense route" on which Mecca was a station.

The volume of the Meccan caravan trade can be gauged by reports quoted in reliable Arabic sources such as Ṭabari's mention of a caravan of 2,500 camels,[21] while the Meccan caravan which caused the battle of Badr in 624 numbered 1,000 camels.

According to *sūra* 106 of the Koran, the Meccans sent out two great trade expeditions *(riḥla)* each year, in winter and in summer. Other sources reveal that the winter venture was to Yemen, the summer one to the north, to Palestine, Syria, Egypt and sometimes Irak. These expeditions were organized by the rich élite of the Quraish tribe, who lived in Mecca, but any Meccan, however limited his means, could participate. The leaders were of course the richer citizens of Mecca, who dominated the economic life of the city. The value of the caravan which Mohammed tried to rob, leading to the battle of Badr, was assessed at

50,000 gold pieces, of which 5,000 had been invested by members of the Quraishite clan of Umayya and one or two thousand each by some rich merchants. The leader of a caravan, at the time of the rise of Islam always somebody prominent among the rich men of Mecca, was usually a member of the then dominant clan of Umayya.

The larger Meccan caravans had guides and an armed escort. The camels, their drivers and the hands for loading were recruited amongst the bedouin of the neighborhood. Experienced guides were well acquainted not only with the routes and crossroads but also with the watering places and pastures for camels. The leader of a caravan, in the course of his journey, maintained communication with Mecca by sending off messengers on fast dromedaries. Certain "holy" months had been established in which the Ḥijāzis and Najdis made their pilgrimage to the Ka'ba. During these months, bloodshed or the squaring of accounts in blood feuds was prohibited. Mecca and its vicinity were proclaimed "holy territory"—*ḥaram*—wherein no murder or act of violence would be tolerated; there is an allusion to this in the Koran, where it is said in the name of Allah: "Do they not see how we have given them a sanctuary of safety, while all around them terror holds its reign?" (XXIX, 67).

The Meccans lived by commerce, for in this city, as the Arabs said, "he who is not a merchant does not possess anything." An influential Meccan told Ya'qūbi: "The life, the prosperity and the future of our city depend on commerce,"[22] while Wāqidi describes the Quraishites as "a tribe of traders."[23]

In the *jāhiliyya* period, prior to the rise of Islam, such future Moslem leaders as Abu-Bakr, 'Abbās, 'Omar ['Umar], 'Uthmān and Ṭalḥa are referred to in the sources as "traders" or "merchantmen." Khadīja, when she was still a widow before becoming Mohammed's first wife, was independently engaged in the caravan trade, and 'Ā'isha, daughter of Abu-Bakr, who married Mohammed after the death of Khadīja, took part in the slave trade. A certain Abū-Jahl also made much money out of the incense trade.

Pre-Islamic Mecca did not have its own currency; the coins in circulation were Byzantine gold pieces, Sassanid silver and

Yemenite (Himyarite) money. Payments were also made in gold dust, which was imported from Africa and the Yemen where it was sifted from river beds. Silver ingots were also used for exchange, while the language clearly reflected the use of broken, worn and pierced coins accepted by weight: for instance, the Arabic verb *wazana lahu*—literally "to weigh for him"—meant "to pay him." Fraudulent weighing was a common occurrence, and was severely judged in the Koran: "Woe to him who weighs falsely, who when he measures for himself takes in full but when he measures or weighs for another defrauds him" (LXXXIII, 1–3).

Usury *(ribā')* was also widely practiced in Mecca, for in order to participate in the profitable caravan trade many a Meccan who had only a modest income had to resort to usurers; despite the high interest, he could hope to benefit after the safe return of the caravan. The richer merchants were both traders and usurers; 'Abbās, for instance, "had much money owed him by his tribesmen,"[24] while one of Mohammed's companions, in Medina, was worried about the money he had lent on interest to Meccan merchants.[25] Money lenders usually took a dinar for a dinar, a dirhem for a dirhem, in other words, 100 per cent interest. In the Koran (III, 125), Allah, addressing the faithful, prescribes: "Do not practice usury doubled twofold." This could mean that interests of 200 or even 400 per cent were demanded. The nets of Meccan usury caught not only fellow-citizens and tribesmen of the usurers, but also members of the Ḥijāzi bedouin tribes active in the Meccan trade. As in ancient Athens, "the principal means of oppressing the people's freedom were . . . money and usury."[26]

The inhabitants of Ṭā'if, or at least the élite of the local tribe of Ṭā'if, the Thaqīf, were important regular contributors to the Meccan caravan trade. Economic relations between Mecca and Ṭā'if were so close that the two towns were known as *Makkatāni,* "the two Meccas." The people of Ṭā'if supplied the Meccans (who had neither gardens nor orchards) with fruit and vegetables. The richer Meccans had their villas in or near Ṭa'if, where they took refuge from the summer heat.

In Mecca, commerce and usury hastened the process of decay of primitive-communal relationships. As in ancient Greece prior to the rise of classes, the money economy burnt up the clan and tribe regime like some strong acid, such a regime being "absolutely incompatible with money economy."[27]

The élite of the Quraish tribe of Mecca had developed, both economically and socially, much faster than the leadership of other tribes. Among the ten clans of this tribe, the Umayya clan had gained preponderance, including most of the richest merchants and usurers, who appointed the leaders of major trade caravans from among themselves and enjoyed influence and real power among their fellow-citizens and among those Ḥijāzi tribes who were economically dependent on Mecca. Such rich and influential Meccans lived in the houses surrounding the Ka'ba, in the central area of the city known as al-Baṭḥā', "open space, plaza." They were thus singled out by the honorary title of "Quaraishites of the Center."

The Quraish leadership possessed not only money and merchandise, but also farmland, slaves and livestock. Certain *himā* sanctuaries in northern Ḥijāz belonged to members of the Umayya clan; these *himā* included artificially irrigated fields and date groves, cultivated by slaves, and in some of them pedigree horses were bred.

Besides the rank-and-file of the Quraish tribe, who were dominated by their own tribal élite, another section of the Meccan population was the *aḥlāf* or "sworn allies," newcomers from other tribes, who settled in the big commercial town as protected residents and thus in a way "adopted brothers" to the native population. Their participation in the commercial activities of the Quraishites gave them sufficient means of subsistence. A similar social category existed, under the same name, in Ṭā'if. The least secure among the inhabitants of Mecca were those who dwelt in the suburbs or "outskirts" (ḍawāḥi), chiefly bedouin, outcasts who had fled their own tribes and who probably included many *"s'alūks"* and *"ṭarīds."* They had been attracted to the big town where there was money in the caravan traffic, working as packers, stevedores or unqualified workers in some trade, or as self-taught veterinaries, herdsmen and sometimes caravan drivers; they were troublesome and often criminal. Moreover, many foreigners from neighboring countries lived in Mecca as wandering traders and craftsmen or as innkeepers; being Christians, Jews or Zoroastrians, they had some ideological influence upon the Meccans and the neighboring bedouin.

The Quraish tribe was organized on the same lines as other Arabian tribes. In Mecca, however, the process of decay of primitive-communal relationships was much further advanced than among other tribes. In this town we can already see the incipient transformation of the tribal élite into a dominant class, with embryonic state institutions: the big merchants, usurers and slave-owners formed a separate group known as the *mala';* they had a police of slaves (Abyssinians), the *aḥābish*, and there was a "House of Assembly" and a council of elders.

The term *mala'* means "assembly" and also "the aristocracy." Thus, to the Arab mind, the angels are *al-mala' al-a'la,* the "Highest Assembly." In the Koran, the term also means "aristocracy" or "tribal leaders" (XXIII, 34), applying to the noblemen around an ancient Egyptian Pharaoh (XXIII, 48; XXVI, 33). The Quraishite *mala'* would assemble by the walls of the Ka'ba to discuss matters concerned with the dispatch or reception of a trade expedition, or other public affairs. This Meccan "aristocratic" assembly may be compared to the ancient Athenian Areopagus, at least in its incipient form.

According to tradition, the "House of Assembly" *(dār an-nadwa)* was founded by the legendary Quṣayy ibn-Kilāb (a descendant of Quraish himself). Ṭabari wrote that Quṣayy arranged for meetings to be held in his own house, the door of which faced the Ka'ba temple: "Both women and men of the Quraish tribe celebrate marriage only in the house of Quṣayy ibn-Kilāb; they (the Quraishites) confer on any affair which happens to concern them only in his house, and (it is in this house) that they display the standard of war against another tribe."[28]

The Quraish aristocracy believed that they had inherited their duties and privileges from the legendary Quṣayy: "The inhabitants of Mecca had given power to Quṣayy . . . and he indeed possessed a power to which his tribe submitted; and he had the *ḥijāba,* the *siqāya,* the *rifāda,* the *nadwa,* and the *līwa.*"[29] The *ḥijāba* was custody of the keys to the Ka'ba, the *siqāya* the obligation to provide water for pilgrims to this temple, the *rifāda* the collection of alms for needy pilgrims, (the *nadwa* the calling of the Assembly,) and the *liwā'* a piece of white cloth which was attached to the point of a spear in the event of war with another tribe and handed over to the *ra'īs*, the war leader.

In the early Islamic period, these privileges were those of the élite of the Umayya clan, who thus exerted a constant influence on the pilgrims who came from the nomadic territories of the bedouin, bringing meat and milk produce and game in exchange for the products of urban craftsmanship and merchandise imported from abroad.

The *aḥābish* are an interesting and characteristic phenomenon. Lammens, working from detailed documentation, [30] gave ample proof that these African slaves were owned by rich Quraishites who were members of the *mala'* and who used them as an armed escort for caravans and as a police force for the protection of the Ka'ba (where the Quraishite treasury was kept), as well as for guarding their own homes which were threatened by the dissatisfied suburban mob and by indigent pilgrims. The theory of the aḥābish as some group of people outside any tribe is quite unfounded.

Further note should be made of the term *īlāf*, used in the Koran (CVI, 1–2), which Sablokov translated by an archaic Russian word meaning "accord," while Krachkovskii gave it the wider meaning of "alliance." The term is probably best rendered as "confraternity" or "concord" in the sense that the Quraishites were capable of concerted action, a necessary prerequisite for any major commercial venture: Arabic sources appear to refer to the *īlāf* as diplomatic trade treaties concluded by the Quraishites with foreign rulers.

HANĪFISM AND ISLAM

Hanīfism, which was fully developed as a religious and ethical doctrine in agricultural Yamāma, also spread to western Arabia, where the ideas of monotheism and ascetism were already known by the relatively large number of people who had been influenced by the monotheistic religions of Christianity and Judaism, some even having converted to these religions. In Mecca, however, one of the main strongholds of Arabian polytheism, the spread of *Hanīfism* was impeded by the well-organized cult of the Ka'ba. This idolatrous cult was closely connected with the economic activities of the Quraishites and lent a halo of sanctity to their dealings with the bedouin tribes, so that the Quraishite aristocracy strove hard to preserve polytheism and idolatry.

Nevertheless, the epoch of polytheism was drawing to its end in Arabia. Elements of new class-relationships appeared in the decaying primitive-communal society, so that the ideology was bound to change from polytheism to monotheism. In particular, the formation of tribal alliances expressed a striving toward the unification of Arabia, the rise of a central power which could be reflected and sanctified only by monotheism.

Hanīfism, the Arabian form of monotheism, began its fight against polytheism firstly by opposing the latter's grossest expression, idolatry; by countering the tribal and local deities with the help of their One God *Raḥmān* (the "Merciful")*, the Ḥanīfites introducing the concept of a pan-Arabian religion. In Mecca, they were faced with a particularly severe struggle, since here polytheism was more solidly grounded than in other tribes and the idolatrous cult was far better organized.

The *Sīra* quite definitely describes Mohammed, at the start of his religious activity, as a typical Ḥanīfite. The doctrine of the Meccan Ḥanīfites is expounded in the "Raḥmānic" *sūrāt* of the Koran. In the earlier parts of the Koranic collection, which European investigators group together as the "poetical" *sūrāt,* there are fantastic theories of the imminent end of the world, the Last Judgment and existence after death; the idea of monotheism is prevalent in these documents and is preached with particular insistence. The "poetical" *sūrāt* (except for spells of witchcraft pertaining to the heritage of polytheism) are thus very similar to Ḥanīfite doctrine, though the influence of Judaic and Christian sects is more marked in the *sūrāt* than in Ḥanīfism, the members of such sects being quite numerous among the foreigners who came to visit or even dwell in pre-Islamic Mecca.

* [Actually, *Raḥmān* is a Hebrew term borrowed from Judaic theology; it was already in use among the Judaizing Himyarites.]

From the earliest *sūrāt* onward one interesting and important detail stands out, namely that the One God appears under the name of "Allah," the tribal deity of the Quraishites,* while the cult of the Ka'ba as the "House of Allah" is retained. Certain rites are also prescribed which had already been practiced in this cult.

The Meccan form of Ḥanīfism, attributed to Mohammed by both Moslem historical tradition and European "bourgeois" Islamology, could never become widespread, not only because of the opposition of the dominant Quraishite leadership, but also, and far more important, because of social causes restricting its spread in Mecca. The socio-economic contradictions in this city had become much more acute than in the tribes (of Arabia outside Mecca). The Meccans certainly wanted to rid themselves of the tyranny of their leadership and to escape the bondage of usurious debts, while the slaves yearned for liberation, but Meccan Ḥanīfism was in no position to attract the needy and oppressed, offering as it did an unattractive prospect of universal doom while directing the eyes of the faithful toward a world beyond the grave and promising a better existence only after death. Threats of the forthcoming cosmic catastrophe and of torments in the Gehenna could hardly impress the Arabs of that period with their widespread scepticism of any afterlife and their Meccan businesslike common sense.

Caught in this impasse, under the stress of the social needs of the population, Meccan Ḥanīfism underwent a second stage of development; it is this that we must interpret as the birth of a new religion, which became known as "Islam." The doctrine corresponding to the incipient phase of this religion found expression in the Meccan "prophetic" *sūrāt,* where a no less important dogma than that of the unity of Allah is that of the apostle or messenger *(rasūl)* of Allah, who claims to be the sole intermediary between the supreme being and mortal men.

The "prophetic" *sūrāt* give increased attention to certain material things. Firstly they condemn and absolutely prohibit usury, which plagued Meccan economic life; the population of Mecca

* [In fact, *Allah,* contracted from *al-ilah,* means simply "the god" in Arabic.]

and the neighboring bedouin tribes suffered greatly from the avarice of the usurers. "That which you seek to increase through usury, so that it should grow from the substance of other men, fails to grow in the sight of Allah" (XXX, 38).

Commerce, on the other hand, is considered quite licit and even praiseworthy. A slave-holding Allah is described as a typical merchant, reflecting all the features of the trading community of Mecca. It appears from the *Sīra* that when Mohammed began his career as a religious preacher he still continued his interests in commercial affairs. The Quraishites, who cast doubt on his prophetic mission, mockingly exclaimed: "What kind of prophet are you? You go on your rounds through the markets as anyone else among us!" The answer can be found in a verse of the Koran where Allah says: "Also before your time, we never sent an apostle who did not eat food and did not go through the markets" (XXV, 22).

The "prophetic" *sūrāt* contain particularly insistent calls to keep the right measures and weights and thus be honest in one's commercial and usurious dealings: "And you should be honest in your measures when you measure, in your weights when you weigh" (XVII, 37). Side by side with the prohibition on squandering the possessions of orphans, one finds the following injunction: "Use measure and weight according to righteousness" (VI, 153). The mythical prophet Shu'aib,* addressing his Midianites, exhorts them to adore only the One Allah and "not to diminish measure and weight." "Oh my people," he repeats, "give just weight and measure in all fairness!" (XI, 85–86). The action of Allah the Creator is cited as an irrefutable example: "He raised the heaven on high and set the balance of all things, so that you should not transgress it" (LV, 6–8). The Koranic conception of the Day of Judgment is that day on which the "right scales" will be established to weigh the deeds of men, for it is announced in the name of Allah: "Our reckoning shall suffice" (XXI, 48).

These and similar appeals and prescriptions express the personal interests of Meccan traders, who continually suffered under the lack of commercial honesty among the leaders of caravan traffic

* [Popular name of the Biblical *Yitrō* (Jethro), "father-in-law" to Moses.]

and of usury.* We have already stressed the Koran's condemnation of those who cheat in weighing (LXXXIII, 1–3).

Historical tradition places Mohammed and nearly all his Meccan followers in the middle class or the needy strata of the population, who suffered personally from the exactions of the "Quraishites of the Center." Mohammed himself was of the Hāshim clan which was neither rich nor influential, so that it is understandable that both he and his entourage should become steeped in the preoccupations of the middle-class merchants and small traders of Mecca.

The activities of the first Moslems in Mecca ended in complete failure. There is no reason to believe that they set up any kind of organization in their native city. Besides faith in the religious teachings of the Koran, they had to perform two practical duties: the *ṣalā* and the *zakā,* "praying" and paying a "purifying" tax. Mohammed was not always able to preach publicly; his followers had to gather secretly somewhere in the suburbs or even in "deep clefts" to hear him and to pray, for fear of persecution. According to the *Sīra,* the Moslems found themselves in such dire straits that Mohammed was forced to send some of them away to seek protection with the Christian Negus of Ethiopia. Those remaining in Mecca under Mohammed's leadership were placed under a boycott by the Meccans, who refused to intermarry or to transact business with them. A significant point was the inability of the families of the Moslems to offer them any aid or comfort, for the economic dependence of Meccans upon the "Quraishites of the Center" was stronger than any ties of kith and kin.

The main reason for the failure of Islam in Mecca is to be sought in the social essence of this religious doctrine. Inequality in property and social status is represented in the Koran as the very order established by Allah, which thus could not be abolished or tampered with. Slavery too is considered as a permanent social institution.** To settle accounts with the rich and powerful is a

* [Quite a different view on this question is taken by W. Montgomery Watt, *op. cit.,* pp. 296–299.]

** [For a much more detailed and more nuanced treatment of this problem, see R. Brunschvig's article "Abd" in the *Encyclopedia of Islam* (new edition), Vol. I.]

task relegated to the imaginary world beyond the grave. Once they enter Paradise, the just will be free from the sorrows of earthly life and of any material needs, but in order to become a righteous one on earth and a dweller in the celestial realms after death, it is mandatory to be always "obedient" and "patient." These virtues, according to the Koran, are just as essential as faith in Allah and in his apostle.

The early *sūrāt* of the Koran preserve certain verses decrying riches and the rich, who are typically greedy, mean and cruel; they "devour" the property of orphans and drive away the poor with insults. This type of protest against inequality in property attracted a few slaves and needy freemen to the new religion, but, as the Koran shows, they were to be disappointed: the prophet of Islam proposed no transformation of the existing socio-economic conditions, promising an improvement in the afterlife only. The existing inequality and tyranny are justified in the Koran, in the name of Allah, as follows: "And thus, in each township we made the notables the sinners thereof, who would continue in their crooked ways therein" (VI, 123).

Islam had failed to gain social support in Mecca, either from the town's inhabitants or from the bedouin of the adjacent districts. Moreover, the "Quraishites of the Center" were in direct opposition to the new religion, and persecuted its followers.

According to tradition, Mohammed began his life as a prophet in the year 610 A.D. It took him twelve years to become convinced of the utter impossibility of success in his native city. The attempt to gain a following in neighboring Ṭā'if also miscarried; indeed, he was met with a hail of stones by its inhabitants. Tradition states that, on his way back to Mecca, Mohammed preached to a crowd of jinns in order to regain his self-control.

The first Moslems found the solution to their problem in deciding to emigrate to Yathrib, Medina. This migration *(hijra)* occurred in the autumn of the year 622.

Yathrib (which was probably also known as Medina prior to the *hijra*) was an extensive oasis in which the arable land was limited to the east and west by *ḥarra* areas and to the north and south by spurs of a mountain range. On the plain of the oasis were scattered several local tribes and a number of *diyār* (a *dār* being a group of dwellings inhabited by members of a clan), separated by cultivated fields, gardens, orchards and palm groves. The basic population of Medina consisted of its three so-called Jewish tribes, the Quainuqā‘, the Quraiẓa and the Naḍīr, and of two Arab tribes, the Aus and the Khazraj. There were also other small tribes and clans of a similar status to the Meccan and Ṭa'ifite *aḥlāf*. The ancient tradition of the Medina "Jews" as direct descendants of settlers from Palestine, who had left their homeland in the first century A.D., after the (first) Jewish War, is doubtful. The Medina "Jews" (at least the majority) were actually native Arabs practicing the Judaic religion. They spoke Arabic, perhaps in some local dialect which included Hebrew words and idioms, and were connoisseurs of pre-Islamic Arabic poetry, some of them being Arabic poets themselves. Their clan and tribal organization was the same as that of the Arabs.

The Medinese "Jewish" tribes were counted as the most ancient settlers of Yathrib, while the Arab tribes of Aus and Khazraj were genealogically connected with the south Arabian tribes and had arrived in the oasis later, when much of its area (perhaps most of it) was already occupied by the "Jews." The "Jews" were mainly agriculturalists, though some were craftsmen; their jewelry was highly prized, as was the work of the Medinese "Jewish" armorers, bought chiefly by bedouin. Certain sources report that the "Jews" had a more advanced irrigational and agricultural system than the Arabs in their gardens and fields, were more industrious and reached a higher standard of living.

It may be assumed that the Aus and Khazraj, who were also farmers, felt a need for more arable land, though we have no data to show that they suffered for the lack of it, for the oasis proper, as well as the areas between the *ḥarras,* contained sufficient arable land, though it was difficult to cultivate and particularly to irrigate. The two Arab tribes of Aus and Khazraj were in frequent conflict, which sometimes resulted in prolonged fighting. Success in such battles frequently depended on support given by one or other of the "Jewish" tribes.

Militarily, the Medinese "Jews" were weaker than the Arabs and thus reconciled to the status of seeking the alternate protection of either the Aus or the Khazraj. Like all followers of Judaism, however, they awaited the advent of the Messiah, when their power and State would be restored, in a none too distant future. The Medinese Arabs presumably felt these expectations of the "Jews" as a threat to themselves, and therefore accepted the Meccan Mohammed as their own prophet who might well play the part of an Arab Messiah. Such speculations, however, hardly correspond to historical reality and are simply theories of European scholars.

In fact, even prior to the rise of Islam, a certain sect of Christianity was common among the Arab tribes of Medina. It is known that there were monks among these tribes, some of whom played an active part in the armed conflicts between the Aus and Khazraj. The very name *anṣār,* given to the Medinese followers of Mohammed, is from the root *n.ṣ.r.,* as is the name for the Christians, *Naṣāra*.*

Moslem tradition itself acknowledges the *anṣār* as active in Medina for several years before the *hijra.* Like the Christian sectarians, they did not recognize the divinity of Christ and merely considered him an outstanding prophet. They could therefore accept Islam with its dogmas of a One God and a Last Judgment, and negotiations between Mohammed and the *anṣār* began two or three years prior to the *hijra.*

The Medinese Arabs were hostile to the dominant élite of the Meccan Quraishites, probably due mainly to the usurious practices of the Meccans, already reaching out to Medina. The Medinese were therefore quite disposed to accept in their midst the prophet of monotheism who was at odds with Mecca's leaders. A

* [Modern western research holds that the name *"ansār"* dates only from the time after Mohammed's arrival at Medina, though its choice could have been influenced by the similarity of the word *"nasāra."*]

point of some importance may also have been the fact that Amīna, the mother of Mohammed, was herself a native Medinese.

By emigrating to Medina, among tribes who were far from friendly, the Meccan Moslems broke all their ties with their tribe and kinsmen, and became their foes. In order to avoid the unenviable position of being *"ṭarīds"* in Medina, the Meccan emigrants performed a formal act of voluntary severance of all blood relationship with their own tribesmen. This act is represented in the *Sīra* as permitted to Mohammed by his uncle, 'Abbās. The Meccan emigrants were known in Medina as *muhājirūn*, people who had accomplished the *hijra*, whereas the Medinese who accepted the religious authority of Mohammed retained their name of *anṣar*.

The *muhājirūn* and the *anṣār* together formed an organization known as the "Community of the Faithful" *(umma),* distinguished from other groups in Arabia firstly by the fact that all its members belonged to one religion. The leader of the *umma* was a man whose authority derived from the fact that he was a religious teacher and thus in constant touch with Allah. This body was above any tribe or clan limits and membership was open to all who accepted its tenets.

The Moslem *umma,* grouping the faithful, was a theocratic organization; its members believed that Allah himself was their ruler through the mediation of his apostle, who assured them that he was receiving orders and instructions from Allah concerning not only political and public affairs but also his own personal behavior (in such matters as his wives).

According to the *Sīra,* Mohammed arrived in Medina at the invitation of representatives of the Khazraj tribe and became a guest of this tribe. However, he was by no means simply a *dakhīl,* a man under the protection of some foreign tribe. On the contrary, he at once assumed an independent status, which tradition recounts that he achieved by concluding a treaty, in his position as the leader of the *muhājirūn* and of the first *anṣār,* with the Medinese Jews and with the Arab tribes, before these had become subjected to his power.

No more than a few years after the *hijra* the entire Arab population of Medina were members of the Moslem community, and the Jewish tribes had been expelled and in part exterminated. As a religious teacher in constant communion with Allah, Mohammed fulfilled the task of ruler of Medina as well as judge and war leader.

The *umma,* the Moslem community, united the "faithful," *mu'minūn,* of whom the upper section, the *muhājirūn,* provided the leaders of the community, while the *anṣār,* who were in the majority, remained in a subordinate position. In the Koran, the "faithful" or *mu'minūn* are contrasted with the *muslimūn,* the merely obedient or those who submit, who were politically dependent on the community, obeying the leadership and paying the *zakā* to the communal treasury.

The Koran considers yet another category of people who seem to have played a role of some importance in the political life of Medina, the *munāfiqūn,* usually rendered as "hypocrites," though it can also mean "waverers" or "doubters." They are mentioned with obvious antipathy: "Hypocrites spring from each other; they enjoin what is evil, forbid what is just, and tighten their purse strings. They forsook Allah and Allah forsook them. In truth, the hypocrites are loose people. Allah has promised the hypocrites, male and female, and the unfaithful, the fire of Gehenna, where they will dwell forever ... And Allah has cursed them" (IX, 68–69). *Sūra* LXIII, entitled "the Hypocrites," is concerned solely with denouncing them and warning the community against their intrigues. In this *sūra* we learn that the *munāfiqūn* stood against the leadership of the *umma,* voicing doubts as to the authenticity of Mohammed's prophetic mission and opposing material aid for his cause. They were former members of the *umma* who had left it later: "They believed and then renounced their faith" (LXIII, 3).

The Medinese *sūrāt* give particular attention to property and protection of owner's rights. Crimes against property were severely punished: "Thieves, male and female, should have their hands cut off in reprisal for what they have stolen and as a warning from Allah" (V, 42). The rights of a successor to property left after death are detailed, and the laws concerning division of inheritance forsee all degrees of kinship and marriage relationship, with precise definition of the share to which each relation is entitled (as, for instance, in IV, 8–15). The same *sūra* displays concern for the property interests of young orphans: their guardians are forbidden, under pain of punishment in Hell, to appropriate what belongs to the orphans or to squander it, or to replace "what is of good quality with things that are worthless (IV, 2). The guardians of minors or the feeble-minded are directed to feed and clothe them, and to treat them well ("give them good advice," IV, 4).

In family relationships, the Koran sanctifies the dominant position of man. Woman, although not totally without rights, is subjected to man and dependent upon him. "Men have authority over women because Allah has made the one superior to the other, and because they spend their wealth to maintain them" (IV, 38); "men are above women in degree" (II, 228).

The Koran shows no trace of any survival of matriarchy or polyandry—the family is always patrilocal—but sanctifies, and confirms in law, the well established custom of polygamy. Permission to marry several wives is related to the protection of female orphans: "But if you fear to be unjust to an orphan, then marry such as seem good to you; marry two, three or four women. But if you fear to lose equality among them, marry one, or else marry those that have come into your possession by your own right hand" (IV, 3). This rather ambiguous verse of the Koran gave occasion to the broadest interpretations, but one should note that it expresses approval of monogamy, which corresponded entirely to existing relations of property and to the best interests of the "faithful."*

The Koran sanctifies another widely accepted usage, concubinage with slaves, which was actually preferred to marriage with a woman of another religion: "The believing slave is better than the idolatress (wife)" (II, 220). A child of the slave, recognized by the father, had the same rights as children born from lawful wives.

Corporal punishment is prescribed for adultery: "As to the adulterer and the adulteress, each should get one hundred strokes"

(p. 199)

* [For another view on Mohammed's attitude toward polygamy, see W. Montgomery Watt, *op. cit.*, pp. 274–277.]

(XXIV, 2). The culprits could then marry only their own kind, or else polytheists. Accusation of adultery, however, had to be sustained by four eyewitnesses. Non-Soviet biographers of Mohammed maintain that only false witnesses would thus be possible. Those "who cast an accusation of immodesty" and cannot produce the four witnesses are considered guilty of calumny and given eighty strokes of the lash. If a husband accuses his wife of infidelity and cannot produce witnesses, he must call four times on Allah as a witness and declare that the curse of Allah be on his head if he lies, while the wife is free from accusation and punishment if she herself calls upon Allah four times to witness her innocence, and likewise declares that the curse of Allah be on her if she is lying (XXIV, 3–9). *Sūra* XXIV—the "*Sūra* of Light"—and its prescriptions as to the conduct of women is explained in Moslem tradition by reference to a curious adventure of 'A'isha, the young wife of the aging Mohammed. Following him on one of his campaigns, she disappeared unnoticed when the troops were breaking camp and about to continue their journey, returning to Medina only the next day in the company of a young Arab who, according to her story, had found her on the way and lifted her onto his camel. To stop the rumors and comments aroused by this, Mohammed brought down a proper revelation by Allah, embodied in this *sūra*.

Some orientalists (outside the USSR) remark that the Koran's attitude to women is that of a jealous husband. Authors hostile to Islam (especially Christian missionaries) explain the marriage and family laws of the Koran as due chiefly or even solely to Mohammed's sensuality, which, they say, became pathological toward the end of his life. Actually, as historical tradition shows, most of his marriages were politically expedient: his more influential wives were the daughters of two of his closest and most active companions, Abu-Bakr and 'Omar. His marriage to Zainab, the divorced wife of his adopted son Zaid, was similarly useful, as were those marriages into tribes with whom he concluded alliances or which he brought under his power. In Medina, Mohammed was married simultaneously to nine women,[31] and his polygamy could well indeed have been due to his position as ruler of this considerable city.

The Koran gives the husband the paramount right of divorce, the initiative being his. The wife has neither the right nor the opportunity to rid herself of an unwanted husband, but can only lodge complaints against him. However, as the Koran pays far more attention to protection of property than to that of the person, some interest is shown the property of the divorced wife: "And give the wives their bridal price as a free gift"; if the wife chooses to leave some of this to the husband, though, lawfully it is his (IV, 3). This last was later the excuse for many a husband to extort property and money from his wife. The husband has no further claim to anything which he has given to a wife, but the immediate reservation is made of "Allah's restrictions," which permit a husband to stipulate a price for agreeing to divorce his wife (II, 231).

Exact determination of paternity is particularly important in the Koran. There are elaborate rules determining the time a divorced wife must wait before remarriage, so that she is in a position where she is unable "to hide that which Allah created in her womb" (II, 228). These delays, encumbent upon both divorcees and widows, were such as to ensure exact knowledge of the paternity of any child, as well as the precise determination of any property heirs.

The Koranic legislation assures the dominance of men both in the family and in the wider society. Obstinate or refractory wives may and in fact should be reprimanded, beaten and deprived of conjugal intimacy: "Those (wives) whose insubordination you fear, admonish them and leave them (alone) in their beds, and even strike them" (IV, 38).

Unfaithful women ("those that commit the loathsome thing"), provided that their unfaithfulness has been attested by four witnesses, are to be dealt with as follows: "Keep them indoors until death has calmed them down or until Allah has arranged a way for them" (IV, 19).

Marriage is prohibited not only between blood relations but also between foster brethren; a man may marry neither his mother, sister or daughter nor his foster mother or her daughters, nor two sisters at the same time (IV, 26–27). This law also was to protect property owners as consanguineous marriages led to complications in questions of inheritance. Also the Arabs of course realised the degenerative effects of consanguineous marriage.

THE POLICIES OF THE MEDINESE COMMUNITY

The leader of the Medinese Community of the Faithful was "the apostle of Allah," who enjoyed unquestionable authority as the sole representative of Allah on Earth, transmitting to mortals not only divine truth but also the decrees and instructions of Allah on current political and public events and even on the personal affairs of individual believers. Moslem interpreters of the Koran *(mufassirūn)* related the several *sūrāt* and verses to definite historical happenings; these interpretations were also accepted by European biographers of Mohammed and historians of Islam, even though they are quite subjective, since the Koran contains no clear reports of events, only hints (themselves often nebulous). Nevertheless we may assume that some of the divine revelations in the Koran were faithful expressions of the thoughts and intentions of the community's leaders, among whom Moslem tradition places foremost Mohammed's two closest companions, Abu-Bakr and 'Omar. This influence upon the prophet is represented as so active and effective that Sprenger thought it possible to single out 'Omar as the true "founder of Islam"; at all events, the leading "triumvirate" of Mohammed, abu-Bakr and 'Omar wielded by far the greatest power in the Medinese community.

The chief manifestation of foreign policy on the part of this community was its struggle with Mecca for the Meccan sanctuary and for predominance over western Arabia. According to the *Sīra,*[32] in his first year in Medina Mohammed was already sending out his followers to attack the Meccan caravans on the trade routes. At first these raids were probably aimed simply at obtaining booty for the homeless and needy *muhājirūn,* but the very next year the leadership of the *umma* embarked upon economic warfare against Mecca. Attacks on Meccan caravans promised not merely rich booty but also interference with the normal commercial activities of the Meccans, their principal means of subsistance. Very soon the Meccans were complaining that "Mohammed and his followers have made our commerce one-eyed,"[33] that is to say, reduced it by half.

In 624, the Medinese "faithful" carefully prepared a raid on a large Meccan caravan arriving from Syria, but the experienced and cautious leader of this caravan, Abu-Sufyān, guessed the intention of the Medinese and sent message of the threat to Mecca. The Meccans sallied out to protect their merchandise, and encountered Mohammed's forces near the wells of Badr. The caravan had escaped, abu-Sufyān having taken it by an alternative route along the Red Sea coast to Mecca, but battle was meanwhile joined at Badr and the Meccans defeated.

The next year, the Meccan Quraishites, with their bedouin allies, set out on a campaign against Medina. At that time the Community of the Faithful was in discord and the "hypocrites" had renewed their activities, so that part of Mohammed's army deserted him on the march out of Medina. The fight at Oḥod (Uḥud) ended in disaster for the Medinese troops.

In 626, the Quraishites, wishing to exploit their victory and their numerical superiority by dealing a decisive blow to the *umma,* marched against Medina a second time with their bedouin allies. Fearing another defeat, the Medinese Arabs refrained from taking the field and resorted to a defensive strategy. Arabic historical tradition attributes exceptional importance to a new tactic inaugurated by the Medinese: following the advice of a Persian, Salmān al-Farisi, a former slave who had turned Moslem, they dug a trench in which they positioned their archers, thus depriving the Quraishites, by this hitherto unheard of mode of defence, of the use of their bedouin cavalry.

The siege of Medina continued indecisively. The winter rains and a harsh north wind (according to tradition) caused suffering among the besiegers; the Meccans, and especially the bedouin, started grumbling. The most important factor, however, was the success of Medinese agents in rekindling the old grudge of the bedouin against their Meccan overlords, the Quraishites, who had led them in this thankless and profitless venture. Secret negotiations between Mohammed's representatives and the chieftains of the powerful Ghaṭafān tribe resulted in the withdrawal of the bedouin from the camp of the besiegers. The Meccans alone were not numerous enough to win and thus had to raise the siege.

Following this Meccan failure, the leaders of the *umma* became more active among the bedouin tribes, securing their support for Medina.

Meanwhile, the more far-sighted and realistic of the leaders of the Quraishites had formed a more correct estimate of the true balance of forces and of the respective potential of the contending sides, with the consequent development of a desire to reach some form of agreement with the Community of the Faithful and thus with Mohammed.

In 628, the Medinese faithful made a very important move with far-reaching political consequences. In the season of pilgrimage they went on a *ḥajj* (pilgrimage) to Mecca, thus demonstrating that the Ka'ba was still the most revered shrine for them too, where the performance of traditional religious rituals remained obligatory. In other words, the followers of the new religion and members of the new religious organization were not trying to reduce the importance of Mecca as a religious center; this attitude would reassure the Quraishites as to their material interests.

In the valley of Ḥudaibiya, not far from Mecca, an armed detachment of Quraishites blocked the road of the Medinese pilgrims. Perhaps the Quraishite leadership feared incitement of the Meccan population and dangerous disorders if the unexpected pilgrims were let in. However, a written agreement was reached in Ḥudaibiya according to which the Medinese would be allowed to perform the *ḥajj* the following year; the Meccans promised to leave their town while the Medinese made their pilgrimage in it.

This agreement or "armistice" (as it is sometimes described) in Ḥudaibiya was interpreted by Moslem tradition as an outstanding diplomatic victory for Mohammed, for the leadership of Mecca had recognized the Community of the Faithful as an equal party, an organization existing both *de facto* and *de jure*.

By the time the Ḥudaibiya agreement was concluded, the Community of the Faithful was already in possession of the entire territory of the Medina oasis. The *muhājirūn,* who formed the upper and most influential stratum of the community, had received the lands, dwellings and property of the three despoiled

"Jewish" tribes. Moslem feudalistic historians gave much attention to the religious disputes between the Medinese rabbis and Mohammed. The rabbis accused the Arabian religious teacher of lack of knowledge of the "Torah"—his preachings on biblical themes would often provoke their malevolent scorn—but Mohammed found a way out by accusing the Judaic scribes of falsifying the holy writ. The Koran bears clear traces of typical religious disputations between representatives of rival religions: "Among these are simpletons who do not know the Scripture, only lies and their own fancies. Woe to those who write the writ with their own hands, and then say: 'It is from Allah'" (II, 73).

Religious disputes and disagreements, although they strengthened the mutual antipathy, were not the sole or even the principal cause of the expulsion and partial extermination of "Jewish" tribes from the Medina oasis. The main reason for the hostile attitude of the leadership of the Community of the Faithful towards the Medinese "Jews" was that they possessed well-cultivated lands, fortified settlements and valuable property, while many of the *muhājirūn* were still indigent, living in the homes of their adopted Medinese brothers without even weapons of their own. Moreover, the feud between the faithful and the "Jews" was not merely religious but also political, for the "Jews" would not participate in the campaigns and battles of the faithful, sympathizing with the Meccan Quraishites and maintaining friendly relations with them in secret.

The first to be assailed by the faithful in Medina was the "Jewish" tribe of *Quainuqā'*. After the battle of Badr, Mohammed, in his strength and confidence, accused the tribe of violating the treaty concluded in the year of the *hijra* by holding secret negotiations with the head of the Meccan Quraishites, Abu-Sufyān. The Qainuqā' tribe offered no armed resistance and emigrated, [seeking asylum] with their coreligionists at first in *Wādi-'l-Qura* (in Ḥijāz) and then in Adhri'āt* in Syria. The dwellings and cultivated fields of the Qainuqā' were given to the needy *muhājirūn*. The booty included many swords, spears, shields and mail manufactured by armorers of the expelled tribe whose ex-

* [Actually, Biblical Edre'i, in the Bashan.]

pulsion, however, was now to result in lack of sufficient new weapons in Medina. The attempt to teach slaves to manufacture arms proved quite unsuccessful.

A second victim of the same policies was the "Jewish" tribe of *Nadīr* expelled from Medina six months after the battle at Mt. Oḥod. It was accused of the same crime as the Qainuqā' tribe, but was made to suffer even more, being forced to leave behind nearly all its movable property. The *Nadīr* emigrated to Khaibar (in Ḥijāz) and perhaps also to Adhri'āt, where the Qainuqā' had already settled. Their dwellings and lands were handed over to the last among the needy *muhājirūn*.

A tragic fate was reserved for the third of Medina's "Jewish" tribes, the *Quraiẓa*. After the siege of Medina, the Quraiẓa were accused of treason and of secret dealings with the enemy, and submitted to cruel reprisals. After a fortnight of siege in their fortified settlement, the tribe surrendered unconditionally. The men were slaughtered, the women and children sold into slavery: some were exchanged against weapons provided by the Najd bedouin. The property of this tribe was confiscated by the leadership of the Community of the Faithful.

The *umma* had now become the strongest and most numerous organization in the Medina oasis. The importance of the political opposition of the "hypocrites" was much reduced after the expulsion of the "Jewish" tribes. At Ḥudaibiya, Mohammed faced the Meccan Quraishites as the leader of a group which had to be reckoned with for both its military strength and its political influence.

In less than two years—after the Ḥudaibiya understanding and prior to the Moslem takeover of Mecca—the army of the Medina community sent out seventeen warlike expeditions; for most of these we have no details, but we know that each raiding party was a few hundred strong.

In spring 628, a campaign was launched against Khaibar, where there were "Jewish" farmers who had given aid and comfort to the Naḍīr after their expulsion from Medina. This was a raid for booty. Khaibar lay some 150 km northeast of Medina and was an agricultural oasis. Its population dwelt in seven *burj* (fortified townships), each consisting of a separate group of fortified dwellings. They were taken, one after the other, by the Medinese army, after a short siege. Another version of the tradition recounts that the Khaibaris quickly reached an agreement with Mohammed, promising to hand over each year half of the crops from their fields and palm groves in exchange for their freedom and possession of their lands and homes.

There was no question of dividing the lands of Khaibar among the raiders, and no desire to settle in Khaibar and farm it. The well-cultivated oasis was considered merely as common booty for all the faithful; the receipts in nature which it provided were divided, by the head of the community, in the same way as the *zakā* and *ṣadaqa* [alms]. The wives and retainers of the prophet were of course included in the distribution.

The agriculturalists of the Fadak oasis (whom unfounded tradition counts among the Arabian "Jews") did not wait to be attacked but approached Mohammed with a treaty similar to the one he had concluded with the Khaibaris. The income in nature from Fadak became the private property of Mohammed, since it was considered that the people of Fadak had submitted to him personally and had not been conquered "with the help of horse and camel."[34]

Some modern Moslem historians assume that Mohammed had developed a quite definite "northern policy," consisting of plans for Syria and Palestine, which he followed in his practical enterprises. It is true that soon after the unsuccessful siege of Medina by the Meccans there were some minor raids northward from Medina toward Syria and Palestine, but there is no reason to believe that these conform to any preconceived plan of conquest outside the boundaries of the Arabian Peninsula.

More important action was that taken against the large Hawāzin tribe, which roamed far and wide in the region of Ṭa'if. In order to ensure success in the forthcoming decisive struggle with Mecca, the Medina Community of the Faithful had to establish their influence over this tribe and make use of the political situation in Ṭa'if. In the Thaqīf tribe, which constituted the population of that city, there was a struggle between the two groups of the Banū-Malik and the Aḥlāf, the former being staunch partisans of economic and political cooperation with Mecca, while the latter opposed such pro-Meccan policies and could be considered as potential allies of Medina.[35] The Medinese pattern of gaining control over the tribes of northwestern Arabia as well as over the Hawāzin tribe and the city of Ṭa'if may be considered as the expression of a policy of encirclement of Mecca. For the same purpose, relations were furthered with Yamāma, where the Ḥanīfite prophet Musailima was then active.

Two years after Ḥudaibiya, many former bedouin allies of Mecca had become dependent on the Medina community. Some of these bedouin tribes paid the *zakā* tax, and in case of conflict with the Meccans were to take the field as allies of the Medinese.

The Koran represents these new allies in a definite though subordinate role in the military and political events of the time. "The bedouin said: 'We have come to believe.' Say: 'You did not come to believe,' but you may assert: 'We have submitted' because faith has not yet entered your hearts. But if you will obey Allah and his apostle, Allah shall in no way detract from your deeds" (XLIX, 14). This verse defines quite exactly the difference between "faith" *(īmān)* and "submission" *(islām)*. The "faithful" *(mu'minūn)* were the members of the Medina community, whereas the *muslimūn* (literally the "Moslems") were merely those who had "submitted" and accepted the leadership of the *umma*. At that time, not all such "Moslems" had been converted to the new religion; many were simply following the guidance of the Medina Community of the Faithful.

After Ḥudaibiya, the balance of forces shifted more and more in favor of the Medina community. As Mecca lost its hold on the Ḥijāzi tribes the more realistic among the Meccan Quraishites began to side with the Medinese. Historical tradition has it that the year after Ḥudaibiya, when *muhājirūn* and *anṣār* performed the *ḥajj* to Mecca, certain prominent Meccans secretly became members of their community; among these were Khālid ibn-al-Walīd, who had commanded the Meccan cavalry at the battle of Oḥod and was to become one of the outstanding war leaders in the period of Arab conquests, and also 'Amr ibn-al-'Aṣ, who was also to become a prominent commander and political leader.

By this time, the leaders of Mecca, correctly estimating the new situation, decided to start negotiations for a final agreement with their counterparts in the Medina community. Abū-Sufyān visited Mohammed in Medina and made a pact with him (secret for the time being) to surrender Mecca on condition that the city be the religious center of the new religion. To celebrate the success of his negotiations, Mohammed married a daughter of Abū-Sufyān, and this marriage, as was customary at that time, was the formal expression of political alliance. Thus, in 630, the Medinese *mu'minūn,* accompanied by their bedouin *muslimūn,* marched on Mecca and "conquered" the city. The "victory" was simply a military demonstration, a kind of parade of the *umma's* armed forces, which nobody had the slightest intention of opposing.

The *Sīra* relates that when the Medinese army camped near Mecca early that morning Abū-Sufyān entered Mohammed's tent to confirm the already concluded treaty. Of course the *Sīra,* which was written at the order of the Caliph of Baghdad, attributes to Mohammed's uncle 'Abbās an exaggerated role of intermediary and protector of Abū-Sufyān, whom 'Omar and other influential *muhājirūn* apparently wanted dealt with very harshly.

As the leader of the Meccan Quraishites, Abū-Sufyān is portrayed, significantly, in the *Sīra* as displaying a political cynicism both prior to and after the final agreement with Mohammed near Mecca. Though gladly accepting the dogma of Allah's unity—indeed, the tribal deity of the Quraishites was known by the name of Allah even before Islam—the shrewd, experienced leader and representative of Mecca treated the other dogma, that of Mohammed's divine and prophetic mission, with obvious irony.

The surrender of Mecca, in the eyes of the leading group of the Quraishites, was far from being an unconditional surrender. This well thought out agreement not only preserved the religious significance of the city but also enhanced and enlarged it, as it was to become the center of a fast-spreading new religion for which the Ka'ba was the main shrine and pilgrimage to it (the *ḥajj*) a fundamental obligation for all Moslems. The Meccans thus expected new and still greater profits from the numerous visitors to their city. The idols that stood around the Ka'ba were declared insignificant and removed; some European researchers doubt the existence of such idols in pagan Mecca, but tradition, again unproved, asserts that there were nearly as many as the days of the year. Even after the abolition, if any, of idols, however, the famous fetish of the "Black Stone," an object of cult and reverence, continued.

The main and most important point of this agreement, though, was the inclusion of the Meccans in the Community of the Faithful as *mu'minūn,* members on a status with the *muhājirūn* and the *anṣār*. Moslem tradition asserts that Mohammed gave preferment to these neophytes in the division of loot, replying to the grumbling of his Medinese companions by explaining that they should "attract their hearts" to the new faith.

Moslem feudalistic historians obviously simplify events, speeding up their sequence, when they claim that nearly all Arabian tribes were converted to Islam during the "year of delegations." According to this concept, delegations of tribes from all regions of Arabia, near and far, streamed toward Medina after the "conquest" of Mecca, announcing that they had embraced Islam. Mohammed then sent his representatives to these tribes to explain the tenets of the new religion and to exact the *zakā* tax collected for the benefit of the treasury of the faithful. This simplified picture of events does not agree even with historical fact as related by the same Moslem historians; the entire concept was simply a representation of the belief that Mohammed was "the prophet of the Arabs," and, therefore, as such, the entire population of Arabia must have come under his power and under his influence (if not in reality, then at least in the imagination of later generations).

After Mecca's surrender, the dominion of the Medino-Meccan community extended rapidly over the neighboring tribes, then over the district of Ṭa'if, and lastly over the town of Ṭa'if itself. The Thaqīf tribe of this town marched out together with the Hawāzin tribe and encamped in the valley of Ḥunain. In order to boost the low morale of his army, the ra'īs of the Hawāzin ordered the wives, children and cattle of his warriors to be placed behind their ranks. Many of these warriors, however, were against resisting Mohammed, and, with the support of the Aḥlaf of Ṭa'if, took to their heels at the very start of the fighting. The Banū-Malik also retreated very soon, taking refuge behind the walls of their city, so that women, children and cattle became the booty of the victors.

Tradition estimates some 20,000 bedouin to have taken part in the battle of Ḥunain valley under the leadership of the Meccan-Medinese community against the tribes of Thaqīf and Hawāzin; this battle was thus considered the first in which bedouin sided in large numbers with the *umma*. After the fight and a short siege, Ṭa'if was taken and the shrine of the local goddess *al-Lāt** destroyed.

Thereafter, a few raids were launched northward, in which, tradition has it, Mohammed concluded treaties with the inhabitants of various settlements, the conditions of which coincided with the obligations accepted by those countries conquered later by the Arabs, in the time of the "orthodox" Caliphs. It is quite possible that Mohammed's treaties were simply later forgeries to justify the taxation policy adopted in the days of the first Caliphs by attesting the Prophet's authority.

Balādhuri relates that in the last two years of his life Mohammed concluded various agreements with the populations of Tabūk, Aila (The Biblical Elath), Maqna, Adhruḥ and Jarbā', in which the inhabitants were to pay a poll tax. The "Jewish" inhabitants of the township of Maqna** received a charter from Mohammed stating, *inter alia*, that the finery, slaves, horses and mail of the inhabitants were to be his, except such as he would leave at their disposal. "Moreover, you must provide one quarter of the yield of your palm trees, one quarter of the fish you catch. and one quarter of what your women spin."[36] The authenticity of this charter, however, which did not survive even in copy, is open to gravest doubts.

Thus Islam arose in Arabia, a new ideology reflecting considerable changes in Arab society, namely inequality in property, slavery and development of exchanges. The rise of this new ideology was due to the formation of a slave-holding regime within a decaying primitive-communal society.

* [*Allāt,* contraction of al-ilāt, "The Goddess."]

** [Like those of the oases of Adhruḥ and Jarbā, the others being Christians; cf. Philip Hitti, *History of the Arabs,* p.119, quoting Balādhuri.]

With the new ideology appeared a new organization, the Community of the Faithful, the very principle of which was in opposition to any tribe and clan grouping. This community became the organizational basis of the Arab State, giving clear confirmation of the thesis that "the first attempt to form a State consists in the severance of tribal and clan connections."[37] The main aim of the newly formed Arab State was now to ensure by armed might the economic subservience of the laboring majority to the wealthy minority.[38]

[1] *Le Coran. Traduction selon un essai de reclassement des Sourates par Régis Blachere,* Paris, 1949-1951.

[2] A. Krymskii, *Istochniki dlya istorii Mokhammeda i literatura o nem* (Sources for the History of Mohammed, and Literature about Mohammed). Moscow, 1902. *Historians of the Middle East,* ed. by B. Lewis and P.M. Holt, pp. 23–34. London, 1962. [The Materials used by *ibn-Ishāq,* by W. Montgomery Watt.]

[3] J. Fück, *Die arabischen Studien in Europa,* pp. 4–6, Leipzig, 1955. I. Kritchen, *Peter the Venerable and Islam.* Princeton, 1964.

[4] L. Caetani, *Studi di storia orientale,* Vol. I, pp. 35 – 45. Milan, 1911.

[5] A. Sprenger, *Das Leben und die Lehre des Mohammed,* Bd 1–3. Berlin, 1861–1869.

[6] For more details see: *Proiskhozhdenie islama.* Khrestomatiya, sost. Evg. Evg. Belyaev ("The Origins of Islam." An Anthology ed. by. E. Belyaev), pp. 121–126. Moscow-Leningrad, 1931.

[7] W. Muir, *The Life of Mahomet,* Vols 1–4. London, 1856–1861.

[8] H. Grimme, *Mohammed.* Münster, 1892.

[9] F. Buhl, *Das Leben Muhammeds.* Heidelberg, 1955.

[10] W. Montgomery Watt, *Muhammad at Mecca.* Oxford, 1953; *Muhammad at Medina.* Oxford, 1956.

[11] M. Gaudefroy-Demombynes, *Mahomet.* Paris, 1957. [Of greater significance, perhaps, is an earlier work by the same author: *Le Monde Musulman,* in *Histoire du Monde,* sous la direction de E. Cavaignac, tome VIII, pp. 29–451. Paris, 1931.]

[12] L. Caetani, *Studi di Storia orientale,* Vol. III, p. 1

[13] V.V. Bartol'd, *Museilima* (Musailima). – "Izvestiya AN SSSR" (Bull. of the Academy of Sciences of the USSR), No. 12 – 15, p. 486. 1925.

[14] I.Yu. Krachkovskii, *Tākhā Khusein o doislamskoi poezii arabov i ego kritika* (Ṭāhā Ḥusain on the pre-Islamic Poetry of the Arabs and his Criticism). – Izbrannye sochineniya (Selected Works), t. III, pp. 189–222. Moscow-Leningrad, 1956.

[15] Cf. N.A. Smirnov, *Ocherki istorii izucheniya islama v SSSR* (Essays in the History of Islamic Studies in the USSR), pp. 79 – 80 Moscow, 1954.

[16] *"Ateist"* ("Atheist," a periodical), No. 58. Moscow, 1930.

[17] S.P. Tolstov, *Ocherki pervonachal'nogo islama* (Essays on Primitive Islam). – "Sovetskaya Etnografiya" (Soviet Ethnography, a review), No. 2. 1932.

[18] Cf. *Voprosy istorii i literatury stran zarubezhnogo Vostoka,* sb. statei ("Problems of History and Literature in the Lands of the non-Russian Orient," a collection of articles), pp. 136–156. Moscow, 1960.

[19] L. Klimovich, *Sushchestvoval li Mokhammed?* (Did Mohammed Exist?) – "Voinstvuyushchii ateism" (Militant Atheism, a publication), No. 2–3. 1931.

[20] K.Ch. Snouck Hurgronje, *Mekka in the Latter Part of the 19th Century.* London, 1931.

[21] *Annales quos scripsit abu Djafar Mohammed ibn Djarir at-Tabari cum aliis, ed. M.J. de Goeje,* Lugduni Batavorum, Vol. I, p. 1271. 1879. (Quoted henceforward as *Ṭabari.*)

[22] H. Lammens, La Mecque à la veille de l'hégire, p. 174. Beirut, 1924.

[23] *History of Muhammed's Campaigns by Aboo Abdallah Mohammad ibn Omar al-Wakidy,* ed. by A. Kremer, p. 196. Calcutta, 1856. (Quoted henceforward as *Wāqidi.*)

[24] Ṭabari, p. 1339.

[25] *Ibidem,* p. 1586.

[26] Friedrich Engels, *The Origins of the Family, Private Property and the State* (in Russian) *Proiskhozhdenie sem'i, chastnoi sobstvennosti i gosudarstva* in *K. Marks i. F. Engel's Sochineniya* (Marx and Engels, Collected Works), 2nd ed., t. 21, p. 111.

[27] *Ibidem.*

[28] Ṭabari, pp. 1097–1098.

[29] *Ibidem,* p. 1097.

[30] H. Lammens, *Les "Aḥabis et l'organisation militaire de Mecque au siècle de l'hégire,*–"Journal Asiatique," Volume VIII. Paris, 1916.

[31] M. Gaudefroy-Demombynes, Mahomet, pp. 242–253.

[32] *Das Leben Muhammed's nach Muhammed Ibn Ishâk bearbeitet von Abd el-Malik Ibn Hischâm.* Aus den Handschriften zu Berlin, Leipzig, Gotha und Leyden herausgegeben von Dr. Ferdinand Wüstenfeld, Bd. 1–2, pp. 416–432. Göttingen, 1858–1860. (Designated henceforward as *ibn-Isḥāq.*)

[33] Wākidi, p. 196.

[34] Ibn-Isḥāq, pp. 776–777.

[35] H. Lammens, *La cité arabe de Ta'if à la veille de l'hégire,* Ch. VIII. Beirut, 1922.

[36] N.A. Mednikov, *Palestina ot zavoevaniya ee arabami do krestovykh pokhodov po arabskim istochnikam* (Palestine from its Conquest by the Arabs until the Crusades, According to Arabic Sources), t. II.—"Pravoslavnyi Palestinskii sbornik" (Orthodox Collection on Palestine), t. XVI, vyp. 2, pp. 40–41. St. Petersburg, 1897–1903.

[37] Friedrich Engels, *The Origins of the Family, Private Property and the State,* in Russian, *Proiskhozhdenie sem'i, chastnoi sobstvennosti i gosudarstva,* in *K. Marks i Engel's Sochineniya,* 2nd ed. 5. 21, p. 111.

[38] Cf. K. Marks i. F. Engel's Sochineniya (Collected Works), 2nd ed., t. 36. p. 9.

CHAPTER III

THE FORMATION OF THE CALIPHATE

The vast dominion which became known in Europe as the "Caliphate"* was formed in the seventh century and much enlarged in the course of Arab conquests in the eighth, when the Arabs subjected the civilized countries of the Near and Middle East and North Africa to their rule.

SOURCES

The main sources for this period are the works of Ṭabari (died 923) and Balādhuri (died 892). The first, in his "History of Prophets and Kings"[1] *(Ta'rikh al-rusul w-al-mulūk),* expounded a "universal history" as understood by Arab-Moslem historians, who, beginning from the "Creation," told those myths traditionally connected with the names of Biblical patriarchs and prophets. These were followed by legendary and historical information on kings of ancient Iran and on Sassanid *shahin-shahs,* from Iranian sources, and lastly the history of the Arabs and the origins of Islam were given. As we have already noted, the events connected with Mohammed's activity are obscured by many myths and miracle tales; only after his death are the accounts free of the superstitious notion of constant interference of supernatural forces in human affairs. Starting from the year of the *hijra,* the "universal history" of Ṭabari assumes the shape of a chronicle, enumerating military and political events according to the years of the Moslem era. Since he wanted to collect the maxi-

* [Arabic *khalīfa* means merely the "lieutenant" or "successor" (of the Prophet), and as applied to a territorial structure or a regime it is indeed a European misnomer.]

mum amount of data, Ṭabari quite freely included mutually incompatible reports on one and the same event, in such cases leaving it to Allah to decide what is authentic and what not by adding the sacramental formula: "Allah knows best." Ṭabari indicates his sources exactly and cites the *isnād,* the list of those authorities who have transmitted the information, sometimes over a number of generations, starting from the testimony of an eyewitness or a contemporary report.

Besides the data he himself collected, Ṭabari made conscientious use of the compilations of historical tradition made by earlier authors (abu-Mikhnaf and others). In sheer abundance of information, his work ranks foremost among those sources for the history of the Caliphate in the seventh to ninth centuries; unfortunately, however, it consists of raw materials, never intended for submission to criticism or even to mere generalization. In its many volumes, Ṭabari's history served as a source for the European Arabists of the nineteenth century, and is still tremendously important today.

Balādhuri is an older contemporary of Ṭabari, but is a historian as well as a compilator, dealing critically with his data and drawing conclusions from them. In *Futūḥ al-Buldān* (The Conquest of the Lands),[2] which deals with the history of Arab conquests, Balādhuri not only related political and military events, but gave serious attention, particularly important to us, to some very valuable data on the economic and social conditions of the countries conquered by the Arabs.

The two authors are the most important early medieval Moslem historians in the Arabic language. Two further compilations of Moslem "universal histories" from the same period are *Kitāb al-akhbār al-ṭiwāl* (The Book of the Long Narratives) by Dīnawari (died 895) and the "History" (Ta'rīkh of Ya'qūbi (died 897)),[3] which include events and phenomena not mentioned in the more extensive historical works.

The works of Mas'ūdi provide a particularly interesting source. An outstanding historian, geographer and traveler (died 956), those books of his that have reached us—*Murūj al-dhahab wa-ma 'ādin al-jawhar* (Placers of Gold and Mines of Gems)[4] and *Kitāb al-tanbīh w-al-ishrāf* (Book of Warning and of Revision)—include much varied information on the culture, customs and beliefs of various peoples within the Caliphate and of countries having economic and political relations with the Caliphate.

Since all these historical writings are narrative in character, European orientalists have often pointed out that the abundance of data in such sources does not compensate for the almost complete lack of documentation. A happy exception is Egypt, where many papyri of official documents and business deeds of this period have been preserved, mainly from Upper Egypt with a few from the Delta, and none at all from Alexandria.

Medieval histories written by chroniclers in the conquered lands and those adjacent to them are useful as complementary works to those of Arabic historians, though themselves far inferior to the latter in the amount and value of their historical information. The most important of these are the chronicles in Greek, Syriac (Christian Aramaic) and Armenian.

MODERN LITERATURE

A specialized and comprehensive work on the history of the Arab conquests and the formation of the Caliphate, making careful use of Arabic sources, is that by Dennett.[5] Few books have been published on the conquest of each of the several countries, however, though of these the richest in factual data is Butler's work on the conquest of Egypt.[6]

Histories of the Arabs and Islam gave considerable attention to the problem of Arab conquests and the formation of the Caliphate. Factual military-political histories of the period of the four "orthodox" Caliphs are given in Gustav Weil's *History of the Caliphs,*[7] William Muir's *The Caliphate, Its Rise, Decline and Fall,*[8] August Müller's *Islam in the Orient and Occident,*[9] Clément Huart's *History of the Arabs*[10] and Philip Hitti's book of the same title.[11]

The "Annals of Islam" *(Annali dell'islam)* by Leone Caetani is a vast compilation of data taken from the works of Arabic-language historians. Ten volumes cover the period 622 - 661. Caetani translated his Arabic sources into Italian and compared and critically analyzed them. He also used the works of former

European orientalists dealing with the history of incipient Islam and the period of the four "orthodox" Caliphs, criticizing them severely and selecting the few he considered valuable. An "idealist" historian, he gave no particular attention to socio-economic phenomena.

A further large compilation of data from Arabic-language sources, translated into Russian, is the outstanding work by N. A. Mednikov, *Palestina ot zavoevaniya ee arabami do krestovykh pokhodov po arabskim istochnikam* (Palestine from its Conquest by the Arabs until the Crusades, According to Arabic Sources), in which the source material, from Arabic historians and geographers, is prefaced by a thoroughly detailed introduction including a critical review of the sources and a comparison of their data on historical events. This voluminous work contains exhaustive extracts from all the medieval Arabic historical and geographical literature published in Europe and in the Orient by the end of the nineteenth century. Mednikov concentrated particularly on information from medieval authors on the history of Syria, Lebanon and Palestine, and partly Egypt, in the period of Arab conquests and the formation of the Caliphate.

Still valuable to Russian readers is Bartol'd's scientific vulgarization, *Musul'manskii mir* (The World of Islam) (Petrograd, 1922), even though written from the standpoint of European bourgeois orientalism.

THE "RIDDA"

Mohammed died in Medina in 632, in the month of *rabīʿ al-awwāl*[12] (exact date unknown). At the news of the death of the prophet, one of the clans of the Medinese *anṣār* congregated at Saqīf banu-Ṣāʿid and indicated their readiness to swear obedience to their own chieftain, most probably as a demonstration of their dissatisfaction with Mohammed's friendly policy towards the newly converted Quraishites of Mecca.

At this gathering, the *anṣār* demanded equal rights and equal power with the Quraishites: two *amīrs* (commanders) should be placed at the head of the community, one from the *anṣār* and the other from the Quraishites. The *muhājirūn,* however, wishing to maintain the *anṣār* in a subordinate position, refused any greater concession than the election by the *anṣār,* from among their midst, of a *wazīr,* assistant, who would help the *amīr* chosen by the leaders of the community, though as soon as the old inter-clan rivalry manifested itself again among the *anṣār,* the *muhājirūn* at once withdrew even this concession.

Abu-Bakr, Mohammed's closest companion, was proclaimed chief of the community, taking the title of *khalīfa,* meaning "successor" or "lieutenant." The situation in Arabia was very confused and tense. Local prophets, and one prophetess, appeared in a number of regions, manifesting the separatism of various tribes who were against recognition of the supremacy of Medina.

Later Moslem writers described this tribal movement as the *ridda,* giving the term the specific sense of "apostasy" from Islam. Those tribes who had been converted to Islam were actually in the minority; other tribes had merely recognized the political rule of the Medina community or had been exposed to its influence while still clinging to their old beliefs (polytheistic, ḥanīfite or Christian) and the corresponding religious rites. In some tribes groups had formed in favor of following the lead of Medina and embracing Islam, while there were other tribes who never felt the influence of the Medinese community and had no notion at all of the new religion.

Caetani divides the tribes of Arabia into four categories according to their relation to the Community of the Faithful. The first includes those tribes directly subordinated to the leadership of the Medino-Meccan community and converted to Islam, who dwelt in the regions of Medina and Mecca and between those towns: the Juhaina, Muzaina, Balī, Ashja', Aslam, Hudhail, Huza and some lesser tribes. The second category comprises the tribes of central Arabia, the Hawāzin, 'Āmir ibn-Ṣa'ṣa'a, Ṭayyi', and Sulaim, who were strongly influenced by the Community of the Faithful but contained active groups in opposition to any submission to Medina. The third category is that of those tribes only beginning to feel the influence of the Community of the Faithful, among whom Moslems (muslimūn) constituted only a negligible minority of the membership; these were the tribes of Asad, Ghaṭafān and Tamīm. The fourth category consists of the tribes which retained their political and ideological independence, namely the Ḥanīfa in Yamāma, the ‘Abd al-Qais, the Azd, and most of the tribes of the Yemen and Ḥaḍramaut. Moreover, the Community of the Faithful exerted no influence at all on those Arab tribes which had become largely Christianized, the Kalb, Quḍā‘a, Bahrā’, Ghassān, Bakr ibn-Wā’il, Tanūkh and Taghlib; the polytheistic tribes of Mahra, Ḥaḍramaut and the Yemen should also be included in this category and the strong influence of Judaism in the Yemen taken into account.

Local prophets expressed not only the political but also the ideological independence of the several tribes. Some of these prophets had started on their careers while Mohammed was still alive. The most stubborn opposition to the policies of the leadership of the *umma* was encountered in the Yemāma, where the local preacher Musailima, the most resolute proponent of Arabian monotheism, Ḥanīfism, was active as a religious teacher and organizer. Not even the Moslem tradition could deny his influence on Mohammed in his Meccan period; holding similar views, their relations were friendly. Musailima substantially helped Mohammed when the Medinese army was preparing to march upon Mecca: using his religious authority, he intercepted in Yamāma a caravan loaded with a considerable shipment of wheat for Mecca. Although an ideological ally of Medina, however, Musailima still stubbornly opposed any submission of the Yamāma to the leadership of the Medinese Community of the Faithful.

An ally of Musailima was a woman by the name of Sajāḥ, who claimed to be a prophetess and a soothsayer, though nothing definite is known of the contents of her prophecies. By her father she belonged to the Tamīm tribe, by her mother to the Taghlib. Perhaps she was a Christian, for she was certainly acquainted with Christianity, which was widespread among those tribes. Arriving with an armed detachment from Mesopotamia, Sajāḥ intervened in the feuds of the Najd tribes, and her followers twice suffered defeat. She then attempted to make a military alliance with Musailima; later Moslem tradition, which distorts the figure of this Yamāma preacher, presents this alliance in an obscene light.

In the Yemen, even within Mohammed’s lifetime, there was

opposition to the policies of the Medinese leadership, the head of this local opposition being Aihala, or Abhala, known as al-Aswad (The Black) or as *Dhu-l-ḥimār,* (The Veiled One). A representative of Yemenite Ḥanīfism, sometimes described as the "Yemenite *raḥmān*" (apostle of the Merciful) just as Musailima was termed the "Yamāmite *raḥmān*," al-Aswad headed a revolt against Iranian overlordship in the Yemen. The rebels quickly overran the Najrān and took the city of Ṣan'ā too, so that the representatives of the Medina community in Yemen had to flee, some of them back to Medina and some to Ḥaḍramaut. Soon after, al-Aswad was killed (possibly by a supporter of Iranian rule).

In central Arabia, in the Asad tribe, a certain Ṭulaiḥa rose to be war-leader and soothsayer, but apparently made no claim to be a prophet. His military and political activities, directed against the Medino-Meccan community, began during Mohammed's lifetime. After Mohammed's death Ṭulaiḥa gained the support of the Fazāra tribe and of part of the Ṭayyi', but the army of Khālid ibn-al-Walīd eventually beat his followers and dealt with them with great cruelty: many who refused to accept Islam were burned alive. Ṭulaiḥa himself succeeded in fleeing, and soon after became a Moslem and took part in the Arab campaigns of conquest.

The *ridda* was thus by no means a religious "apostasy"; indeed, the majority of Arabia's population remained unconverted to the new religion in Mohammed's lifetime and even refused to accept the political supremacy of the Medina Community of the Faithful. The *ridda* was in fact a process of subjection of Arabian tribes to the rule of the Medino-Meccan *umma,* followed by their utilization in war. This subjection or so-called unification of all the tribes of Arabia was completed only in the reign of the second "orthodox" Caliph, 'Omar ibn-al-Khaṭṭāb (634–644).

THE ARAB CONQUESTS

Even prior to the final submission of Arabia, the armed forces of the Medino-Meccan community, with the support of bedouin tribes, had begun to invade the neighboring civilized countries. The Arab conquests, which by the seventh and eighth centuries resulted in the establishment of Arab domination over vast territories of Asia, Africa and Europe, were accomplished in several stages. The first of these took place during the rule of the first three "orthodox" Caliphs, Abu-Bakr (632–634), 'Omar (634–644) and 'Uthmān (644–656).

In the autumn of 633 (or spring of 634), three Arab troops of 7,500 warriors each invaded Palestine and Syria through the Syrian desert (Bādiyat ash-Sha'm). As more Arabian tribes became subject to the Medinese Caliph, reinforcements were dispatched. The first encounters with Byzantine forces occurred in *Wādi al'Araba* (to the south of the Dead Sea) and in the district of Gaza. The weak Byzantine garrisons, stationed in a few settlements, and the hastily raised local militia could put up no effective resistance against the Arab invaders. As early as the summer of 634 the Arabs took Buṣra (in the Ḥaurān) and defeated the Byzantine troops at Ajnādain and Fiḥl. The inhabitants of Palestinian and Syrian fortified towns were reluctant to help in defending their towns against the Arabs, despite the Arab's ignorance of siege and assault techniques, preferring to parley with their war leaders and to surrender the townships "on condition of preserving their life, property and children against payment of a poll tax."[13] The Byzantine armies were far inferior in battle to the Arabs; they were always beaten and driven to take refuge behind the walls of the major cities. One exception is the fight at Marj al-Ṣuffar in February 635, but the details we have of the battle are sheer exaggeration, as, for example, Balādhuri's account of the Byzantines fighting "with such ferocity that the blood flowed into the stream and brought the water mill into motion."[14]

The eruption of the Arabs into southern Irak, in the form of raids in the border region of Ḥīra, took place even prior to the war in Yamāma. The resistance of the Yamāma Ḥanīfites broken, Khālid ibn-al-Walīd, who retained some 500 Medinese and Meccans under his command, succeeded in rallying the tribe of Bakr ibn-Wā'il and with their help took Ḥīra.

The Bakr ibn-Wā'il were a numerous and powerful tribe who roamed central Arabia from the Yamāma to the northwestern shores of the Persian Gulf. A considerable part of the tribe were

Christians of the Nestorian sect, so that the Moslem faith would not serve as a motivation for conquest for them. The tribe had had long experience of sudden raids into southern Irak, however, seeking booty there quite often even before the rise of Islam; in 610, their raiding parties had inflicted a defeat on the Iranian army at Dhū-Qār.

In March 634, Khālid, at the head of 500–800 cavalry, was ordered by Medina to march on Damascus, across the desert. The Arabs occupied the Ghūṭa, the orchard district around the city, but were quite at a loss when they reached the city walls, for they had neither the technical means nor the experience required to storm a fortified township. After six months of siege, in September 635, the commander and the bishop of Damascus were forced by the pressure of the populace to surrender the city. Not a single ladder could be found in the camp of the besiegers to scale the walls, the gates being blocked from the inside with stones and logs, so the victors had to borrow a ladder from one of the monasteries in the Ghūṭa.

Realizing that the inroads of the Arabs were becoming a major invasion, the Byzantine high command, headed by the Emperor Heraclius, concentrated a large army in northern Syria. Beside the Greeks *(Rūm)* ["Romans" in Arabic], this army included units of Syrians, people from the Jazīra (Upper Mesopotamia) and Armenians, and, according to the quite exaggerated estimate of Arabic historians, was 200,000 strong. The same historians accordingly clearly underestimated the number of Arab warriors, whose total was set at only 24,000. As the Byzantines approached, the Arabs abandoned Damascus and other cities and retreated to the Yarmūk River, an eastern tributary of the Jordan. Here, on 20 August 636, battle was joined. The Byzantines suffered a crushing defeat, with losses estimated at 70,000 dead. The effectiveness of the Byzantines in combat had been impaired by quarrels between their Greek and Armenian units, which had actually fought against each other on the eve of the battle, while the Syrian Arabs, commanded by the Ghassānid king *(malik)* Jabala ibn-al-Aiham, had gone over to the Arab side during the fighting.[15]

This rout of the Byzantines on the Yarmūk saw the Arab

conquerors become the complete masters of Syria. Tradition recounts that the Emperor Heraclius, leaving this country for ever, exclaimed on reaching the narrow cleft marking its border: "Farewell, Syria! What a splendid land for our enemy!"

The Arabs again occupied Damascus, and subjected the whole of northern Syria. In 638, after two years of siege, Jerusalem was surrendered, and in 640 Caesarea, after a siege of seven years. This long siege was due not so much to the technical ineptitude of the Arabs as to the constant help sent by sea from Byzantium to the port; at that time, the Arabs possessed no means of hampering the Byzantine fleets.

In Irak, after the capture of Ḥīra, the Arabs suffered several setbacks in battles with the Sassanid armies, and were forced to relinquish this city and the region around it. The bedouin were terrified by the Iranian battle-elephants, the sight of which was a new and awesome experience for them. But from the end of 635 onwards, victory belonged to the Arabs as they defeated the Iranians at Buwaib on the Euphrates, retook Ḥīra, and on 31 May or 1 June 637 emerged victorious over a large Iranian army at the battle of Qādisīyya. Two or three weeks later, they entered the Sassanid capital of Ctesiphon, known among the Arabs as Madā'in, whose inhabitants opened their gates to the Arabs after the flight of *shahin-shah* Yazdagird III and his court

The armistice concluded by the Arab war leaders with the Iranian military command was soon broken by the latter (or so the Arabs asserted), upon which the Arab army marched north, took Mosul in 641 and inflicted defeat upon the Iranians in the big battle of Nehavend (Nihāwand), near Hamadan (Hamadhān). In 644–645, Arab detachments penetrated through Baluchistan to the Indian borders and in 649 took Iṣṭakhr (ancient Persepolis). In 651, Yazdagird III was killed at Merv (Marw); this year is considered as marking the end of the Arab conquest of Irak (in the sense of all Iran), and the same year saw the Arabs at the Amu-Darya River.

The Arabs had already invaded Armenia in 640, soon after the conquest of Syria, and taken its capital, Dvin. In 654 they reached Tbilisi [Tiflis].

As soon as their success in arms seemed assured in Syria, the

Arabs started on their conquests in Africa. The first incursion into Egypt, by a small Arab party commanded by 'Amr ibn-al-'Aṣ, took place in December 639. The old story according to which Ibn-al-'Aṣ was dissatisfied with his subordinate command in Syria and undertook the campaign into the Nile valley on his own initiative is completely irrelevant; the invasion was actually due to the urgent need for the grain and other victuals of fertile Egypt in Ḥijāz. The demand for Meccan consumer goods increased considerably after the unification of Arabia with the tremendous increase in the number of Moslem pilgrims; the population of Medina, now the capital of the Arab Caliphs, also expanded.

In January 640, the troops of 'Amr took Faramā (Pelusium), advanced to the Nile and forced a crossing, proceeding to raid the Fayyūm. In June, with reinforcements, the Arab army defeated the Byzantines near Heliopolis. In September 640 they besieged the fortress of Babylon [Bābalyūn of Egypt], which surrendered in April 641, and then followed the Nile downstream to begin the siege of Alexandria. November 641 saw the Patriarch Cyrus (known to the Arabs as *al-Muqawqis*) conclude an accord with 'Amr by which he surrendered this strong, otherwise impregnable city. By the terms of the treaty the Egyptian capital was to be yielded to the Arabs after an armistice of eleven months, required for the evacuation of the rich and noble Greek citizens. The evacuation completed, the Arab army entered Alexandria in September 642, at which time other Arab detachments had already penetrated into Upper Egypt. In the year 645, a Byzantine fleet entered the harbor of Alexandria and landed troops. These forces ousted the Arabs from the city; however, the Arabs besieged Alexandria once more and took it by storm in the summer of 646.

From Egypt, the Arabs raided neighboring Libya, where the local Berber tribes offered no resistance and the Byzantine garrisons were defeated. In autumn 642 the Arabs took the town of Barqa and subdued the entire region of Cyrenaica [also known as Barqa in Arabic], whence they penetrated southward to the Fezzan and westward to the city of Tripoli, which was captured in 643. In 647 an Arab army commanded by the viceroy of Egypt,

'Abdallah ibn-Sa'd, raided Ifriqiya (present-day Tunisia) and defeated the Byzantines near the fortress of Sbeitla.

In two decades, then, the Arabs had conquered the extensive territories of the Byzantine Empire in Asia and Africa and subdued the entire Iranian realm, marking the end of the independent political existence of this great power. The search for the reasons as to the relative rapidity and ease of these conquests still continues among European historians of Arab lands and Arabism.

The basis of the military successes gained by the Arabs was undoubtedly the economic exhaustion of Byzantium and Sassanid Iran, and in particular the social contradictions that had quite suddenly become more acute in both these states. Oppression and exploitation of the working people were rife in those countries and regions invaded by the Arabs, so that the population tended to consider them as deliverers from the heavy yoke of Byzantium and Iran. Moreover, the Arabs offered terms which were definitely preferable to their present existence. Thus most of the people in the conquered lands made no resistance against the Arabs, sometimes actually acting as their allies.

The dwindling material resources of Byzantium and Sassanid Iran moreover resulted in their military weakness, both in numbers and in the quality of their forces, while many defensive facilities and fortifications were neglected.

The old hackneyed explanation of the Arab successes as due to religious fanaticism has by now been rejected as completely untenable, for the bedouin, who formed the bulk of the Arab army, most certainly knew nothing, and could not have known anything, of the tenets of the new religion. Indeed, the composition of the Koran, the first product of Moslem religious literature, was begun only in the mid-seventh century, when the first stage of Arab conquests was reaching its completion.*

* [For a much more comprehensive (and somewhat more balanced) evolution of the causes of Arab success, see: M. Canard, *L'expansion arabe: le probleme militaire,* L'Occidente e l'Islam nell'Alto medioevo, vol. 1, Spoleto 1965, pp. 37–63, 309–335.]

THE ADMINISTRATION OF THE CONQUERED TERRITORIES

The socio-economic relationships and the forms of ownership which the Arabs found in the lands they had conquered were as yet unknown in Arabia and seemed quite incomprehensible to the conquerors. Wherever early-feudal conditions prevailed, the Arabs failed to show any interest in land as a means of production, simply considering all the cultivated land which fell under their dominion as the property of the Moslem community. The conquerors, busied with their loot (including prisoners and hostages, who were enslaved) and with the exaction of tribute and contributions, could not and did not interfere with the social production of the subject population, and made no attempt to modify the existing regime. The lands remained in the possession of local feudals, clergy and other landowners, the former exploiters retaining all their rights and privileges over the peasants who tilled the land. Landowners had merely to pay the land tax to the treasury of the Moslem community, while the holdings of the Byzantine emperor and the Greek Byzantine nobility and of the Sassanid *shahin-shah* and the Iranian royal family, as well as the lands of feudals who had fallen in battle or fled their estates, became the property of the Moslem community and were administered directly by the *bait al-māl* ("treasury"), to which the peasants working the land had to pay tribute.

As they were at an earlier stage of social development than the conquered civilized peoples, the Arabs could not at first manipulate the complex apparatus of administration and exploitation. Nor did they deem it necessary, being quite content with the seizure of booty and the collection of tribute from the subject population. They left untouched both the socio-economic regime and the administrative-fiscal apparatus in the lands they had conquered, and became merely an upper, dominant stratum superimposed on the local feudal society.

Throughout the period of the four orthodox Caliphs, the Caliphate, the vast territories conquered by the Arabs in Asia and Africa, remained a collection of regions with different systems of land tenure and exploitation of the subject population. In the

Sawād (southern Irak), the Arabs found no less than four categories of land. The first of these consisted of estates of local feudal lords or *dihqāns* ("village lords"). These *dihqāns* received rent and collected the state taxes from the laboring population of their estates and villages, also fulfilling certain administrative and judicial functions. The conquerors left such lands in the possession of the *dihqāns* and confirmed their rights and privileges: nothing was changed, the only difference being that the tribute now went to the Moslem *bait al-māl* instead of to the Sassanid treasury. The Arabs aimed at obtaining the same amount of taxes from the Sawād as that exacted by the Sassanids, for which purpose the old Sassanid cadaster was used, with the active cooperation of the *dihqāns*.

The second category of land covered the possessions of the *shahin-shah* (the royal domain), his kinsmen and his courtiers, as well as the estates of such *dihqāns* as had been killed in battle or had fled their lands. This land *(ṣawāfī),* left lordless, was turned over to the Caliph as the head of the Moslem community, and the peasants tilling the land paid their taxes directly to the *bait al-māl*.

Lands unsuitable for cultivation or those left uncultivated because of the disruption of the irrigation system formed the third category. Under the last Sassanids, with constant Byzantine invasions and court revolutions, the Iranian government had sadly neglected natural production: dikes had been broken and dams destroyed, so that entire agricultural districts were rendered useless and became known in Moslem law as "dead land." Both the landlords and the government strove to "bring them alive," to repair or reconstruct the irrigation facilities so that the land should again become fit for agriculture.

The fourth category consisted of lands belonging to the urban population, such as the land around Ḥīra and many other Iraki cities, whose inhabitants made an agreement with the Arabs on the payment of a stated yearly tribute, the conquerors guaranteeing the citizens' safety and property in exchange. The inhabitants of these cities retained the right to dispose of their possessions as they wished: they could sell their land, mortgage it and also bequeath it.

The rural and urban populations which came under Arab rule paid both a poll tax, *jizya,* and a land tax, *kharāj.* These terms, borrowed directly from the Iranian fiscal terminology, were more or less synonymous during the first hundred years of the Caliphate, meaning simply "tribute," although even then the two words were sometimes given distinct meanings.

Taxation in the Sawād immediately after the Arab conquest was in complete disorder. In practice, only a single system of assessing and levying tribute was used, not only because of the Arabs' inability to comprehend the Sassanid fiscal system, including special agreements with urban and rural localities, but also because of the shrewd dealings of the Iranian *dabirs* ["scribes"] and *dihqāns,* ["village lords"], who gladly undertook fiscal functions in order to pursue their own interests, sometimes hiding substantial objects of taxation from the Arabs. For instance, in the year 22 of the *hijra* (642/643), the Arab commander Mughīra discovered that besides the land under wheat and barley, which paid tribute, there was much land under other agricultural crops which was not taxed at all. Taxation of this land began only after this "discovery," more than ten years after the conquest.

In Syria (which then also comprised Palestine and Lebanon) the Arabs pursued the same fiscal policies, their commanders being willing to conclude treaties with those who would submit, represented usually by the local Christian clergy. The main point in each such agreement obliged the population to make regular payments of the stipulated tribute, in money and in produce, in return for which the Arabs promised to respect their life and freedom (that is, not to enslave them), to prohibit looting by the warriors, to leave untouched those buildings reserved for religious cults and not turn them into mosques, and to let religious services and rituals proceed without interference. The taxable population of the conquered regions of Syria was thus considered as being under the protection of the Arab conquerors, so that, the story goes, when the Arabs were forced to retreat from Damascus and Ḥimṣ at the approach of Heraclius' army, they returned their recently exacted tribute to the inhabitants of these cities and their vicinity, naively justifying this hitherto unheard of behavior (quite incomprehensible to the Syrians) on the grounds that they were no longer in a position to protect their tributaries.

The estates of the Byzantine emperor and of the Constantinople noblemen, and those lands abandoned by their proprietors, constituted a land reserve at the disposal of the Arab authorities.

In medieval Arabic historiography and jurisprudence, the formation of the Caliphate—that is, the transformation of conquered territories into an allegedly centralized state—is attributed to the "orthodox" Caliph 'Omar, represented as an outstanding statesman of exceptional political wisdom, with an iron will and tireless energy. He was especially idealized by many subsequent generations of Moslems for his modesty, sagacity, avoidance of luxury, indifference to comfort, high sense of duty and selfless service in the interests of Islam and the Moslems. Even in the present century, Oriental historians and publicists who remain faithful to traditional Moslem values describe this Caliph as a "democratic ruler" who should stand as a model in all the lands of Islam.

In fact, 'Omar's historical role was as a true exponent of the interests of the leading stratum of the Medino-Meccan Community of the Faithful. The interests of the "companions" of Mohammed—both *muhājirūn* and *anṣār*—coincided with the aspirations of the headmen of the bedouin tribes, subject to the guidance of the Moslem community; such bedouin formed the bulk of the invaders.

There is of course no reason to suppose that the first Caliphs and the Arab war leaders who obeyed them had any preconceived strategic plan of conquest. Their military successes astounded them, at times, no less than they astounded the conquered peoples. The initiative in concluding treaties and in drawing up the stipulations of such treaties was more often than not taken by the representatives of the local population overrun by the Arabs. For instance, "the inhabitants of Fiḥl [near the Jordan River] manned their fortifications; the Moslems started besieging them until they asked for *amān* (mercy),* offering to pay a poll tax

* [In fact, protection or treaty of protection; they sued for a negotiated surrender that would ensure their lives, property, etc.]

as well as *kharāj* for their lands. And the Moslems granted them *amān,* with the promise not to lay their hands on them or on their property, nor to destroy their (city) walls."[16] When the Arab army commanded by Abū-'Ubaida marched within sight of Baalbek *(Ba'lbakk),* the inhabitants of this city "asked for mercy and peace." Abū-'Ubaida "made peace with them, with the proviso that he spare their lives, property and churches."[17] Under the same commander, this army approached Ḥimṣ (on the Orontes), and "the people of Ḥimṣ concluded peace with him, upon condition that he would spare their lives, their property, the walls of their city, their churches and their water mills."[18]

The amount of taxes in money and produce and the methods and delays of payment all varied so much in the different treaties that it was impossible to assess or to distribute it fairly. In search of some kind of order in Arab relationships with the conquered population, the Caliph 'Omar journeyed from Medina to Jābiya (in southern Palestine), where he conferred with Arab war leaders and tribal chieftains active in Syria. The story that 'Omar came to Palestine mainly in order to sign an agreement on the conditions of the surrender of Jerusalem is merely a tendentious later invention.

The evidence of Arabic historians giving the most detailed information on the progress of the conquests (chiefly Balādhuri and Ṭabari) is not sufficient to establish any detailed sequence of fiscal policies practiced by the Moslem leadership, though the main tendency, towards increasing the burden of taxation, is clear. According to Balādhuri, "at first the poll tax in Syria was exacted in the amount of one *jarīb* (measure of wheat) and one dinar per head. Thereafter 'Omar ibn-al-Khaṭṭāb decreed that the poll tax should be from possessors of gold in the amount of four dinars, and from possessors of silver forty dirhems; he divided the tax into categories according to the richness of the rich, the poverty of the poor, and the modest income of the moderately well-to-do." The historical tradition passed on by some relates that the treaty concluded by Khālid ibn-al-Walīd with the people of Damascus allowed for "each man to contribute one dinar of poll tax and one *jarīb* of wheat, as well as vinegar and olive oil for the provisioning of the Moslems." Later, 'Omar ordered all adults to be taxed ("all those who had shaved") at 40 dirhems or 4 dinars, and they were further obligated to make a monthly provision of two *mudya* of wheat and three *qisṭ* of olive oil, as well as some quantity of fat and honey,[19] for every Arab warrior in Syria and the Jazīra [upper Mesopotamia]. The warriors in Egypt could demand three days billeting per month from the local population, as well as an *ardabb** and a piece of clothing for each warrior.

Our sources are less definite on the extent and system of Arab taxation in Egypt than in Syria and Irak, though it seems clear that at first the Arabs took a sum of two dinars a year from each adult Egyptian. Women, children and old men unable to work were exempted from the tax.

Monks who lived in monasteries run by their own work, and part of the secular clergy, were also presumably exempt from any tribute, though later, when the Arab authorities realized that the monks lived in ease and idleness at the expense of dependent peasants and on the gifts of numerous devotees, they too were taxed, the more so since these monasteries possessed considerable reserves of money and precious goods.

In addition to the poll tax, the Egyptian landlords had to pay a tribute of produce from each planted *faddān,* which was used for the upkeep of Arab warriors garrisoned in Egypt. The local population had also to provide these warriors with a stated amount of clothing and footwear each year, and for this purpose a census of Arabs in Egypt was carried out.

It is not clear whether, in addition to the poll tax and the tribute in produce, the landowners had also to pay land tax in money, though certain information indicates that for each *jarīb* of cultivated land, besides the tribute of produce, one dinar had also to be paid.

The Arabs took further contributions from the people of certain cities they had conquered; for instance, the Patriarch Cyrus (of Alexandria) was forced to pay the sum of 13,000 dinars in one installment.

The estates of the Byzantine emperor and his noblemen (like

* [A measure of wheat, about 198 litres.]

the *sawāfī* lands in the Sawād) became the poperty of the Community of the Faithful, in other words State-owned lands, their tillers paying taxes to the State's tax collectors.

In all the lands conquered, the following classes of people were exempt from taxation: women, minors, paupers, lunatics and paralytics, and also monks living by the work of their own hands. At first, before the cultivated area had been assessed, the tribute was collected according to the numbers of the adult male population. Tax collection was entrusted to local landlords, municipal authorities and the clergy, who were also responsible for the exact payment of taxes and execution of obligations.

Just as they left social production untouched, the Arabs also left the organs of local administration, including judicial institutions and the police, it being the task of the population to take care of welfare in towns and cities and to mend roads, bridges and wells.

The officials of the [pre-Arab] fiscal administration were entrusted with the task of preparing lists of the taxable population and of registering the produce of taxes entering the *bait al-māl:* they even registered its distribution among the Arabs. As before the conquest affairs were transacted in the Persian language in the Sawād, in Greek in Syria, and in Coptic (as well as Greek) in Egypt.

A *dīwān* was compiled in the days of 'Omar—the word is Persian in origin and meant, at that time, "list" or "register"—including the names of persons and tribes who had a recognized right to money from the taxes exacted. The first generation of Moslems assumed that all the receipts from tax payers belonged in their entirety to the victors; indeed, they saw no difference between booty taken on the battle field and the produce of exploitation of conquered people, for the conquered lands, worked by the subject and tributary population, and the tribute exacted from this population were both known as *fai',* which was taken to be synonymous with *ghānīm* ("booty") and *kharāj* ("land tax"). In the Moslem view, everything obtained from the conquered should be distributed among the conquering Moslems.

The first lines of the *diwan* held the names of the Prophet's wives, headed by 'A'isha, later to be called the "Mother of the

Faithful." Each of these women received an annual sum of several tens of thousand dirhems from the treasury. The next names were those of the "Companions of the Prophet" *(aṣḥāb* or *ṣaḥāba)* [sing. *ṣāḥib*], first the *muhājirūn,* then the *anṣār,* after whom were enumerated the tribes who had participated in the conquests and were stationed within the conquered territories.

The Medina treasury and each provincial *bait al-māl* received one fifth of the assessed booty, tribute and contributions. A large part of these sums and goods was appropriated by the viceroys, war leaders and tribal chieftains, who thus very rapidly grew rich and acquired a taste for luxury and dissipation. As additional loot, the Arab tribal aristocracy took many captive warriors and peaceful inhabitants and made them slaves.

Another kind of "live booty" were the Moslem neophytes themselves, who became known as *mawlā* (plural *mawālī*), those among the native inhabitants who had become converted to Islam. But acceptance of Islam, the religion of the conquerors, did not make them the equals of the Moslem Arabs, who, whether settling in the conquered lands or continuing to wage wars, retained their clan and tribe organization and kept fresh their old intertribal feuds. A local inhabitant who turned Moslem forfeited his own community but, not being an Arab, could have no blood relationship to the conquerors and thus could not become an equal member of any Arab clan or tribe. According to ancient Arab custom, still retained, such a man could enter the clan and tribe organization only as somebody seeking protection. Thus the non-Arab Moslem neophyte usually became the protégé of some influential member of an Arab tribe, his *mawlā*, the designation for a slave who had been freed but who remained under the protection of his former master or of members of the latter's family. As applied to the non-Arab Moslem the word *mawlā* had the connotation of "freedman" or "client" (to use the terms of Roman slave-holding legislation); he had to bring gifts, from time to time, to his master, or serve him in his professional capacity. Arab tribal aristocrats usually went on a campaign surrounded by a crowd of *mawālī* who catered to all their needs, including all kinds of craftsmen and men of liberal professions, among them physicians, scribe-secretaries, astrologers and even poets.

The Arab rulers and war leaders considered all such people as part of the booty which Allah had granted them.

Military service was considered by the Arabs as their own exclusive right and duty. The "Islamic army" consisted of levies of Arab tribes, and its means of subsistence, besides loot, consisted of the produce provided as tribute by the local population and brought into the camp, as well as subsidies in money from the *bait-al-māl*. As they lived at the expense of the subject population, most of the Arabs who settled in conquered lands did not perform any productive work, and were extremely reluctant to resort to agriculture: Arab settlers who became farmers in the conquered lands were highly exceptional.

The Arab clan and tribe organization protected the conquerors against intermixture with the subject peoples, which would have seen the Arabs dissolved in the mass of the conquered. The Arabs preferred to dwell in their own military camps, each of which was a circular area enclosed by an earthen wall with four gates, usually oriented according to the cardinal points. Straight roads led from the gates to the center, converging on a square. Within the sectors delimited by the roads were the tents of the members of the several clans or minor tribes: as in a bedouin encampment, neighborhoods coincided with kinship groups. The earthen wall was an innovation borrowed from those Arab tribes who had served in the Iranian and Byzantine armed forces. Large camps of this type were Baṣra (Bassora) [637 or 638] and Kūfa (636) in Irak, Fusṭāṭ in Egypt (640) and Qairuwān (Kairouan) in Tunisia (670).

The unsanitary conditions in these military camps, where Arab warriors lived with their families and cattle, turned them into foci of epidemic diseases. The plague inflicted far higher losses on the Arabs than the bloodiest battles. The infamous plague of 639 started in the 'Amwās camp, midway between Jaffa and Jerusalem, and caused the death of no less than 20,000 Arabs.

Some of the local inhabitants, attracted by the easy money to be gained by servicing the Arabs—the latter had an enormous amount of booty and also much money—began to settle near the Arab military camps, outside the walls. Suburbs soon arose peopled with craftsmen, shopkeepers, money-changers and *Lum-*

penproletariat, including many crooks, thieves and prostitutes. Later, the wall was replaced by brick fortifications and the tents gave way to permanent dwellings and public edifices. The commercial and artisanal suburbs soon merged with these towns, and new cities arose to become important economic, political and cultural centers, proving especially attractive to the Moslem neophytes, who left their own communities.

In the old cities which had surrendered to the Arabs or had been taken by force of arms, the conquerors settled down in certain quarters abandoned by the inhabitants, sometimes expelling the citizens to provide dwellings for their warriors.

The Arabs usually would not admit recruits from the native population into their armed forces, even if they had embraced Islam, but those Arab tribes that had emigrated from Arabia in pre-Islamic times and were converted to Christianity by their new neighbors joined at once in the military campaigns of the new conquerors from Arabia: the Christian Arab tribes of Syria and Jordan played an especially important military-political role in the first hundred years of the Islamic era. The conquering Moslems were quite tolerant in matters of faith, not only towards Christians and Jews, termed in the Koran *Ahl al-Kitab,* "people of the Book" (provided with divine revelation), but also towards Zoroastrians, Manicheans, Ṣābians* and other "polytheists." This tolerant attitude had a quite realistic motivation, for converts to Islam, in the early days, were sometimes freed from the poll tax, which meant diminished receipts in the treasury.

The earlier conception of a mass conversion of conquered people to Islam as early as the first caliphs must now be considered a gross exaggeration, for the conversion of the non-Moslem population of the Caliphate was in fact a lengthy process which only reached its conclusion in the twentieth century in certain countries of the Arab Orient. For instance in the ninth century the overwhelming majority of the people of Egypt remained Christian (Copts); the Moslems did not gain numerical preponderance until the thirteenth century, though Egypt has still retained a considerable Christian (Coptic) minority even today.

* [A term variously applied to the Mandean Gnostics of Irak and to the unrelated star worshippers of Harrān in Upper Mesopotamia.]

Jordan also has its Christian minority, not only among the sedentary farmers and city folk, but also in some of the local nomadic tribes, direct descendants of those Arabs who embraced Christianity prior to the rise of Islam. In present-day Lebanon no less than half the population is Christian, of several denominations which, in the Arab Orient, date from pre-Islamic times. In those countries which had previously been Christian, most of the people turned Moslem in the Middle Ages (after the completion of Arab conquests), but very few cases of conversion from Islam to Christianity have ever been observed.

The conquests and the establishment of Arab rule in civilized countries hastened and made more complex the process of economic and social development in Arab society, the upper stratum of which, holding military and political power, acquired a disproportionate share of booty and tribute, whereas many rank-and-file warriors gained only hardship and suffering in the campaigns.* As early as the time of the Caliph 'Omar, an Arab poet exclaimed: "We participate in the same campaigns, and when we come back—why do some live in abundance while we remain destitute?"[20]

The sums of booty and tribute from the conquered lands were so enormous at times as to astonish 'Omar himself, for whom such resources at his disposal were entirely new. When his viceroy in Baḥrain returned to Medina and declared that he had brought with him 500,000 dirhems, the Caliph asked: "Do you really understand what you are saying?" "Yes," came the reply, "five times a hundred thousand." Much of the booty and tribute remained in the coffers and purses of the viceroys and war leaders. Soon after the conquest of Egypt, the Caliph 'Omar wrote to 'Amr ibn-al-'Aṣ, his lieutenant in this rich country: "There are rumors that you possess produce, slaves, utensils and cattle which you did not have when you were appointed regent of Egypt." At that time, the receipts from the tributary Egyptians were estimated at 2 million dinars and later rose to 4 million. Under 'Uthmān, the successor of 'Omar, in the year 27 of the *hijra* (647/648), Ifrīqiya [that is, Tunisia] provided a tribute of two and a half

* [This view seems to be much exaggerated and to rely on evidence no more reliable than the poetic exclamation cited below.]

million dinars. Under 'Omar the Sawād yielded 80 million dirhems per year, and the inhabitants of Kūfa and perhaps Baṣra were ordered to pay an annual sum varying from 20 to 30 million dirhems.

Enslavement of prisoners also enriched the Arab tribal aristocracy; moreover, increasing the number of slaves from the native inhabitants of townships (especially if there was armed resistance to the invaders) was among the commonest methods of establishing Arab domination. The war leader Khālid ibn-al-Walīd, a typical representative of the Arab aristocracy, used this method, as we have seen, for crushing the resistance of the Yamāma Ḥanīfites; also, in his conquest of southern Irak, having taken 'Ain al-Tamr by force of arms, he ordered some of the population to be slaughtered and the rest to be sold as slaves. Balādhuri reports that "the number of captives in Caesarea reached four thousand. And when Mu'āwiya sent them to 'Omar ibn-al-Khaṭṭāb, the latter ordered them to be placed in al-Jurf, and then gave them as a gift to the orphans among the *anṣār,* while appointing some of them as scribes in Moslem institutions dealing with the tribute, so as to profit the Moslems."[21] Nūba surrendered to the besieging Arabs on the condition of providing them with 400 slaves each year. Provision of slaves was actually one of the forms of tribute in some of the conquered regions. At that time, slaves still played an important part in social production, especially in the formerly Byzantine provinces.

Foremost in the acquisition of riches and power were the members of the Meccan Umayya clan, who at one time were engaged in a bitter struggle against the Medinese Community of the Faithful, only to join it later on advantageous terms. The Umayyads already exerted great influence within the leadership of the *umma* during Mohammed's lifetime, and after his death they were very active in the conquering expeditions.

Under 'Omar, members of the Umayya clan received Syria as their dominion, where Yazīd, son of Abū-Sufyān, held the post of chief war leader. After his death from the 'Amwās plague, his brother Mu'āwiya became viceroy of Syria.

In 644, after the murder of 'Omar at the hands of an Iranian slave, 'Uthmān ibn-al-'Affān, also an Umayyad, became Caliph.

In his youth, before the rise of Islam, 'Uthmān had been very rich and gained much money from profitable usurious transactions. He was known in Mecca as a great connoisseur of perfumes, thoroughbred horses and young slave girls. He became one of the early followers of Mohammed: tradition relates that he was in love with one of the prophet's daughters, whom he later married, and after her untimely death married another of Mohammed's daughters, thus receiving the honored title of "twice son-in-law to the Apostle of Allah."

'Uthmān's acquisitiveness and business talents gained full scope when he became Caliph. He built himself a stone house in Medina with doors of precious wood and acquired much real estate in that city, including gardens and water sources. He had a large income from his fruit plantations in *Wādi al-Qurā,* Ḥunain and other places, valued at 100,000 dinars, besides large herds of horses and camels on these estates. The day 'Uthmān died his personal treasury was found to contain 150,000 dinars and one million dirhems.[22]

Multiplying his riches at the expence of the Moslem treasury, 'Uthmān also gave free use of the latter to some of the closest companions of Mohammed, attempting to justify his illegal actions by associating these most authoritative veteran Moslems with his own depredations. The "companions" applauded the Caliph 'Uthmān for his generosity and magnanimity, no doubt for solid reasons of self-interest. Zubair ibn-al-'Awwām, for example, one of the better known amongst them, built tenement houses in Kūfa, Baṣra, Fusṭāṭ and Alexandria. His property was estimated at 50,000 dinars, in addition to which he possessed one thousand horses and one thousand slaves. Another "companion," Ṭalḥa ibn-'Ubaidallah, built a large tenement house in Kūfa and acquired estates in Irak which brought in a daily 1,000 dinars; he also built a luxurious house of brick and precious wood in Medina. 'Abd-al Raḥmān ibn-'Auf, also an outstanding "companion," also built himself a rich and spacious dwelling: his stables contained 100 horses and his pastures 1,000 camels and 10,000 sheep, and one quarter of the inheritance he left after his death was valued at 84,000 dinars. Such acquisitiveness was widespread among the companions of the Prophet and 'Uthmān's entourage.

This rapid accumulation of riches appears to have given rise to quite exaggerated rumors as to their size; there were some, for instance, who asserted that Zubair's heritage amounted to 35 million dinars, while others put the amount at 52 million.[23]

The undisguised plunder of the Moslem treasury met with protests from those few companions of the Prophet who deemed that all receipts belonged to the Moslems and should be divided equally between them. The most outstanding of these opponents of inequality of wealth was Abū-Dharr al-Ghifārī. In the period of conquest, this old "companion," whom, according to tradition, Mohammed set as an example to other Moslems, had gone to Syria, where he publicly decried the viceroy and the war leaders for appropriating booty and tribute which in his opinion was "the property of Allah," belonging to all Moslems. Mu'āwiya asked the Caliph 'Uthmān to remove this dangerous agitator, who was becoming increasingly popular among the rank-and-file, from Syria. Recalled by 'Uthmān, Abu-Dharr settled in Medina, but, on learning there that the Caliph had given generous gifts out of the Moslem treasury to his nephew Marwān ibn-al-Ḥakam, while granting 300,000 dirhems from the same source to another nephew, Ḥārith ibn-al-Ḥakam, and 100,000 dirhems to one Zaid ibn-Thābit, he began to criticize him sharply, promising all four, on the strength of the Koran, punishment in the flames of Hell. Pursuing his criticism, this irreconcilable and incorruptible tribune declared that rich men increase their riches by despoiling the poor. The Caliph 'Uthmān ordered the "trouble maker" deported to an out-of-the-way place, where he died in extreme poverty, leaving his widow without even the means to pay for his modest burial.

During the rule of 'Uthmān (644–656), his relatives, members of the Meccan slave-holding aristocracy, seized governmental posts and landed estates in the conquered countries. Historical tradition assigns a particularly pernicious role to the Caliph's nephew Marwān, who, profiting from his uncle's senility ('Uthmān became Caliph at the age of nearly seventy), took over the actual power of government in Medina and connived in every way with the arbitrary deeds of his avid, plundering relatives. These kin of the Caliph, members of the Umayya clan, had been appointed by 'Uthmān as viceroys and war leaders; they began first to appropriate those lands considered the property of the Moslem community and as such at the disposal of the Caliph. In the Sawād, these Umayyads took over part of the *ṣāwāfi* lands and very soon reinstituted those methods of feudal exploitation which had been in practice there earlier. In Syria, they seized state lands and cultivated them by means of slave labor.

Such seizures of land, together with the spoliation, blackmail and violence committed by these rulers, gave rise to a growing discontent, expressed most forcefully by those friends of 'Omar who had been displaced from their influential and lucrative positions. Their displeasure was shared by Arab tribes (especially in Irak) whose material interests suffered from the arbitrary dissipation of state funds at the hands of 'Uthmān's appointees.

The Caliph 'Uthmān himself set the example of misuse of governmental receipts for the benefit of his own family; when his daughter was married to 'Abdallāh ibn-Khālid, for instance, 'Uthmān granted them 600,000 dirhems out of the Baṣra *bait al-māl,* while when 'Abdallāh ibn-Abī-Sarḥ sent 3,000 *qanāṭīr** of gold from Ifrīqiya, he ordered this gold to be given to the family of al-Ḥakam.

This discontent was expressed in active protest by representatives of Moslems from Kūfa, Baṣra and Egypt, who arrived in Medina under the guise of pilgrimage. With the support of the Medinese, the protest soon assumed the character of an uprising: the rebels surrounded 'Uthmān in his house and murdered him.

The new Caliph chosen was 'Alī, cousin and son-in-law to Mohammed, husband of Fāṭima, Mohammed's daughter. Proclaimed by the rebels, this Caliph was opposed, however, by an influential group of enriched "companions" and of course by the kinsmen of his murdered predecessor. The first group, the "companions," was headed by Ṭalḥa and Zubair and further supported by 'Ā'isha, Mohammed's widow. Thus began a bitter struggle for power, which soon turned into armed conflict. 'Alī suppressed this group of opponents quite easily, as they had no strong forces at their

* [*Qinṭār,* plur. *qanāṭīr* = "hundredweight, talent" (equal to 1000 or more dinars).]

disposal and did not enjoy any widespread social support: the army of Ṭalḥa and Zubair was defeated in 656 at Khuraiba near Baṣra, both "companions" killed, and 'Ā'isha taken prisoner. The encounter was known as the "Battle of the Camel," as 'Ā'isha rode in her palanquin on a camel.

Far more serious resistance was encountered from the Umayyad aristocracy, which had acquired both power and riches under 'Uthmān. In its struggle against 'Alī's partisans, this aristocracy was headed by Mu'āwiya, viceroy of rich and civilized Syria, who had very large forces and abundant means at his disposal.

Against this mighty opponent, 'Alī could count on the Arab tribes of Irak, who claimed to be the bearers of communal-democratic ideas and policies identified with the personality and activities of the Caliph 'Omar. As Caliph, 'Alī proclaimed that he would rule in the spirit of 'Omar's policy, and began to dismiss the viceroys appointed under 'Uthman and to confiscate the landed estates which had been usurped. Since he lacked sufficient forces and means in Arabia to pursue the struggle, and in the hope of better military and social support in Irak, 'Alī transferred his residence to Kūfa.

In 657, at Ṣiffīn in the Jazīra, on the right bank of the Euphrates, battle was joined between the Syrian armies of Mu'āwiya and the Iraki armies of 'Alī. Neither side gained a decisive advantage. Arabic historians relate that the shrewdness and perfidy of 'Amr ibn-al-'Āṣ, in Mu'āwiya's camp, deprived the warriors of 'Alī of their victory: forseeing certain defeat for the Syrian army, 'Amr, the "conqueror of Egypt," ordered the warriors of Mu'āwiya to raise folios of the Koran manuscript on their spears and swords to signify that the opponents should desist from bloodshed and their dispute be resolved peacefully according to the prescriptions of Holy Writ. Reluctantly bowing to the demands of certain of his influential partisans, 'Alī accepted this proposal. There are grounds, however, for doubting this sequence of events; some military historians consider it quite impossible that the enemy could be appealed to during battle, especially in such a manner.[24]

Soon after the battle of Ṣiffīn, the Khārijites, considered the first sect to arise among the Moslems, broke away from the camp of 'Alī. The traditional Moslem concept of the rise of this sect is quite naive: Arabic historians described the first generation of Khārijites as the most zealous Moslems, stubborn proponents of the celebrated "equality" which was supposed to have existed in the Community of the Faithful in the days of Mohammed and his first two successors. The Khārijites actually called themselves "men of fasting and prayer," following the Koran strictly. They saw 'Alī as transgressing one of its main tenets, one of the "Words of God," by having accepted secular arbitration in a question affecting his right and dignity as Caliph. The Khārijites adopted the slogan, *lā ḥukma illā li-llāh* ("Only Allah may judge!"), thus calling themselves *muḥakkimūn,* those that proclaim this slogan.

These decided adversaries of 'Alī's policy of concessions, which they regarded as appeasement, left the military camp of the Caliph near Kūfa and marched toward Baghdad, then a small township on the left bank of the Tigris. The departure of these troops, numbering some 12,000 men, and their rejection of 'Alī's command, served to accredit the widespread but incorrect explanation of the name of the Khārijites (Arabic *khawārij*): many historians still believe that the stem is the verb *kharaja* in the sense of "go out" or "go away," whereas the nickname was in fact given to the Khārijites by their opponents and is derived from the same verb followed by the preposition *'alā,* which alters the meaning to "to go forth against somebody" or "to rebel." The true sense of the word "Khārijites" is thus "insurgents."

The Khārijite movement arose in response to the growing contradictions within Arab society. The social condition and property status of rank-and-file tribesmen, who formed the armed forces of the Caliphate, were constantly and rapidly deteriorating while the riches and power of the Arab tribal aristocracy increased. Military discipline under this aristocratic leadership helped to worsen the position of the Arab masses; the Arab tribes, as long as they roamed their native Arabia, had hardly any notion of discipline, but in the circumstances of ceaseless warfare, subjection and looting, however weak and relative this discipline was, it gave the tribal leaders an additional hold on their tribesmen.

The companions of the Prophet, belonging to the oldest generation of Moslems (such as the Caliph 'Omar), had endeavored to practice a policy of "tribal democracy," but after 'Uthmān, under whom the Arab tribal aristocracy had become firmly entrenched, other "companions" (such as 'Alī), who had to take into account the real balance of forces and who had moreover become rich themselves, were inclined to come to terms with the aristocracy, with the inevitable result of discontent and protest among both the Arab masses and the working masses of the conquered population.

The Khārijite movement at its inception was actually a continuation of the revolt which had caused the death of the Caliph 'Uthmān. Among the first Khārijites were many "readers of the Koran" formerly in the ranks of 'Alī's army; these "readers" were propagandists of early Islam for whom prayer, fasting and religious preaching was a profession, but, contrary to some assumptions, they were by no means at the heart of the Khārijite troops. An envoy of the Caliph 'Alī, sent into the Khārijite camp at Nahrawān, described these sectarians: "I saw among them men whose foreheads were covered with scratches and wounds from too many prostrations (in prayer), and whose arms were like the thongs of a camel harness; but they were dressed in clean shirts, and all seemed to rush somewhere in a hurry."[25]

In fact it was neither prayer nor fasting that attracted the working masses to the Khārijites but their militant support of democratic principles. The first point of their political program was the sovereignty of the Community of the Faithful, of the community of all Moslems. A Caliph receives the supreme power from the community, and solely by right of election, but if he fails in his mission, if his policies are not in the best interests of the community, the latter's representatives have the right to depose him or even to kill him. A Caliph most certainly does not have to be from the Quraish tribe, the tribe of Mohammed, but, in the opinion of the Khārijites, may also be an Arab of some other tribe or a non-Arab or even "an Ethiopian slave," always provided that he is known as a pious Moslem.

The menace of the Khārijites made it impossible for 'Alī to renew military operations against Mu'āwiya when the attempted arbitration in 658 failed to yield any result. That year, then, 'Alī marched his army to Nahrawān to annihilate the Khārijite threat:

he called for an end to armed resistance and granted an amnesty to all Khārijites, thus shaking their fervor so that many (perhaps the majority) left the military camp of their *amīr,* Ibn Wahb, to join the army of 'Alī, to return to Kūfa, or to go to Iran, or to Mecca. Only 2,800 of the more stubborn Khārijites remained with Ibn Wahb. Promising each other the "meeting in Paradise," they flung themselves against 'Alī's army and were destroyed almost to the last man in bitter fighting. Even after this defeat, however, the Khārijite movement continued; those Khārijites who had returned to Kūfa soon left it again and, together with the Khārijite detachments in Irak and Iran, renewed the struggle against 'Alī's partisans.

The traditional story is that the Khārijites in Mecca decided to kill 'Alī, Mu'āwiya and 'Amr ibn-al-'Āṣ in order to clear the way for their own appointee. In 661, 'Alī died of wounds inflicted by a Khārijite with a poisoned dagger as he was entering a mosque in Kūfa, but attempts to assassinate the other two failed.

Khārijite ideologists formulated some tenets of their faith justifying intolerance and fanaticism. A particularly important point, which acquired great practical significance, was their dogma of salvation; they believed that faith in Allah and the performance of religious rites would not in themselves guarantee salvation, bliss in Paradise after death. This could be achieved only by a practical manifestation of faith, by which the Khārijites meant the use of constant armed struggle to apply their principles against the Caliph and any authorities appointed by him.

The Khārijites excluded all Moslems who refused this dogma from the Community of the Faithful, considering them as *kāfirs* ("infidels") against whom the *jihād* (Holy War) must be waged. This uncompromising ideology sometimes saw peaceful workers the victims of Khārijite fanaticism, but nevertheless the socio-political principles of the Khārijites, expressing the aspirations of the working masses towards liberation from the oppression, violence and exploitation of both the local feudals and the Arab authorities, appealed to the downtrodden rural and urban population, who often gave their support to these tireless fighters. The social base of the Khārijite movement broadened considerably under the rule of the Umayyads, when the Khārijites became extremely active in the military and political field in nearly all the countries of the Caliphate.*

* [Modern western research offers a somewhat different interpretation of this movement. See F. Gabrieli, *Salle origini del movimento Ḫarigita,* Prendiconti della Reale Accademia dei Lincei (Class di scienze morali filologiche), ser. VIII, Vol. III (1941), fasc. VI, pp. 110–117; L. Veccia Vaglieri, *Il conflito ʻAli-Muʻāwiyya e la seccessione Kharigita riesaminati alla luce di fonti ibāḍite,* Annali dell' Instituto Universitario Orientale di Napoli, N. S. IV (1952), pp. 1–94.]

[1] "Annales quos scripsit Abu Djafar Mohammed ibn-Djarir at-Tabari cum aliis ed. M.J. de Goeje," Lugduni Batavorum, 1879 – 1901.

[2] "Liber expugnationis regionum, auctore Imámo Ahmed ibn Jahja ibn Djábir al-Beládsori . . ," ed. M.J. de Goeje, Lugduni Batavorum, 1866. (Henceforward *"Balādhuri.")*

[3] Abû Hanifâ ad-Dînaweri, Kitâb al aḫbâr et-tiwâl, publié par V. Guirgass, Liede, 1888. — Ibn Wādhih qui dicitur al-Ja'qubī, *Historiae,* ed. M.Th. Houtsma, pars 1–2, Lugduni Bavatorum, 1883.

[4] The title of this work has been incorrectly rendered as *Meadows of Gold. . .*

[5] D.C. Dennett, *Conversion and the Poll Tax in Early Islam.* Cambridge (Mass.), 1950.

[6] A. Butler, *The Arab Conquest of Egypt and the Last Thirty Years of the Roman Dominion.* Oxford, 1902.

[7] G. Weil, *Geschichte der Chalifen,* Bd. I–V. Stuttgart, 1846–1862.

[8] W. Muir, *The Caliphate, Its Rise, Decline and Fall.* Edinburgh, 1924.

[9] A. Müller, *Der Islam im Morgen—und Abendland,* Bd. I–II. *Berlin,* 1887.

[10] Cl. Huart, *Histoire des Arabes,* t. I – II. Paris, 1912 – 1913.

[11] Ph. Hitti, *History of the Arabs,* 5th ed. London, 1953.

[12] *Rabīʻ al-awwāl,* 11th year of the *hijra* = 27 May – 25 June 632.

[13] Quoted from N.A. Mednikov, *Palestina ot zavoevaniya ee arabami do krestovykh pokhodov po arabskim istochnikam* (Palestine from its Conquest by the Arabs until the Crusades, According to Arabic Sources), t. II. — "Pravoslavnyi Palestinskii sbornik," t. XVI, vyp. 2, p. 47. St. Petersburg, 1897–1903.

[14] *Ibidem,* p. 54.

[15] H. Lammens, *La Syrie. Précis historique,* t. I, p. 56. Beirut, 1921.

[16] Quoted from N.A. Mednikov, *Palestina. . .,* t. II, p. 50.

[17] *Ibidem,* p. 68.

[18] *Ibidem,* p. 70.

[19] *Mudya* is a measure of dry weight equal to 19 *ṣāʼ,* the *ṣāʼ* being slightly more than 2 kg; the *qisṭ* is half a *ṣāʼ*.

[20] Quoted from *Vsemirnaya istoriya* (Universal History), t. III, p. 112. Moscow, 1957.

[21] Quoted from N.A. Mednikov, *Palestina. . .*, t. II, p. 82.

[22] Macoudi (Mas'ūdi), *Les prairies d'or*. Texte arabe et trad. par C. Barbier de Meynard et A. Pavet de V. Courteille, t. IV, p. 263. Paris, 1865.

[23] Taha Ḥusain, *Al-fitna 'l-kubra* (The Great Civil War). [In Arabic, no date.]

[24] Hans Delbrück, *Geschichte der Kriegskunst,* t. III. p. 220. Berlin, 1907.

[25] Aḥmed Amin, *Fajr al-islām* (The Schism of Islam). [Cairo, 1935.]

CHAPTER IV

THE UMAYYAD CALIPHATE

SOURCES

In dealing with the sources used for the history of Arab lands in the period of Umayyad rule (660–750), one should take into account the fact that Arabic-language historiography started only in the ninth or tenth century under the dynasty of the 'Abbāsids, whose particular religious-political claims found expression in these historical works. In them we find a tendentious, preconceived attitude towards the Umayyads, considered as lay rulers upholding the traditions of the *jāhiliyya* in contradistinction to the 'Abbāsids who were "a dynasty blessed by God." The historians we shall deal with here lived and worked in Irak, and gave preference to the data of pro-'Abbāsid (thus anti-Umayyad) historical tradition.

The most abundant and varied information can be found in the "History" of Ṭabari and in two works by Balādhuri, *Futuḥ al-buldān* (The Conquest of the Lands) and *Ansāb al-ahsrāf* (Genealogy of Noblemen). The reports of Maṣ'ūdi are also important.

Geographical writings in Arabic are valuable as a historical source, especially their data on the economic history of Arab lands in the Middle Ages. Exhaustive information on this literature may be found in Krachkovskii's *Arabic Geographical Literature.*[1]

Most abundant (though not exhaustive) material on this subject, ordered by years of the Moslem era and provided with valuable bibliographical and historical notes, was collected by Caetani in his *Annals of Islam,*[2] in Italian translation.

An important book for any study of the Umayyad period is Mednikov's *Palestine from its Conquest by the Arabs until the Crusades, According to Arabic Sources,* which provides, in Russian translation, data from Arabic-writing historians and geographers pertaining to Syria, Lebanon and Palestine (Israel and Jordan), the translations being preceded by a comprehensive and valuable investigation of sources.

Compared with those sources in Arabic on the Umayyad period, historical works in other languages are much less valuable. Byzantine, Armenian, Syrian (Syriac) and west European writers provide little information on this period, the information there not being always reliable.

MODERN LITERATURE

The Umayyad period (in its chronological entirety) has been the object of special study by both Wellhausen and Lammens. The first of these two major orientalists is the author of *The Arab Kingdom and its Fall,*[3] until recently considered the best, indeed the classical, work on the history of the Umayyad Caliphate. Although in the last two or three decades certain of Wellhausen's major findings and deductions (particularly those pertaining to economic history) have been found incorrect (cf. the work of Denett and others), his monograph is still considered as of value by non-Soviet orientalists; neither can we neglect it, for it contains factual data taken from Arabic-writing historians.

The work of Lammens has defects typical of this learned Catholic missionary, who is, moreover, biased in favor of the Syrian Umayyads, with whom he particularly sympathizes for the stubborn fight of the father of the founder of the dynasty, Abū-Sufyān, and his relatives against "the founder of Islam." Lammens' works are nevertheless extremely valuable due to the extraordinary erudition of this author, who uses Arabic and other sources in a quite exhaustive way, as well as the data of west European orientalist literature; his numerous works are rendered still more attractive by the exceptionally rich and varied factual material collected in them. The following deal especially with the Umayyads: *Essays on the Reign of the Umayyad Caliph Mu'āwiya I, Essays on the Century of the Umayyads,*[4] and several articles in the *Encyclopaedia of Islam*. In his general history of Syria,[5] Lammens wrote extensively and very sympathetically on the Umayyad period.

Every "History of the Arabs" written in western Europe of course includes a chapter on the Syrian Umayyads, but as a rule such chapters are not devoted to scientific research. More specialized works are that of Gabrieli on the reign of the Caliph Hishām[6] and the valuable research of Carl Becker on the socio-economic history of Egypt under the Umayyads.[7]

Important work in Russian on the history of the Umayyads was done by Bartol'd in his research papers *Khalif Omar II i protivorechivye izvestiya o ego lichnosti* (Caliph Omar II and the Contradictory Information about his Personality, in *Khristianskii Vostok* (Christian Orient), t. VI, vyp. 3, 1922) and *Épokha Omeiyadov po noveishim issledovaniyam* (The Umayyad Period According to Latest Research, in *Novyi Vostok* ((New Orient), No.2). Bartol'd also gives a general description of the dynasty of the Syrian Umayyads in his article *Khalif i sultan* (The Caliph and the Sultan, in the journal *Mir islama* (The World of Islam), t. I, St. Petersberg, 1912, No. 2). Even greater attention should be given A. Yu. Yakubovskii's *Irak na grani VIII veka* (Irak on the Verge of the Eighth Century, in *Trudy Pervoi sessii arabistov* (Proceedings, First Session of Arabists), Leningrad, 1937), but A.E. Krymskii's chapter on the Umayyad Caliphate in his *Istoria arabov i arabskoi literatury* (History of the Arabs and of Arabic Literature) is by now outdated and gives the impression of superficiality.

Publications by present-day historians in Arab lands are by no means as valuable as those of European orientalists, for their information on the Umayyad period derives not so much from Arabic sources as from selective use of the books of European scientists. Moreover, the methodology of twentieth-century Arabic historians is based on the Arab-Moslem tradition, which detracts from their scientific value.

Two of the briefer yet more comprehensive of these studies on medieval Arabs and Islam are the *Political History of Islam* by Ḥasan Ibrāhīm Ḥasan[8] and the *General Islamic History* by Dr. 'Alī Ibrāhīm Ḥasan,[9] but these and similar works are of no interest whatsoever for the reader who can acquaint himself with the research of west European orientalists. Today, the Arabic historian conceives of "Islam" not just as the religion but as including the political life and culture of the Moslem "feudalistic" Orient. Among the few Arabic books dealing particularly with the period of the Syrian Umayyads are *Irak under the Rule of the Umayyads* by Kharbūṭlī and the *Reforms of ʻAbd-al-Malik*.

THE FORMATION OF THE UMAYYAD CALIPHATE

The singling out of the ninety years of rule of the Umayyad dynasty (660–750) as a separate period in history may be justified not only by the political fact (stressed by Wellhausen) that the Umayyads personified Arab domination in the conquered lands that formed the extensive Caliphate—for with the fall of this dynasty Arab hegemony ceased over the various subject peoples of Asia, Africa and Europe—but yet more important by the socio-economic changes which took place in the Caliphate during their rule and which resulted in the triumph of feudal relations among all the peoples of the Caliphate, including the Arabs. Under the influence of feudal conditions in the conquered lands, this period saw a process of transformation of the slave-holding tribal Arab aristocracy, which now became the dominant class of feudals in the Caliphate*; thus we can justifiably consider the military and political preponderance of the Umayyads as a transitional period in the history of the multi-national society of medieval "Arab" lands.

Properly speaking, the first Umayyad was the Caliph ʻUthmān, his successor being Muʻāwiya ibn-abu-Sufyān, proclaimed Caliph in Jerusalem by the Syro-Arab tribes faithful to him. At all events the Umayyad dynasty must be dated from the year 660. For more than a year, the two Caliphs, ʻAlī and Muʻāwiya, fought for supreme power, but unless we abide by Moslem orthodox tradition there is no reason to assign the year 661 as the first year of the Umayyad dynasty simply because the fourth "orthodox" Caliph, ʻAli, was murdered in that year.

The Umayyad Caliph Muʻāwiya rested on far stronger eco-

* [Modern western research describes the development of the Muslim feudalism in quite a different manner, and *inter alia* does not consider the Umayyad period to be the decisive phase of this development. see Cl. Cahen, "L'évolution de l'igtāʻ du IXe. au XIIIe. siecle, Annales (S–E–C)", VIII (1953), pp. 25–52.]

nomic foundations and possessed more trustworthy armed forces than his political opponents. He had become the all-powerful permanent viceroy of rich and civilized Syria as early as the days of the Caliph ʻOmar, and having spent more than twenty years in this important post, became the recognized leader of Arab tribal aristocracy in Syria; he also knew how to foster good relations with the Syrian population and gain their support.

THE SITUATION OF SYRIA UNDER THE SUFYĀNIDS

Two related branches may be distinguished among the Umayyad Caliphs, the first of which are the Sufyānids, thus named after the *kunya* [Arabic for "surname"] of the father of Muʻāwiya and consisting of Muʻāwiya (660–680), his son Yazīd I (680–683) and his grandson Muʻāwiya II, who died from the plague in 683 a few months after his reign began. The second branch, which replaced the first on the Caliphal throne, are known as the Marwānids after Marwān, the fourth Caliph of the Umayyad dynasty.

While he was still only viceroy of Syria, Muʻāwiya created a strong material base for himself, his kin and his military following, becoming a very big landlord by large-scale seizure of land. By the time the Arabs invaded Syria—a country with developed irrigational agriculture—the cultivated acreage had shrunk considerably and agricultural production had in part decreased due to the spoliation of the Irano-Byzantine wars and also to the fiscal policy of the Emperor Heraclius. Partial disruption of the provincial and communal systems of artificial irrigation, and the flight and death of farmers in many districts, had reduced the numbers of the rural population. Cultivated land, deprived of regular irrigation, turned to wasteland. This abandoned land was first seized by the Arab tribal aristocracy in conquered Syria; the new owners set many thousands of slaves to work on this land, prisoners and hostages enslaved during the conquests which were going on beyond the borders of Syria. Under the guidance of Syrian engineers, specialists in melioration, hydrologists and agronomists, the wasteland was again transformed into fields, gardens, orchards and vineyards.

The landed estates of the Byzantine Emperor and his dignitaries, masterless after the Arab conquests, also fell under the grasp of the new lords of Syria. In this way Mu'āwiya gained a very extensive domain, and became one of the biggest land- and slave-owners in the Caliphate. He also retained his family estates in the Ḥijāz, in which alone he had 4,000 slaves (according to incomplete data).

We can form some idea of the origins of slave-holding among the Arab tribal aristocracy by the following. When, in the seventies of the seventh century (under Caliph Mu'āwiya I), the Arabs captured the city of Bukhāra [in central Asia], their war leader Sa'īd ibn-'Uthmān, *amīr* of Khurāsān, acquired many prisoners and several hostages from among the local landowners. He ordered this "live booty" to be sent to Khurāsān and thence to Medina, where he possessed estates; as related by Nershahi (the tenth-century historian of Bukhāra), when Sa'īd arrived in Medina he ordered his ghulāms ("servants") to strip the hostages of their riches, precious habits and arms and replace them with garments of the plainest cloth, in which the hostages were forced to till the land. Thus the Bukharian landowners complained that they had been reduced to slavery and forced labor.

The Umayyad dynasty rested on the armed support of the Syro-Arab tribes, the best units in their forces. According to traditional genealogies, these tribes were of south Arabian origin and had migrated in the fourth and fifth centuries to Syria, Palestine, Transjordan and Irak, in which countries, during the two or three centuries before Islam, they came into permanent contact with the Byzantine and Iranian administration and army command and entered the service of both Iran and Byzantium as auxiliary forces. Under the influence of the local Aramean [Aramaic-speaking] population they had absorbed some elements of civilization and had become converted to Christianity.

The Syro-Arab tribes belonged to the Kelbites *(Banū-Kalb)* or [so-called] Yemenites, one of the two main groupings of Arab tribes. The other grouping consisted of the Qaisites *(Banū-Qais)* or Nizarites *(Banū-Nizār)*. The feud between these two groups dated from the days of the *jāhiliyya,* the constant struggle for political predominance sometimes assuming the form of bloodshed and civil war.

This struggle, in all the provinces of the Caliphate, was due not merely to old accounts left unsettled and to blood feuds but also to different political ideologies. The Qaisites, as the bearers of old Bedouin traditions and military and political patterns, limited their aim to taking booty and collecting tribute from the subject population; the production and culture of this population they considered a matter of complete indifference, and left it untouched. The Kelbites, however, though disdaining neither loot nor tribute, were in favor of cooperating with the conquered civilized peoples and assimilating their cultures.

The Umayyads, being one of the clans of the Quraish tribe, were genealogically Qaisites, but for political reasons and in view of the actual balance of power in Syria they sought the support of the Kelbites. In order to establish kinship with the latter, Mu'āwiya married Maimūna, a girl from a Kelbite tribe, who became his principal wife, the mother of Yazid the future Caliph, who himself later also married a Kelbite girl.

The Syrian Kelbite tribes formed the élite troops of the Sufyānids. Mu'āwiya ordered higher pay for them, was generous in his gifts to their leaders, invited them to feasts, and gave instructions to his son that on his taking the throne he should not overburden them with garrison duties and should grant them frequent leave so that they might spend more time on their grazing grounds with their wives, thus ensuring more progeny.

The Umayyads, being typical members of the Arab tribal aristocracy, did not interfere in the social production of the subject population, but remained quite content with the taxes and custom dues entering their treasury; they had additional huge incomes from their own estates. True, they sometimes showed interest in artificial irrigation, but only inasfar as this might increase the yield of taxation; on the whole, matters of social production and "increased production" were left entirely to the native population. The local dominant classes retained the functions of jurisdiction and police power as means of subjecting Syria's working masses. The influence of the Syrian Christian clergy was particularly enhanced under Arab domination; with the fall of Byzantine overlordship in Syria, persecution of heterodox Christians, the opponents of Greco-Byzantine orthodoxy, ceased, while on the other hand the Orthodox clergy was freed from the tyranny of the Greek Princes of the Church. This undoubtedly improved the position of the local Churches as well, such as the Monophysites, Nestorians and Maronites. Furthermore, the Christian clergy retained their judicial functions, acted as tax collectors among their flock and guaranteed the taxes (thus enhancing the influence of the clergy and accruing further benefits). Lastly, the clergy was in charge of the schools. The monasteries, moreover, were granted substantial tax reliefs by the Arab-Moslem authorities. Thus the Christian clergy in Syria supported the rule of the Umayyads, especially since many Christians at this time viewed Islam not as a separate religion but as a Christian sect.*

The Umayyads were popular among the native people of Syria, for their rise to power brought about a development of production and exchange in that country. Under Mu'āwiya, who had chosen Damascus for his residence, thus making it the capital of the Caliphate, Syria already enjoyed the advantages of a central region. It was girt by a line of customs posts which protected Syrian produce against competition by products imported from other lands of the Caliphate, while now that the old Irano-Byzantine frontier had been abolished, the well-developed Syrian artisanry sent its products into Irak and Iran.

Economic development of Syria under the Umayyads, however, was only relative. The cultivated area in that country was certainly far more extensive than, for instance, under Turkish rule from the sixteenth to the nineteenth centuries, but this prosperity was limited (cf. Henri Lammens). We know that under the Sufyānids the Syrian population suffered from recurrent famine, which, together with epidemics, resulted in the people dying en masse, especially in the cities. The reasons for these recurrent famine years have not yet been elucidated, but we know that the tax collection system worked without respite, taking no account of either the level of production or the economic position of the population.

* [Compare Cl. Cahen,"Note sur l'accueil des chrétiens d'Oriént à l'Islam", Revue de l'Histoire des Religions, CLXVI (1964), pp. 51–58.]

Under the Sufyānids, the same methods were used to exploit the agricultural population as in the period of conquests. The vast number of slaves sent from the theaters of military operations further enriched the Arab aristocracy, but apparently gave no impulse for a rapid extension of agricultural production. Moreover, the development of feudal relationships was slowed down, even temporarily stopped, after the Arab conquests.

Service in the army was the duty and the right of the Arabs, both Moslem and Christian, and was rewarded by payment and by material privileges provided by the Caliphal treasury, which quite sufficed for a living. Magazines containing ample reserves of produce paid in tribute were established to maintain the large army of nomad tribes, as well as the navy. The Arabs despised handicrafts, however, considering them an occupation fit for slaves. All branches of artisanal production were left in the hands of the tributary native people, who remained in the position of *dhimmis* (tributaries by "covenant"); these people also worked in commerce, usury and other money transactions, some of them as the officials of the state and its fiscal institutions. As before, affairs were transacted in Greek.

The Arabs still had no intelligentsia of their own. The liberal professions and intellectual occupations—architecture, medicine, writing, organizing land management and irrigation—consisted exclusively of members of the native population, Christians and Jews, for the Jews also enjoyed religious freedom, their remote ancestors having settled in Syria at the time of the dispersion, where most of them were now concerned in various branches of artisanal production, and some in commerce.

Those Syrians who had accepted Islam and had become *mawālī* served the Arab aristocracy; thus a literate *mawlā* who enjoyed the confidence of his patron could be profitably employed as a secretary, a treasurer, a butler or an estate manager.

Slaves played a considerable part in production, not merely in irrigational agriculture but also in the handicrafts. Serfdom was widespread: the serf lived and worked outside the home of his master and merely paid him regular money-dues *(darība)*.

The condition of the slaves and peasants under Sufyānid rule was apparently no worse than under the Byzantines; at least we have no reports of any uprisings of the working masses in Syria during this period, and it should be noted that the Khārijites, who were quite active by then in Irak and Iran, found no mass support among the peasantry and the urban plebe of Sufyānid Syria. Here the Caliphs felt themselves fairly safe: they had at their disposal a trustworthy and efficient army of devoted Kelbite tribes, and moreover enjoyed the support of the local landowners, the richer merchants, the Greco-Syrian intelligentsia, the upper stratum of artisans and the Christian clergy.

ARABO-BYZANTINE RELATIONS

Under the Sufyānids, the Arab tribes continued their conquests in Transcaucasia, central Asia and eastern Iran, but had no direct influence on affairs in Syria itself, where the Arab armed forces were fully absorbed in the struggle with neighboring Byzantium. Asia Minor became the arena of ceaseless Arab incursions, with the object of loot. Nearly every summer Arab flying columns penetrated more or less deeply into Anatolia, not merely in search of booty but in order to seize the approaches of Constantinople, for Mu'āwiya I had established as a major policy the capture of this magnificent city. In 668 the Arabs reached the Asian shore of the Bosporus for the first time, but the cold of the winter, their lack of warm clothing or provisions, the plague and dysentery soon decimated their camp. Reinforcements were sent from Syria under the command of Yazīd, the Caliph's son, and the Arabs began a siege of the Byzantine capital. But Constantinople was a first-rate fortress, and the Arabs, ignorant of siege techniques, were unable to storm it; in summer 669 the siege was raised. In 673 the Arabs launched a second, much better prepared, campaign against Constantinople; this time the land army was accompanied by a Syrian war-fleet and the Byzantine capital was blockaded by land and sea. The siege lasted five years, but again had to be raised after the resounding defeat of the Arab fleet by the Greeks.

The Syro-Arab navy was Mu'āwiya's creation; he had grasped its necessity for coastal defence in the face of the total Byzantine naval domination of the eastern Mediterranean, which presented a constant menace. Moreover, the creation (or rather, reconstruction) of a Syrian navy was also in the interests of the influential group of local merchants involved in maritime commerce with western Europe. However, the Caliph 'Omar had strenuously opposed the plan, apparently not wanting to entrust Moslem lives to any "wet, floating planks." The building of a fleet began only under the Caliph 'Uthmān, when Mu'āwiya had become full master of Syria. The shipbuilders were experts from the Lebanese coastland, descendants of the ancient Phoenicians, and they also provided the crews, under the command of local captains. Cedars of Lebanon yielded excellent wood for the ships.

Landed from Syrian ships, an Arab detachment now occupied Cyprus. During the second campaign against Constantinople, the Syrian fleet was to penetrate to the Bosporus and to the Golden Horn, and was later to keep the Byzantine ships at a safe distance from the Syrian and Egyptian coasts.

THE RELATIONS BETWEEN SYRIA AND OTHER LANDS OF THE CALIPHATE

During the reign of Mu'āwiya I, the Caliphate was far from being a unitary state with a centralized administration: the war leaders and viceroys of the various regions acted without any check or control (from the center), and although, as members of the Arab tribal aristocracy appointed to their high posts by the Caliph, they sent one fifth of their war spoils and tribute regularly to Damascus, the remaining four-fifths of course saw them generously provided for. Egypt was given over entirely to 'Amr ibn-al-'Āṣ, to whom the following cynical statement was ascribed: "I have no intention of holding a cow by the horns so that somebody else should milk her." The ruler of Damascus had actually to wage war against Irak, where the Shī'ites ["partisans" of 'Alī] and the Khārijites did not recognize him at all. The Shī'ites, aided by those Arab tribes that had supported 'Alī, chose as their supreme leader or *imām* the son of 'Alī, Ḥasan, whose mother was Fāṭima, daughter to the prophet Mohammed. Mu'āwiya they considered to be a usurper who had criminally seized the supreme power; he in his turn did not recognize ʻAlī as Caliph and ordered that he be cursed in the mosques.

European orientalists often describe the Shīʻites as Moslem "legitimists" because they considered only the direct offspring of the Prophet to be legitimate rulers. Muʻāwiya found it fairly easy to remove Ḥasan, a devout voluptuary who had neither the desire nor the capacity to fight against the Caliph, from the political scene by granting him a sufficient income from *ṣawāfī* lands in Irak so that he could retire to "private life."

The Khārijites meanwhile found widespread social support in Irak and Iran and waged a bitter struggle for the fulfillment of their democratic ideals. They recognized the authority of neither the Caliph from Damascus nor the Shīʻite *imām,* often using terrorist methods, which is probably why Muʻāwiya failed to visit Irak once during his twenty years of rule. The Khārijites were becoming particularly dangerous since they were supported not only by Moslems but also by the working masses of other religions.

The viceroys of Muʻāwiya in Irak and Iran practiced the same policies as he himself in Syria, aiming for the support of the native population, especially the *mawālī,* and improving the discipline among those Arab tribes who helped them against the Khārijites. Muʻāwiya's viceroy in Irak was Ziyād ibn-Abīhi, from the Thaqīf tribe of Ṭa'if, with which tribe the Meccan Umayya clan had maintained close economic and political relations ever since pre-Islamic times. Ziyād was at first named "ibn-Abīhi," meaning "son of his own father," because the actual identity of his father was unknown, though it was rumored that he was really a son of the famous Abu-Sufyān, the father of Muʻāwiya. Appreciating the outstanding intelligence and character of this man, who had successfully accomplished various missions entrusted to him by the Caliph ʻAlī, Muʻāwiya officially recognized him as his brother, and Ziyād thereafter became one of his most devoted and zealous partisans. He was appointed viceroy at Baṣra and then also received the administration of Kūfa and of all the eastern lands of the Caliphate. Enjoying complete administrative autonomy and the full confidence of Muʻāwiya, Ziyād in fact became co-regent with the Damascus Caliph. He had at his disposal considerable armed forces of Arab tribes settled in Iran* and adroitly manipulated the support of the *mawālī* as well as the inaction of the Shī'ites. He governed his provinces with the help of local forces and supplies and requested no military aid from Syria; the successors of Mu'āwiya later found the existence of such a situation quite astonishing.

Underground opposition to the Umayyads was based in the holy cities, in Mecca and particularly in Medina, which harbored the "companions" of Mohammed and their offspring, who had been elbowed out of political life by the Arab tribal aristocracy. Moreover, as the capital of the Caliphate had been moved to Damascus and economic and political importance in these vast dominions had now shifted to the conquered lands, the Ḥijāz retained only a religious significance. The surviving *muhājirūn* and *anṣār,* for want of other business, occupied themselves with works of devotion and hopes of bliss in Paradise. Their unasked-for leisure was filled with religious rites, readings from the Koran and gathering data on the life and activities of the Prophet, which by now began to acquire considerable socio-political meaning and importance. Favorite providers of traditions pertaining to the life of Mohammed, in the form of separate stories *(ḥadīths),* were his widows, companions and other contemporaries. At first, such traditions, which later on constituted the voluminous collections of the *sunna,* were passed on orally (as had been the case, earlier, with the Koran itself and pre-Islamic poetry) by the collectors and connoisseurs of the *ḥadīths* to their pupils; it was some time before the few literate pupils began to write down these traditions.

The "companions" of the Prophet and their successors had a strong inclination to pose as strictly orthodox Moslems, the keepers of the true doctrine, who followed in every way the rules of life established by Mohammed. They set themselves apart from the Umayyads, who had acquired ways of life and views in civilized Syria which made them doubtful Moslems in the eyes of the orthodox Medinese. This hostility towards the Umayyads of course also found expression in the original *sunna,* whose

* [Sic: probably a misprint for Irak.]

composers considered themselves wronged men and nursed this feeling. Later on, members of the Medina "school" of sacred tradition found their way into Irak, and it was here (under the 'Abbāsids) that the orthodox *sunna* was finally elaborated.

Thus, the orthodox Ḥijāzis had hammered out an ideological weapon against the Umayyads and were quite prepared to make use of it whenever possible.

THE REVOLT OF ḤUSAIN AND HIS DEATH

After the death of Mu'āwiya in 680, his son Yazīd became Caliph. He had been proclaimed heir to the throne in his father's lifetime, and Mu'āwiya had used both threats and blandishments to achieve his recognition. The Medina opposition, however, took no account of this, refusing to recognize either the heredity of power or the existence of a new dynasty, whereas for the Syrian Arabs (whose opinion had particular weight) hereditary rule was nothing new, since prior to Islam they had obeyed the *maliks* [kings] of the Ghassānid dynasty.

Caliph Yazīd I had been raised on Arabo-Syrian culture; he despised the orthodox Moslems in the holy cities and neglected the prescriptions of the Koran. He had been educated by Akhṭal, an outstanding Arab poet from the Christian tribe of Taghlib, and was himself a poet, a hunter and falconer, and a lover of music, song and dance. He liked to drink wine, both alone and in gay, profuse company, appreciating the comforts of city life and living in luxury like some Byzantine grandee or rich landlord, or like a viceroy of some important province. Like all his family, he remembered the desert and bedouin grazing grounds only during the recurrent plagues, for the epidemic did not reach the encampments and pastures of the nomads. Thus, in the "black" months or years, the Umayyad Caliphs and *amīrs* would leave Damascus and seek salvation in the Syrian desert.

When Yazīd became Caliph, there was discontent among the people in the holy cities; the principal grudge was not any violation of the merely formal principle of appointment by election, but was contained in the fact that with the establishment of the hereditary power of the Umayyads, the "companions" of the

Prophet and their numerous offspring lost their last hopes of important dignities and profitable posts. Pretenders to supreme power thus arose among these orthodox Moslems, for whom such power was to be gained by rebellion and armed struggle.

The first such rebel was Ḥusain, the second son of ʻAlī and Fāṭima, grandson of Mohammed. At the time of his elder brother's death (Ḥasan died in 669), when Muʻāwiya was still in power, Ḥusain had apparently decided that it would be madness to put forward his claim openly. He went on living peacefully in Medina, near the tomb that was dear to him (as he said), that of his grandfather the Prophet. At Muʻāwiya's death, refusing to swear allegiance to his successor, Ḥusain went to live in Mecca under the protection of the "house of Allah," the Kaʻba. There he was visited by representatives of the Shīʻites of Kūfa, who promised to raise a rebellion in his favor if he would come to their city. Consequently a relative of Ḥusain was dispatched to Kūfa to make preparations for the rising, and received many promises from the inhabitants of this large city, though when he was attacked by an armed troop sent by the Umayyad viceroy of Irak, ʻUbaidallāh son of Ziyād (the adopted brother of Muʻāwiya), he was left to his own fate.

The news of the murder of his agent reached Ḥusain *en route* from Mecca to Kūfa with a small escort of his relatives and personal supporters, less than 300 men. ʻUbaidallāh ibn-Ziyād sent stronger detachments against them, and Ḥusain's party was surrounded and slaughtered near the small town of Karbalā' in 680. In European literature the event is often called "the tragedy of Karbalā'," while later Shīʻites made Ḥusain, who had fallen in this hopeless fight, their greatest martyr, and established the month of *muḥarram* in which the fight had taken place as a time of mourning, fasting and sorrow for them.

THE WAR IN ARABIA

To the Medinese companions of the Prophet, the death of Muʻāwiya was an excellent occasion to rid themselves of Umayyad domination: at their meeting in the main mosque of Medina they refused to recognize Yazīd as the lawful Caliph. Yazīd immediately sent out a punitive expedition from Syria to Ḥijāz, which included troops levied from the Taghlib tribe. The commander of these troops was accompanied by a standard with the picture of Saint Sergius, the patron saint of the tribe.[10] The Medinese issued forth from their city to meet the enemy and suffered defeat at the "Battle of the *ḥarra.*"

Medina thus subdued, the Syrian army marched on to Mecca, which had become the stronghold of ʻAbdallāh ibn-Zubair, the son of that Zubair who had unsuccessfully challenged ʻAlī (with the support of ʻA'isha) and claimed supreme power in the Caliphate. ʻAbdallāh had inherited his father's claim, hoping for the support of the inhabitants of Islam's holy land. He thought himself completely safe in Mecca, as it was *ḥaram,* made inviolable by Allah according to the Koran, but for the Syrian army the notions and injunctions of Moslem Holy Writ held only very relative significance. They surrounded Mecca and used their stone-throwing artillery, positioned on the neighboring hills *(jibāl),* to shoot into it. The holy city and its population suffered heavily under this bombardment and the fires that broke out, which claimed even the Kaʻba, but the seemingly imminent fall of Mecca was delayed by the position in Syria.

During these events, in 683, the Caliph Yazīd had died; the Syrian army thus left Mecca and moved back to Syria in order to take part in the approaching struggle there. After the death of Yazīd, his son Muʻāwiya (II) had been proclaimed Caliph in Damascus. A young man, barely aged twenty, sickly and indecisive, he showed no capacity whatsoever for affairs of state. The Qaisites stationed in Syria refused to swear allegiance to him and preferred ʻAbdallāh ibn-Zubair, who had proclaimed himself Caliph in Mecca. This Meccan competitor of the Damascus ruler was recognized not merely in Arabia but also in Irak, and the Arab tribes of Iran, central Asia and Transcaucasia were ready to follow suit. Only the Syrian Kelbites still supported the Umayyad dynasty: the deep discontent of the Qaisites stemmed from the preference shown the Kelbites by Muʻāwiya I and his successors, who had granted them a privileged position.

In 683 or 684, the Caliph Muʻāwiya II, after an unremarkable rule, died of the plague. The Syrian army which had returned from Arabia then nominated Marwān ibn-al-Ḥakam, who was proclaimed Caliph at Jābiya at a meeting of Umayyad supporters. In the ensuing battle of the Syrian Kelbites against the Qaisites, the latter were decisively beaten at Marj Rāhiṭ, northeast of Damascus; the Kelbites were thus able to retain their former privileged position.

The Caliph Marwān, founder of the Marwānid dynasty, the younger branch of the Umayyads, was already infamous in the days of the Caliph 'Uthmān when he was the *de facto* ruler of the state. During the reigns of Mu'āwiya I and Yazīd, he was their viceroy in Ḥijāz, in his capacity as head of the Umayya clan in that country. When the rebellion against Yazīd broke out in Medina, he fled with his kin to Syria; now Caliph, he married one of the widows of Yazīd in order to establish closer kinship with the older branch of the dynasty. About a year later (according to certain reports), he was strangled by his new wife when he refused to proclaim her son heir to the throne, but other information attributes his death to the plague.

Next in the line of Caliphs were 'Abd-al-Malik (685–705) and Walīd I (705–715), whose reigns saw extensive conquests achieved and important reforms made.

RE-ESTABLISHMENT OF UMAYYAD RULE IN ARABIA AND IRAK

When 'Abd-al-Malik became Caliph, the Umayyads held only Syria and Egypt. The population of western and central Arabia, Irak and the dependent eastern provinces of the Caliphate all obeyed the Meccan Caliph 'Abdallāh ibn-Zubair, whom European orientalists usually designate as the "anti-Caliph," though this description is justified merely from the standpoint of Umayyad legitimism. In fact, as in the last year of the rule of 'Ali, there were actually two Caliphs in power (one in Damascus and the other in Mecca), and their partisans waged a bitter civil war.

Wishing to take advantage of the confusion in Syria, the war leaders of Ibn-Zubair, having put to flight the forces of the Umayyad viceroy Ibn-Ziyād, who fell in battle, led out considerable detachments to invade southern Palestine several times. The armies of the Byzantine Emperor Justinian II operating in Cilicia meanwhile posed a direct threat to northern Syria. Incited by the Byzantine military command, the Mardaites (see below) launched raids into inner Syria. A rebellion of slaves broke out in Damascus: these slaves, as Mas'ūdi writes, together with "the dregs" of the local population and "criminal elements," attacked the citizens of the capital and then encamped on a mountain near Damascus. The inmates of prisons in the city also broke out, forming an additional threat to peaceful citizens. Bedouin horsemen from the Qais tribes meanwhile raided and plundered the districts of Ḥimṣ, Baalbek and the Biqā'.

Hostilities with Byzantium immobilized the best Umayyad troops near the northern frontier. In order to stop the Byzantine menace and gain freedom of movement, 'Abd-al-Malik made slight territorial concessions to the Emperor and agreed to pay him tribute. The improved relations with Byzantium entailed a reduction of the activities of the Mardaites, mountaineers of unknown origin,* who were Christians and had fought on the Byzantine side at the time of Arab conquests in Asia Minor. In the sixties of the seventh century, they penetrated into the less accessible districts of mountainous Lebanon and settled there. The Arabs called them *Jarājima* after the name of their city [Jurjūma, further north, on Mount Amanus]. The Mardaites willingly gave refuge to all those fleeing into the mountains of Lebanon from the burden of taxation and persecution by the conquerors of the plains of Syria. Supported by the Byzantine command, who from time to time provided them with gold and weapons and even with military instructors, the Mardaites launched raids into the lower-lying parts of Syria, sometimes as far as Palestine.

During the various Arabo-Byzantine negotiations, the envoys of the Damascus Caliph insisted particularly on the discontinuation of Byzantine support to the Mardaites. The Caliph Mu'āwiya I had been forced, at times, to pay gold to the chieftains of these warlike mountaineers as a bribe to stop them raiding, and 'Abd-al-Malik now followed the same tactics. By the beginning of the eighth century, some of the Mardaites had migrated into

* [They were Aramaic speakers.]

Byzantine territory, while the remainder merged with the Maronites, the Lebanese Christians.

The viceroy of Irak, over which the Meccan Caliph Ibn-Zubair claimed dominion, was Zubair's brother, Muṣ'ab ibn-Zubair, but he held only very limited sway there, his best units being entirely committed to fighting the Khārijites. These uncompromising sectarians continued their usual policy of obstinacy and ferocity, accepting the authority of neither Caliph, nor that of any Shī'te *imām*. The peaceful population was especially terrorized by the bloody "exploits" of the Azraqis, the extreme sub-sect of the Khārijites [thus named after their first leader, Nufi 'ibn-al Azraq]. These raving fanatics waged "holy" wars against anybody who did not share their insane doctrine; not only were all "unbelievers" to be excommunicated from the Moslem community, but they were to be slaughtered outright. No exception was made for children in the belief that a bad tree could not bear good fruit. The Azraqi gangs spread terror and hatred throughout southern Irak and adjacent Khūzistān, and the bitter fighting between Muṣ'ab and these Khārijiteṣ made it easier for 'Abd-al-Malik to conquer Irak.

The Iraki Shī'ites were also quite active, though not so uncompromising as the Azraqis. With wide social support in Kūfa, the Shī'ites gained considerable though only temporary success, being most numerous at that time in this populous city. Mukhtār, of the Thaqīf tribe, appointed by the Meccan Caliph as governor of Kūfa, declared himself in favor of Mohammed ibn-al-Ḥanafiya, one of the sons of the Caliph 'Ali. Rejecting the rule of Ibn-Zubair, Mukhtār promised the numerous *mawālī,* the "new" Moslems still restricted in their rights, full economic and social equality. His forces were thus increased to the point where he was able to beat the troops of the Meccan viceroy back southward, to the district of Baṣra, and proclaim Mohammed ibn-al-Ḥanafiyya as the Shī'ite Messiah or *mahdī,* who was to reform the existing regime of inequality and oppression. But no perceptible change occurred in this regime during the short period of Mukhtār's activity (685–687); the *mawālī* began to desert him and his movement declined. His followers were pushed back to Kūfa by Ibn-Zubair and most died after a desperate resistance.

In 691, the army of ‘Abd-al-Malik entered Kūfa; Irak was henceforward under the rule of the Umayyads. This rule, however, was far from secure, for the Khārijites continued a stubborn resistance. Hostilities were resumed the next year in Ḥijāz, the population of which was still governed by Ibn-Zubair who, living in Mecca, considered himself Caliph even after the loss of Irak and demanded Moslem pilgrims, on arriving in "the Holy Land of Islam," to swear allegiance to him. To deprive his rival of this propaganda with Moslems outside Arabia, ‘Abd-al-Malik ordered the pilgrimage switched from Mecca to Jerusalem.

An army was sent out against Mecca, levied from Syrian and Egyptian Arabs and commanded by Ḥajjāj ibn-Yūsuf. After five weeks of siege, this army stormed the city. Ibn-Zubair, seeing that resistance was impossible now that the enemy had entered Mecca, asked the advice of his mother, the daughter of the Caliph Abu-Bakr and a sister of ‘A'isha. Despite her great age (she was a hundred years old), she had retained all her mental faculties, her teeth were whole and her hair had not yet turned gray.

Following the advice of this aged woman, the Meccan Caliph perished bravely at the Ka‘ba, fighting the Syrian warriors closing in on him to the last. At the orders of Ḥajjāj, his head was sent to ‘Abd-al-Malik in Damascus, while his body was crucified.

THE RULE OF ḤAJJĀJ IN IRAK

To complete the subjection of Irak to the rule of the Umayyad Caliph, the Khārijite rebellion had to be crushed and the Shī‘ite opposition smothered. A rich country with well-developed irrigational agriculture, Irak held great economic importance for the Arab aristocracy as a wide arena for fiscal exploitation. Its geographical location was also highly favorable, opening the way into Iran and adjacent countries, where the Arabs continued to wage aggressive wars and whence Syria received abundant loot and tribute. The Caliph ‘Abd-al-Malik therefore appointed Ḥajjāj as his viceroy in Irak, Ḥajjāj being entirely devoted to the Umayyad dynasty and having shown, in the Arabian campaign against Ibn-Zubair, boundless energy and complete disregard for the usual preconceptions and conventions.

The new viceroy reached Irak in 694, and until his death in 714 remained sole ruler of the eastern provinces of the Caliphate (like Ziyād ibn-Abīhi in the days of Mu'āwiya I).

Ḥajjāj ibn-Yūsuf was a native of Ṭa'if and a member of the Thaqīf tribe. According to tradition, in his youth he taught Arabic grammar in his home town and then enlisted in the Syrian army, where his career was brilliant. His interest in philology remained with him however: already all-powerful viceroy of Irak, he collaborated with the Ṭa'if scholars in editing the Koran. An important reform in Arabic writing is attributed to him, namely the introduction of diacritical marks and of signs above and below the line (*ḥarakāt* ["short vowels"]). He was also a great connoisseur and collector of Arab folklore.

Many contemporary Arabs considered his first public speech at Kūfa an outstanding example of rhetoric. Having reached Kūfa with 2,000 Syrian (Kelbite) warriors, he went at once to the mosque, where the representatives of the population awaited the new viceroy, for in the Middle Ages a mosque was not only a place of worship but a kind of forum where the decisions of the authorities were announced. Ascending the pulpit of the preacher (the *minbar*), he made a strange declaration, interspersed with verse as was the practice of Arab orators at that time, stating that the people of Kūfa, who were impious and factious, deserved punishment: he would skin them, twist them, beat them as one beats the branches of a *salām* [a kind of thorn tree] with rods until the leaves fall; he would strike them as one strikes a flint until it produces fire; he would pummel them as one pummels a stray camel who has joined an alien herd. He described himself as a valiant man who could not be pressed as one presses figs, nor frightened by the sound of empty skins (referring to the way bedouin drive a timid camel by beating a dried, empty skin bag).

In reply to the loud grumbling and the outcries of anger from the audience, he added that he could already see the streaks of blood that were to flow on the turbans and beards of many among them.

The rule of Ḥajjāj in Irak was one of bloodshed and terror, of which A.Yu. Yakubovskii[11] has written: "This was not accidental episode. It was either Ḥajjāj with his cruel, heavy hand—

or else it was Irak which at any time might overthrow the Umayyads and all their policies." Sometimes the executions proceeded day and night, so many that there were not even enough executioners to behead all the condemned. Witnesses estimated that during the twenty years of Ḥajjāj's rule, no less than 130,000 men and women perished on the scaffold. The prisons were overflowing, and on the day Ḥajjāj died contained 50,000 men and 30,000 women.[12] This pitiless ruler showed himself particularly ferocious with the Khārijites, considering them, quite rightly, as the most irreconcilable foes of the Umayyads. The military expeditions sent against them (especially against the Azraqis) and the bloody repression resulted in an exodus of the fanatic sectarians from Irak into other countries, Iran, Arabia and North Africa. Those Khārijites who remained in Irak (mainly the town dwellers) renounced any armed rebellion for the time being and contented themselves with religious propaganda. Towards the end of the seventh century the Azraqis disappeared from the political scene, and a moderate sub-sect of Khārijites arose, the Ibāḍites [or Abādites],* so that the viceroy of Irak was no longer troubled with ceaseless uprisings.

The main aim of Ḥajjāj and his administration was to transfer the rich resources of Irak to Syria. Considerable contingents of Syrian troops were sent into Irak to maintain it in the position of an occupied country, and were most active in repressing any revolts by the Iraki population. A fortress was built at Ḥajjāj's orders in which the Syrian troops were quartered; this fortress was called Wāsiṭ ("the Median") because of its position midway between Kūfa and Baṣra.

To increase the revenues which Irak yielded to Syria, Ḥajjāj paid some attention to agriculture. In order to increase the amount of cultivated land, peasants and slaves were directed to dig new canals and repair old ones and to build dykes and reclaim marshland. Black slave labor—the *Zanj*, brought by slave traders from East Africa—was brought into use to drain the marshes and clean the salt flats. In order to reduce the influx of rural people into the towns, where they increased the numbers of potential rebels,

* [Thus named after their founder, 'Abdallāh ibn-Ibāḍ.]

and also to combat vagrancy, special detachments were sent out to catch roving peasants, brand them and return them to their original homes. Sometimes villagers who did not move were branded as a precautionary measure, to prevent them from running away. The aim of such measures was to ensure a sufficient labor force for agriculture and to conserve the maximum amount of tax payers, who were also liable to pay the *corvée*. Farmers were forbidden to sell their buffalos, which were the most common form of chattel.

The fiscal policy of Ḥajjāj aimed at the same goal, increasing the receipts of the Caliphal treasury. According to the "law of the year 700," attributed to him, non-Arab Iraki Moslems were no longer exempt from payment of the poll tax *(jizya)*. This caused great dissatisfaction among the numerous *mawālī,* who dwelt chiefly in Kūfa and Baṣra, but the rural population was less affected by this law as most of the peasants in the days of the Umayyads remained faithful to their old religions (principally Zoroastrianism).

The disaffection in the largest cities of Irak broke out explosively as early as the very next year, 701, when the army of Ibn-al-Ash'ath mutinied. This war leader had been sent to Afghanistan at the head of a magnificently equipped "army of peacocks." Levied in Kūfa and Baṣra, this army resorted to active resistance when Ḥajjāj demanded a speed-up of combat operations despite the difficult, unfamiliar mountain terrain. Still commanded by Ibn-al-Ash'ath, the army retraced its steps toward Irak, defeated the reinforcements sent out by the Caliph, and approached Baṣra, where it was met with open arms by the population. New troops had meanwhile reached Irak under the command of a Kelbite war leader; these troops now threw back the rebels (whose ranks had been replenished by many men from Baṣra) toward Kūfa, and Ḥajjāj ordered terrible reprisals against the Baṣra population: it was rumored that he had nearly 11,000 people killed there. In the meantime, the army of Ibn-al-Ash'ath, again reinforced by large detachments from Baṣra and Kūfa, reached a total of 100,000 fighters. The Caliph 'Abd-al-Malik proposed an end to the fighting, promising a pardon to all insurgents, but the latter stood firmly by their resolution to continue the struggle against "the enemy of God and men," Ḥajjāj, and his overlord. This time, though, Ibn-al-Ash'ath's army, despite a desperate resistance, was defeated twice, and dispersed.

MEASURES TAKEN BY 'ABD-AL-MALIK AND BY WALĪD

The name of 'Abd-al-Malik is usually connected with certain "reforms" expressed in the use of Arabic in offices and chanceries and the coining of money with Arabic inscriptions. The business of the fisc had formerly been transacted in the local languages (Greek, Persian and Coptic) by a staff recruited from the subject population. Administration under the Umayyads included collecting taxes, customs, fines and contributions, assessing and distributing war booty, and also armed repression of any active protest on the part of the population. Any concern shown by the Arab rulers for agriculture (as, for instance, by Ḥajjāj in Irak) was merely aimed at increasing the taxable capacity of rural workers.

The introduction of Arabic for administrative and financial transactions was due to the Arab aristocrats' desire to head the administrative apparatus, for it made it possible for them to control the activity of the finance department. The reform was carried out in the days of 'Abd-al-Malik and Walīd I; it involved no change in staff, for the Arabs had no inclination for office work, while the immediate descendants of the conquered population by then included a good number of scribes who had fully mastered the language and script of the conquerors. Arabic became a mother language of the Syrian Arabs, and as early as the time of Mu'āwiya I Syrians were teaching Arabic language and literature to the children of the invaders from Arabia.

Another reform measure was the introduction of a single currency system throughout the far-flung Caliphate. Byzantine gold coins and Iranian silver coins were replaced by Arabic money—the gold dinar and the silver dirhem*—on which, after the Moslem profession of faith, were inscribed the name of the reigning Caliph

* [The dinar weighed 4.25 grams, and was worth some 20 dirhems; one dirhem weighed 2.97 grams.]

and the city in which the coin had been struck, as there were mints in all the principal cities with Arab viceroys, as well as in the capital.

The introduction of a new monetary system testified to the development of trade and economic relations between the various lands of the Caliphate and also expressed the tendency of the ruling dynasty towards centralization and proper management of the fiscal apparatus, though of course any centralization in the Umayyad Caliphate was very limited. The Byzantine government reacted to this new monetary system by opening hostilities against the Caliphate, for the earlier use of Byzantine coins gave some illusion of the Caliphate as politically dependent on Byzantium.

THE CONQUESTS UNDER THE MARWĀNIDS

The second major phase of Arab conquests began during the rule of ʻAbd-al-Malik. Under the Sufyānids the Arabs had already penetrated as far as Tunisia (still known in the old Roman manner as "Africa," *Ifrīqiya*), where they had founded the fortified camp of Kairouan in 670. The native Berbers, however, resisted strenuously and threw back the Arabs, taking and destroying this important stronghold of the invaders in 685. Earlier, in 638, they had ambushed and killed the Arab war leader ʻUqba ibn-Nāfiʻ, under whose command the Arab cavalry had raided deep into the Maghrib [northwest Africa as far as Morocco], but this "campaign of ʻUqba" is possibly merely legend, only remotely connected with historical events.

The real conquest of North Africa took place in the end of the seventh and the beginning of the eighth centuries, after the Syrian armies of the Damascus Caliph had defeated the supporters of Ibn-Zubair and re-established the rule of the Umayyads in Irak. The Berbers still stubbornly resisted the invaders; ultimately this resistance was personified by a Berber female war leader, the *Kāhina*,* a representative of the tribal aristocracy (perhaps a soothsayer or prophetess whom the Arabs knew as the "priestess," *kāhina*). We may assume that she led the resistance

* [At the head of "Jewish" or at least Judaizing Berber tribes.]

of the Berber nomads, for at her behest they ravaged the sown fields, felled tree plantations and filled up the wells with earth to create a defensive desert belt against the invading Arabs. Perhaps this was done at the advice of the Byzantines, who had tried the same tactics, unsuccessfully, in northern Syria. Such measures could not stop the bedouin, however, with their long experience of crossing vast desert expanses, while they only served to incense the sedentary Berbers against their nomadic countrymen, making them firm allies of the Arab conquerors.

At the very end of the seventh century (the year itself is unknown), the Arab armies again appeared in Ifrīqiya (Tunisia), took Carthage and began to rebuild Kairouan. In the early eighth century, the Arab war leader Mūsa ibn-Nuṣair arrived in North Africa to become the first viceroy of the Caliph in this region, which became known in Arabic geography as the "Maghrib," the lands of the "West."

Under the command of Ibn-Nuṣair, the Arab troops conquered the entire Maghrib, reaching the shores of the Atlantic Ocean in 709. The "conquest" was simply a series of big raids, resulting in the nominal submission of various Berber tribes, who were converted to Islam by sheer violence and therefore merely in externals. This policy of hasty proselytizing was due to the Arab conquerors' need to utilize the neophytes as recruits for further conquests in Europe.

In spring 711, Mūsa ibn-Nuṣair sent his *mawlā* (perhaps a Berber by origin), Ṭāriq, to Spain at the head of 300 Arabs and 7,000 Berbers, with the intention of making a thorough reconnaissance within the territory of the Visigothic kingdom. Since the Visigoths were militarily weak, owing to constant struggles between the feudals* and social and religious contradictions which had shaken the very foundations of the state, the reconnaissance became a major conquest, so that the next year saw the peninsula (known to the Arabs as *al-Andalus*) invaded by an Arab army under the command of Ibn-Nuṣair himself. The conquest of Andalusia was completed and Arab rule established over most

* [It is an exaggeration to speak of Visigothic society as feudal; it was at most proto-feudal.]

of the peninsula as far as the mountain range north of Toledo. According to certain data, still unconfirmed, the armies of Ibn-Nuṣair crossed the Pyrenees and raided some places in southern Gaul.

During these extensive conquests in the west, the Arabs were still at war in the Middle East and central Asia. Khurāsān, which they had seized in 644, provided a convenient base for invasions into *Ma-warā'-n-nahr** as the Arabs called Transoxiana. This was a rich land with an ancient civilization, stretching between the Amu-Darya and Syr-Darya rivers. Towards the end of the seventh century, the warlike enterprises of the Arabs in *Ma-warā'-n-nahr* were merely large-scale raids for booty, especially for slaves. Thus, in 673–674, an army commanded by 'Ubaidallāh ibn-Ziyād, Arab viceroy of Irak, crossed the Amu-Darya to capture and ruin Rotiman and the suburbs of Bukhāra. After bitter fighting with Turks and Bukharians, Ibn-Ziyād made peace with the queen of Bukhāra, and the Arabs brought back to Khurāsān a vast fortune in gold and silver coins and vessels, artistically worked weapons and high-grade silk stuffs, as well as some 4,000 captive inhabitants. In 676, the Arab army again crossed the Amu-Darya and approached Bukhāra, at which the queen of Bukhāra paid a ransom of 300,000 dirhems. Not content with this, the Arab war leader took a group of young Bukharian noblemen as hostages, sent them to Arabia, enslaved them and forced them to work on his own estates. Although this army finally suffered defeat near Samarkand, it still came back to Khurāsān with captives and booty.

The actual conquests of *Ma-warā'-n-nahr* occurred at the beginning of the eighth century, under the Caliph Walīd I. The conqueror of this rich and civilized country was the outstanding Arab war leader Qutaiba ibn-Muslim, who was answerable to Ḥajjāj, the all-powerful regent of the eastern provinces of the Caliphate. Qutaiba, by his faithlessness and cruelty, was infamous among the people of *Ma-warā'-n-nahr;* his military successes were actually due to the political fragmentation of that country,

* ["That-which-is-beyond-the-River," namely beyond the Amu-Darya, the classical Oxus.]

where local feudal lords constantly fought each other, so that some of them even sided with the invaders in the hope of triumphing over their opponents with Arab help.

The army of Qutaiba entered *Ma-warā'-n-nahr* in 706 and within ten years had conquered the country. Fresh reinforcements were sent out each year from Merv and from the Arab military camps in Khurāsān, for the stubborn resistance of the native population caused the Arabs heavy losses. Qutaiba had to display not only strategic but diplomatic skill, which for him consisted in perfidy and treachery.

Seeking booty (including captives and hostages) and tribute, Ḥajjāj pursued an aggressive policy in Afghanistan, eastern Iran and India. The plains of Afghanistan once conquered, the Arabs went on to take Kābul. In 708, an army commanded by Mohammed ibn-Qāsim, regent of Karmān, moved toward Sind, the region of the lower Indus River. This army, though less than 6,000 strong, was well-provided with siege and storming equipment. *Ballistae* and battering rams were transported in segments, on camel-back, and with this equipment the Arabs took Daibul and then broke the resistance of the defenders of Multan. Sind, where enormous loot was taken, was incorporated into the Caliphate.

THE UMAYYADS AND THE MAWĀLĪ

The reforms under 'Abd-al-Malik and Walīd I indicated an alteration of Umayyad policy from military occupation to orderly administration of subject countries, which meant direct control of the economic and political life of the population. The social foundations of Umayyad rule thus needed to expand now, to gain the sympathy of many classes and groups of subjects who for various reasons were dissatisfied with the existing regime. The most active enemies of the Umayyads were the Khārijites, against whom the armed struggle required constant use of large contingents, while repression of the political opposition of the Shī'ites also involved large forces and much money. Another category of the discontented were the numerous "new" Moslems [*mawalī*], native people who had embraced Islam and who generally could not improve their social and economic standing even after conversion.

In the Umayyad Caliphate, the viceroys of the Caliph governing the several provinces were completely arbitrary when it came to fiscal exploitation. The prescription of the Koran (IX, 29) on collecting tribute *(jizya)* only from tributary *(dhimmi)* people but not from Moslems was ignored; as we have seen, Ḥajjāj in Irak ordered tribute to be taken from Moslem neophytes as from the infidels (law of 700). 'Abd-al-'Azīz brother of the Caliph 'Abd-al-Malik and viceroy of Egypt from 685 to 704/705, ordered tribute to be collected from the new Moslems and the Christian monks, who had formerly been non-taxable, to be taxed in the same way, while his successor commanded all who evaded the tax to be branded and the dead to be left unburied until their outstanding taxes had been collected. The viceroy of Khurāsān declared that conversion to Islam did not free a man from the land tax, and in North Africa too the Berbers who had embraced Islam were forced to pay the same dues as their non-Moslem countrymen.

Among the Caliphal rulers of all these lands were many admirers and imitators of Ḥajjāj, who believed that bloodshed and terror were the best methods of government.

In Irak, the *mawālī* played a very active part in politics and in cultural life. By language and ethnic origin they were mostly Persian. Kūfa became their center, and as early as the "orthodox" Caliphs no less than half the city's population consisted of Persian traders and craftsmen. Even prior to Islam, the Arabs referred to the inhabitants of neighboring Irak as *'ajām,* "those that speak with difficulty or incorrectly, with improper pronunciation." Both the sense and usage of this word corresponded quite closely to the Latin "Barbarian," and among Arabs also acquired the meaning of "dumb" and even "lifeless." Arab aristocrats in the days of 'Uthmān and the Umayyads used the expression *'ajām* for the *mawālī* as a term of scorn and disparagement.

As we have seen, the *mawālī,* victims of fiscal exploitation, were on a far from equal status with the Arabs. Some historians, both western and oriental, interpret this unequal status as due to the Arabs' haughtiness and "national" pride, but it was in fact due to the survival of the Arab tribe and clan organization, in which a non-Arab could never become the equal of a full-fledged member. Moreover, the Arab conquerors tried to avoid intermixture with the subject population for fear of losing their identity in the mass, and marriage between a *mawlā* (or any other non-Arab) and an Arab woman was therefore considered a crime punishable by death.

The *mawālī* did not even enjoy the same rights as the Arab Moslems in the performance of religious ritual. They had to build separate mosques for themselves, which the Arabs did not enter, but if they prayed together with the Arabs in a mosque or forecourt, they had to stand in the last rows, behind the Arabs. Many Arab Moslems believed that the prayers of the *mawālī* were of doubtful value, "like prayers of donkeys or camels, if such quadrupeds could pray," yet the *mawālī*—many of whom had been Zoroastrians or faithful of other religions with a developed cult and ritual—displayed much greater religious zeal and piety than the Arab Moslems, for the latter were not really terribly concerned with the ritual prescriptions of Islam. For instance, orthodox Moslem tradition holds up the *mawla* Ḥasan al-Baṣri (died in 728), the son of a slave and a convert to Islam, as an exemplary Moslem of the first century of the *hijra*. In addition to the mandatory five (daily) prayers, Ḥasan would often pray throughout most of the day and night; his feet would swell from the frequent genuflexions and prostrations and his eyes were red from his vigils; he looked frightened, as if he beheld the flames of Hell.

The *mawālī,* heirs to Iranian and Aramaic culture, were at a far higher level of civilization than the early Moslem Arabs. The Arabs therefore made use of the *mawālī* wherever literate people were required, in offices, in the army and in private households. Even under the Caliph 'Omar I, far from every *mawla* received his dues from the *bait al-māl,* and what he did receive was much less than the share of an Arab, while under 'Uthmān, with the land-grabbing Arab aristocracy wanting Irak transformed into "a garden of the Quraishites," the condition of the *mawālī* deteriorated sharply. Thus they supported the uprisings against 'Uthmān and sided with 'Ali, who enrolled them in his army.

The establishment of Mu'āwiya's rule in Irak resulted in a revolt of the *mawālī* in Kūfa in the year 43 of the *hijra* (663/664).

After this was repressed, the Damascus Caliph ordered many *mawālī* from Irak to be resettled in the coastal districts of Syria and in Antioch (Anṭāqiya). Ziyād ibn-Abīhi, co-ruler with Mu'ā-wiya, appreciated the importance and strength of the Iraki *mawālī,* however, and tried to attract them to his side, thus being able to govern his provinces just with local forces and without the military support of Syria, though after his death the *mawālī* willingly swore allegiance to Ibn-Zubair (the Meccan Caliph), and later supported the unsuccessful rebellion of the Kūfa viceroy Bishr ibn-Marwān, against his brother, the Caliph 'Abd-al-Malik.

Ḥajjāj earned the hatred of the *mawālī* by humiliating and exploiting them. They stubbornly resisted their enlistment in punitive units sent out against the Khārijites, and both Iraki and Iranian *mawālī* felt particular sympathy for the Shī'ites. They were always ready to back the political claims of the 'Alids, as they accepted as historical fact the marriage of Ḥusain ibn-'Alī to a Sassanid princess, daughter to the last *shahin-shah* Yazdagird III, on the strength of which fact, though not quite authentic, they recognized the descendants of the "martyred" *imām* as the legal successors of the Sassanid kings who had ruled independent Iran.

It is among the *mawālī* that the "shu'ūbiyya" movement arose, the ideological struggle of non-Arab "nations" [shu'ūb] (mainly Persians), in the eastern provinces of the Caliphate against Arab hegemony. Conscious of their cultural superiority over the Arabs, the Persians who participated in this movement demanded equal rights and even privileged positions for Persians and members of other nations more civilized than the Arabs.*

The rising dissatisfaction of the masses under fiscal oppression, expressed in frequent revolts, induced the Umayyads to take measures which they thought might reconcile the "new" Moslems with the ruling dynasty; these measures the principal Arabic-Moslem historians, usually hostile to the Umayyads, see as very closely connected with the personality of the Umayyad Caliph 'Omar II (717–720), son of 'Abd-al-'Azīz and nephew of 'Abd-

* For a different interpretation of the shu'ūbiyya see H.A.R. Gibb, "The Social Significance of the Shuubiya", Studies on the Civilization of Islam, Boston, 1962, pp. 62–72.

al-Malik, whom they single out as an exception, outstanding for his piety. This "pious," "God-fearing" Caliph, according to these authors, strove to rule in strict accordance with the prescriptions of the Koran ("the Book of Allah") and of the *sunna* (tradition) of the apostle.

European bourgeois historians of the Caliphate have accepted the bulk of these Moslem notions, describing 'Omar II as a pious idealist, even a utopian, and explaining the measures taken during his rule by reference to his personal qualities, convictions and moods. Even Wellhausen, the author of the most comprehensive monograph on the history of the Umayyad Caliphate, came under the influence of Moslem tradition.*

The sources and the trend of the relevant scientific literature on 'Omar II's rule being such, then, Bartol'd's "Caliph 'Omar II and the Contradictory Information about his Personality"[13] gains particular significance.

This paper, which makes exhaustive use of sources in the Arabic language, presents the personality and activities of 'Omar II in a historically authentic light. Firstly, Bartol'd revealed a formerly unknown tradition of Arabic literature which differs substantially from the current Moslem orthodox views on the piety and ascetism of this Caliph. It now appears that this Umayyad, prior to ascending the throne, was a totally different character. He was known as a dandy, who spent lavishly on perfumes, clothes and horses; he liked his ease and lived in luxury. By the age of forty he had 14 children (some say 16), including 9 from his favorite slave girl; as Bartol'd remarks, "in any case, this does not point to an ascetic way of life."[14] When he was viceroy of Walīd I in Medina, 'Omar scrupulously carried out all the orders of the Caliph, including those bound to offend the local orthodox, who had appointed themselves custodians of the Koran and the *sunna*. When a son of the former Meccan Caliph Ibn-Zubair dared to voice disapproval at the acts of Walīd I, 'Omar ordered him cruelly punished: the executioner gave him 100 strokes of

* [The author ignores here the revision undertaken by various Western historians in their attitude to this Caliph. See, for example, H.A.R. Gibb, "The Fiscal Receipts of Umar II," Arabica II (1955), pp. 1–16.]

the lash, after which the tortured man was splashed with cold water in bitter winter weather and left thus to die.

On becoming Caliph, ‘Omar II changed his way of life abruptly. His palace now resembled a refuge of beggar monks; he and his courtiers dressed in mourning, with cheap cloth, and practiced abstinence and penitence. The change was the more stupefying as under the preceding Caliph, Sulaimān (715–717), a voluptuary and a glutton, the palace had been the stage of orgies with music, song and dance. Bartol'd believes that the sudden change in the behavior of ‘Omar II is accounted for by the fact that his rule started on the 100th year of the Moslem era (718/719 A.D.), when the subjects of the Caliph underwent a real attack of religious psychosis due to the widespread and absurd belief that the Moslem state was fated to exist for one hundred years and that therefore the end of the world and the Last Judgment were at hand.

The measures taken in the days of ‘Omar II, however, were dictated not by mysticism but by political realism, and were aimed at strengthening the dynasty by widening its social support. Thus the Caliph ordered his viceroys to cease collecting poll tax from the new Moslems, actually declaring himself in favor of including them in the *dīwān,* the lists of Arabs who received permanent subsidies out of the state treasury; it became known thus that conversion to Islam "saves the soul and the money." Land tax was now ordered from all landlords and farmers, without distinction of religion. This "equality of rights" between the descendants of the Arab conquerors and the Moslems of the native population was intended to improve the lot and social standing of the *mawālī,* any such improvement being particularly marked for the numerous *mawālī* in the cities, unconnected with agriculture.

‘Omar II also tried to come to terms with representatives of the Shī‘ites and the Khārijites on a suspension of hostilities. Predictably, the Khārijites rejected outright the peaceful proposals of the Caliph. He was also against the policy of *jihād,* Moslem "holy war," believing that Islam should be propagated among the "infidels" by means of peaceful religious propaganda. The Arab armies were therefore recalled from the walls of Constantinople, the siege of which had been begun under the Caliph Sulaimān in spring, 716, though other sources report that the unsuccessful siege had been raised before the reign of 'Omar II. Despite his peaceful disposition, however, this Caliph took good care of the army, the best prop of his dynasty, and increased its pay considerably.

Thus, a quite realistic policy was carried out under 'Omar II, aimed chiefly at strengthening the rule of the Umayyad dynasty. and certainly not concerned with otherworldly salvation. But this policy failed to enlist any influential support, to such an extent that we even have information (unconfirmed) that 'Omar II was poisoned by his kinsmen. At all events, his successors reverted to the traditional Umayyad policy of fiscal exploitation of the people, which was ultimately to be the downfall of the dynasty.

THE CALIPHATE UNDER THE RULE OF HISHĀM

Under Caliph Hishām (724–743), the son of 'Abd-al-Malik, the fiscal apparatus functioned smoothly and remorselessly, exacting abundant moneys from the subjects to fill the Caliphal treasury. Many Arabic-writing as well as west European historians have accounted for the increased taxation of the laboring masses by the avidity and avarice of the Caliph Hishām, though this ruler led a temperate mode of life, despised luxury and would not tolerate wasteful expenditure, besides which it is ridiculous to account for the worsening condition of the people in the various lands of the extensive Caliphate merely by the bad character of any one statesman. In fact the rising taxes were due to the unwillingness of the Arab tribal aristocracy, especially the members of the now very numerous Umayyad clan (some of whom had become big landlords), to renounce either their privileges or the big subsidies they received from the treasury, for this meant that they were diametrically opposed to any policy of equality among Moslems such as was attempted by 'Omar II, after whose death they renewed the traditional procedures of the Marwānids, that is, increased fiscal pillaging of the masses. Under 'Abd-al-Malik taxation had increased twofold and provoked several peasant uprisings. Now Hishām and his successors ceased to rely on the Kelbites and made the tribes of Qais their support instead, therefore treating Damascus, where Kelbite traditions prevailed, with some contempt. Hishām made his residence in Ruṣāfa, to the north of Palmyra (Tadmor), rebuilding this abandoned and nearly completely ruined town, which under the Byzantines was called Sergiopolis.

The Caliph Hishām, with some of the Umayyad *amīrs* and several Caliphal viceroys, ordered the irrigational system to be restored and enlarged, and cleaning disused ditches and digging new canals proceeded with particular energy throughout his domains, for irrigation meant an expansion of cultivated acreage and thus of the tax-paying capacity of the farmers. For the same fiscal purposes, the tax-collecting administration was put in what was later considered as exemplary order.

The activity of officers of the fisc was approaching its peak, and under Hisham became quite pitiless, even criminal, in its proceedings. Tax collectors considered as a willful defaulter any subject who could not pay his dues at the stated time, and the prisons overflowed with such defaulters. Torture was applied as the surest method to force payment: the victim was pilloried and left for hours under a scorching sun, while the most recalcitrant had boiling oil poured on their heads. Under Yazīd II, Hishām's predecessor, taxes had been imposed on both secular and regular clergy, who formerly had been exempt. Such methods abundantly made up for the decrease in the treasury from "Omar's days."

The organization of increased production by the Caliphal authorities themselves, together with the "exemplary" fiscal administration, were the only means by which the Umayyads could bring to completion those measures taken in the reigns of 'Abd-al-Malik and Walīd I; the reforms of these Umayyad Caliphs may well be considered a kind of end-result of the influence of the feudal relationships in force in those countries conquered by the Arabs upon the slave-holding Arab aristocracy itself. By the start of the eighth century, the ruling stratum of this aristocracy was becoming a dominant class of Arab feudals, but, unable as yet to free themselves of their traditions as conquerors, they did not come into contact with the (native) feudals of subject countries (this particularly in Iran and central Asia).

These economic-political changes were accompanied by a shift in political ideology as in the days of Hishām the regime of the later Sassanids came to be regarded as an ideal of state structure and administration.

During the reign of Hishām, the Arab and Berber troops who ensured the Arabs' dominion in Spain continued to raid deeply into Aquitania (the basin of the Garonne River), whence they advanced from Lyons along the old Roman road toward the northwest. In 732, between Tours and Poitiers, they engaged in battle the Frankish army of Charles Martel, but, lacking success, retreated. Their attempts to renew their raids in the following years also met with failure. In 739 the Berbers of North Africa rose against Arab rule, and this was the sign for Arab conquests in western Europe to stop, especially since the booty from Gaul was intercepted in Andalusia and did not reach Syria, so that Hishām therefore saw no cause to pursue an aggressive policy in Europe.

The increasing fiscal exploitation and the cruel executions [of defaulters] provoked active opposition by the people in repeated rebellion. The most widespread and stubborn revolts occurred in central Asia and North Africa. In *Ma-warā'-n-nahr* [Transoxiana], the rebels allied themselves with the central Asian Turks, thus vastly complicating the task of Arab punitive expeditions. Nevertheless, the uprising of 736–737 was ruthlessly put down by the troops of the Khurāsān viceroy, who made ample use of the alarm of the local feudal lords at the scale of the popular movement.

Not much later, in 739–740, the Berbers rose in northern Morocco. Uncompromising Khārijites were in the van of this rebellion. A Syrian army of 25,000 warriors sent by Hishām to North Africa was defeated and in 742 the uprising engulfed the whole of the Maghrib. The rebels, with the Khārijites in the lead, invaded Ifrīqiya (Tunisia) and threatened Kairouan, but here the Caliphal army, commanded by the viceroy of Egypt, succeeded in beating the rebel troops. Nevertheless agitation and uprisings continued among the masses of the Berbers in the Maghrib, and the Umayyads found it impossible to pacify the countries of North Africa. In Irak the relative calm and order ensuring the ormal productive activities of the population were frequently interrupted, mainly by rebel Khārijites, while in Syria—the stronghold of the Umayyads—the new policy of Hishām and his successors in seeking the support of the Qaisite tribes offended and antagonized the Kalbites, who formed the majority of the Arab population in that country.

HE FALL OF THE UMAYYADS

The active discontent of the working masses in all the lands f the Caliphate resulted in the downfall of the Umayyad dynasty, or it had thus lost all social support. The vast resources accumulated by Hishām in the state treasury were dissipated under his politically inept and inactive successors, and his fiscal administration, considered excellent, and his well-organized army were soon out of order. Within two years (743–744) no less than three Caliphs succeeded each other (all grandsons of 'Abd-al-Malik), the most colorful of whom was Walīd II, who completely neglected affairs of state and spent his days in hunting and falconry and his nights in feasting. He had artistic pretensions and thought himself a poet, competing unsuccessfully with numerous *literati,* dancers, singers and musicians of either sex, who helped him spend the money accumulated by his predecessor Hishām. His neglect of Islamic prescriptions must have exceeded that of all other Umayyad Caliphs, for he was certainly accused more than any other of lack of faith and piety. Some later Arabic-writing historians hostile to the Umayyads accused him of sacrilegious actions: it was said that he used manuscripts of the Koran as targets in archery practice so that "God's books" were pierced with arrows, and that he sent one of his concubines as *imām* to conduct the Friday prayers in the mosque. He resided in a palatial "hunting lodge" built in the desert to the east of Jordan, and finally fell victim to a conspiracy to his own kinsmen.

His contemptible successor, Yazīd III, was nicknamed *nāqiṣ,* "he who decreases," because his empty treasury forced him to decrease the pay of the soldiers. This further demoralized the armies of the Caliphate, and disorders broke out in Syria, complicated by the feud between the Qais and Kalb tribes which was causing great damage to both the rural and urban population. In nearly every *jund* [military district] self-appointed Caliphs arose from among the Umayyad *amīrs,* and the tribute levied by such illegal authorities of course never reached the state treasury.

The disorders continued under the last Umayyad Caliph, Marwān II (744–750), who had seized power at the age of sixty. An energetic and experienced war leader, he had commanded the Arab troops against the Byzantines in Asia Minor and had then become viceroy in Armenia and in Mesopotamia *(Jazīra)*. Now Caliph, he chose for his residence the city of Ḥarrān in Mesopotamia, and transferred both the state treasury and the central administration there. He tried to lean on the Qaisite tribes, thus arousing extreme dissatisfaction on the part of the Kalbite units garrisoned in Syria and Irak.

Both the rural and the urban population of Syria rose several times in rebellion against this Caliph. To subdue the rebels, Marwān II repeatedly went on campaigns in Syria, twice besieged Ḥimṣ, and ordered the fortifications of major Syrian cities to be dismantled in the hope that it would thus be easier to subdue the population. The Syrians were rebelling not only against excessive taxation and arbitrary exaction by publicans but also against *corvées* and other additional duties. Under the last Umayyads, many Syrians were being forced into hard and dirty labor in shipyards and military camps, and to provide squads of laborers to work in military convoys and ancillary services.

In Mesopotamia and Irak, Marwān II was forced into bitter war against the Khārijites, who by that time had acquired much military experience, improving their organization and using more sophisticated tactics, while still retaining their former stubbornness and fearlessness. In the Mosul district, for instance, the Khārijite army waged trench warfare, which much increased their own combat value while complicating the task of the Caliphal army. Meanwhile the hardships of the laboring masses of Irak, whose condition had deteriorated rapidly under the latest Umayyads, provided favorable ground for Khārijite propaganda; even some Kalbites stationed in Irak sided with the Khārijites. At the same time, the Khārijite movement spread quite widely throughout

Arabia, where the last Umayyad Caliph did not have sufficient forces to strike back, the troops at his disposal being exhausted by ceaseless, bitter fighting with the Khārijites in Mesopotamia and Irak and by campaigns against the rebels in Syria.

Large-scale Shī'ite propaganda also took advantage of the general disaffection under Marwān II, who continued the traditional policy of fiscal exploitation. Shī'ite preachers called on the people to bring down the Umayyad usurpers, who had deprived the descendants of the Prophet of their legitimate right to supreme power. This propaganda found a particularly sympathetic audience in Khurāsān and in *Ma-warā'-n-nahr,* where (as in all of Iran) the class struggle of the working people was combined with the desire to oust the foreign rule. The anti-Umayyad rebellion thus found widest scope in central Asia and northern Iran, where the peasants and the urban plebe, who constituted the bulk of the rebels, were joined by many local *dihqāns* (feudal lords) and even by certain Arab tribes. The most outstanding leader of this uprising was Abū-Muslim, a gifted captain and statesman. A Persian from the lowest rungs of the social ladder, he had been a slave in his youth, and thus expressed not only the aspiration toward political independence of the fatherland, but also toward the social liberation of the working masses, among whom he was particularly popular. The *dihqāns,* on the other hand, did not trust him and were afraid of him, but were forced to take account of his growing fame.

The uprising started in 747 in the Merv oasis, where numerous peasant troops from far and near gathered in response to an appeal by Abū-Muslim. The rebellion rapidly spread to western Iran and thence to Irak. The army of the rebels engaged the troops of Marwān II on the Greater Zāb River, a left-bank tributary of the Tigris. The Caliphal army had been levied in a hurry and was of low combat value: it was decisively beaten and soon dispersed. Marwān, at the head of a small band of devoted followers, fled to Syria, but here the army as well as the population were hostile to the Caliph; the citizens of Ḥimṣ, seeing the small numbers of his followers, tried to attack them and capture Marwān himself, but some of his warriors, lying in ambush, sprang on the men of Ḥimṣ from the rear and put them to flight.

Marwān next attempted to raise a new army in Palestine, but this merely provoked one more uprising, and he thus fled farther, to Egypt, and tried to gather forces there to fight off the Khurāsān army which was approaching under the command of ‘Abdallāh ibn-‘Alī. But the Copts and local Arabs rose in rebellion and forced Marwān to retreat to Giza [near present-day Cairo], where even then the Caliph and his warriors proved capable only of misconduct and violence against the local nunnery. As he was preparing to flee thence to the Maghrib, Marwān was finally seized and killed, and his corpse crucified.

[1] I.Yu. Krachkovskii, *Arabskaya geograficheskaya literatura* (Arabic Geographical Literature). Izbrannye sochineniya (Selected Works), t. IV. Moscow-Leningrad, 1957.

[2] L. Caetani, *Annali dell'islām,* I–VI. Milano, 1905–1913.

[3] J. Wellhausen, *Das Arabische Reich und sein Sturz,* Berlin, 1902; English translation: "The Arab Kingdom and its Fall."

[4] H. Lammens, *Études sur le regne du calife omaiyade Moawia I,* t. I–III. Beirut, 1906–1908; id., *Études sur le siècle des Omayyades*. Beirut, 1930.

[5] H. Lammens. *La Syrie. Précis historique,* Vol. 1–2. Beirut, 1921.

[6] F. Gabrieli, *Il califfator di Hisham* [Alexandria, 1935.]

[7] C.H. Becker, *Islamstudien,* Bd. 1–2. Leipzig, 1924–1932.

[8] Hasan *Ibrāhīm* Hasan, *Ta'rīkh al-īslām al-siyāsi.* Cairo, 1935.

[9] ‘Ali Ibrāhīm Ḥasan, *Al-ta'rīkh al-islāmi al-‘alm.* Cairo, 1953.

[10] H. Lammens, *La Syrie*. . . , Vol. I, p. 73.

[11] Cf. *Trudy Pervoi sessii arabistov* (Proceedings, First Session of Arabists), p. 29. Moscow-Leningrad, 1937.

[12] *Ibidem.*

[13] V.V. Bartol'd, *Khalif Omar II i protivorechivye izvestiya o ego lichnosti.*— "Khristianskii Vostok" ("The Christian Orient"), t. VI, vyp. 3. Petrograd, 1922.

[14] *Ibidem,* p. 213.

CHAPTER V

THE BAGHDAD CALIPHATE IN THE EIGHTH TO TENTH CENTURIES

SOURCES

In studying the history of the Baghdad Caliphate during the first century and a half of its existence, orientalists generally use the Arabic-language works mentioned in the preceding chapter. The most complete and reliable narrative source is Ṭabari's *Universal History,* but we may add here the remarkable chronicle by Ibn al-Athīr (1160–1233), *al-Kāmil fi-l-ta'rīkh* (The Complete Collection of History), which is a successful reworking of Ṭabari's book, with additions. In comparison with Tabari and Ibn al-Athīr, the *Kitab al-'ibar* (Book of Instructive Examples) by Ibn-Khaldūn (1332 – 1406) is less important for the history of the Asian provinces of the Baghdad Caliphate and of Egypt, though it is exceptionally valuable for the history of the Maghrib. There is also some quite interesting and valuable information in the works of Mas'ūdi.

Besides the narrative source material in Moslem authors' "general histories," important information can also be found in those works by scholars and historiographers who were high officials of the central administrations of the Caliphate and courtiers of the 'Abbāsid Caliphs.

Geographical studies in Arabic are highly significant for any study of the productive activity of the working masses in the Baghdad Caliphate and also for their coverage of the far-flung commerce between the provinces of this extensive empire and between the latter and foreign countries. These works have been published by M. J. de Goeje in the series "Bibliotheca geographorum arabicorum." Exhaustive information on this geographical literature can be found in Krachkovskii's "Arabic Geographical Literature."[1] Data on Arabic-writing geographers dealing with Syria (in the wider sense of the term) may be found (in Russian translation) in Mednikov's "Palestine from its Conquest by the Arabs until the Crusades, According to Arabic Sources" [see below, footnote 2].

Particularly important sources are the special "books on taxation," written as manuals for rulers and civil servants of financial administrations. Orientalists (including Soviet Arabic medievalists) regard the "Book Concerning the *kharāj* Tax" *(Kitāb al-kharāj)* by Abū-Yūsuf Ya'qub al Anṣāri (731 – 798) as especially valuable. This was a report written on the orders of Hārūn al-Rashīd, who apparently wanted to understand something of the complicated and intricate system by which his subjects were being fiscally exploited. The author of the "report" held the important post of Chief Judge of Baghdad under the Caliphs Mahdi, Hādi and Hārūn al-Rashīd. He was the favorite pupil and zealous follower of the celebrated jurist Abū-Ḥanīfa, the founder of one of the four orthodox Moslem *madhhabs* ["rites"], and himself also acquired a reputation as an outstanding and authoritative jurist. His moral character, however, was hardly such as to ensure impartiality and objectivity in his judgments, for he was a careerist who retained his exalted position for such a long time only because he had gained the favor of three successive Caliphs by his pliancy and ingenuity in applying his wide erudition in Moslem law to justify any action by those in power.[2]

The content of Abū-Yūsuf's *Kitāb al-kharāj* is abundant and varied. The author deals firstly with the various forms and methods of fiscal exploitation and examines the various categories of land tenure and land management within this context. His concepts are clearly tendentious: like all other orthodox jurists, he attributes the origin of all contemporary agrarian relations, which were the result of historical development, to the times of the prophet Mohammed and the Caliph 'Omar I, the only other historical figure to be mentioned being 'Omar (II) ibn-'Abd-al 'Azīz, the Umayyad. To confirm his own opinions and conclusions he quotes Moslem tradition (of the *hadīth* category), whose authenticity he blithely accepts. European medievalists use the work of Abū-Yūsuf frequently, but not once have any of them submitted it to scientific criticism.

In its original, the *Kitāb al-kharāj* is accessible only in its Oriental *(Būlāq)* edition, of which Fagnan made a good French translation provided with notes.[3] Short passages have been translated from the Arabic original into Russian by Mednikov and by Yakubovskii.[4]

A similar source is the *Kitāb al-kharāj* by Yaḥya ibn-Adam, the Arabic original of which has been edited by the Dutch Arabist Juynboll in 1896, and translated into English in 1958 by Ben Shemesh.[5]

MODERN LITERATURE

Scientific and popular scientific literature on the history of the Baghdad Caliphate includes many books and papers of varying size and quality. In every "History of the Arabs" from Weil's to Hitti's, this Caliphate takes up several chapters. The outstanding work of non-Soviet bourgeois orientalism in this field is the book by von Kremer on the "Cultural History of the Orient under the Caliphs,"[6] a most comprehensive study including interesting and still informative data on the economic and social history of the Caliphate. The material on the Baghdad Caliphate in this book has been summarized in the article "The 'Abbāsids" in *Kniga dlya chteniya po istorii srednikh vekov* (Anthology on the History of the Middle Ages), edited by Prof. P. G. Vinogradov, vyp. I, 3rd. ed., pp. 363–382, Moscow, 1901. Carra de Vaux's "The Thinkers of Islam"[7] and Reuben Levy's "An Introduction to the Sociology of Islam"[8] are much weaker than Kremer's work in content and scientific level, but they do contain certain data which complement those of Kremer.

Under the direct influence of Kremer, and making wide use of his data, a book appeared in Arabic by Jirjī Zaydān, *Ta'rīkh al-tamaddun al-islāmi* (History of Islamic Civilization), Part Four of which has been translated into English by D. Margoliouth.[9]

The works of two outstanding Russian scholars—the Arabist Mednikov and the Byzantologist Vasil'ev—are of exceptional scientific value. Mednikov, in his book *Palestina* . . . (Palestine . . . Until the Crusades, According to Arabic Sources), in addition to research on political and military events in Syria and Egypt, includes translations from historians and geographers writing in Arabic on the Baghdad Caliphate.

Vasil'ev's book *Vizantiya i araby* (Byzantium and the Arabs) consists of two monographs: *Politicheskie otnosheniya Vizantii i arabov za vremya Amoriiskoi dinastii* (The Political Relations between Byzantium and the Arabs in the Days of the Amorian Dynasty, St. Petersberg, 1900) and *Politicheskie otnosheniya Vizantii i arabov za vremya Makedonskoi dinastii* (The Political Relations Between Byzantium and the Arabs in the Days of the Macedonian Dynasty, St. Petersberg, 1902), both of which include appendices of Russian translations of those passages from Arabic sources quoted by the author.

Bartol'd's scientific vulgarization *Musul'manskii mir* (The World of Islam) published in Petrograd in 1922, is still informative, unlike two Soviet works on the history of the Caliphate which are by now outdated: Krymskii's *Istoriya arabov i arabskoi literatury* (History of the Arabs and of Arabic Literature, Moscow, 1911) and the Russian version of Müller's "History of Islam," *Istoriya islama* (St. Petersburg, 1895).

Non-Soviet popular science containing data worth attention includes the relevant chapters in the French "General History of Civilizations"[10] and in the books of Bernard Lewis[11] and Gaston Wiet.[12]

Non-Soviet literature on the early period of the Baghdad Caliphate is sparser than the general descriptions included in "Histories of the Arabs" and in works of scientific vulgarization. The best product of this literature is still the research by von Kremer, *The Budgetary Receipts in the 'Abbāsid Empire,*[13] but another work which deserves attention is Dominique Sourdel's *The 'Abbāsid Vizirate from* 749 *to* 936.[14] Some information on the historical geography and economics of the Baghdad Caliphate may also be obtained from the work of le Strange.[15]

Certain semi-scientific and semi-literary books by western orientalists such as Levy's[16] are also interesting, while the manuals by Pfanmüller and Sauvaget are very useful aids containing bibliographical data on books and articles in the field.[17]

The relevant articles in the "Encyclopedia of Islam" (t. I–IV; 2nd edition, t. I, II) deserve particular attention; many papers, especially in the first edition, such as "The Barmakids" by Bartol'd (t. I, pp. 663–6), are reports of basic research with valuable source references and bibliographical indications given. Although outstanding non-Soviet orientalists also participated in the "Encyclopedia," not all the articles are on a high scientific level, some, such as the paper on the 'Abbāsids (2nd ed., t. I, pp. 15–23), being weak and superficial.

Publications of twentieth-century Arabic historians are generally intended for Arabic and Moslem readers who have no access to European and American orientalist literature, and are mainly mere scientific vulgarization, written largely on the basis of west European scientific literature. One example is the book by Dr. 'Alī Ibrāhīm Ḥasan, *Al-ta'rīkh al-islāmi al-'amm* (General Islamic History), where, besides recording military and political facts, the author reviews some phenomena of the social and cultural history of the early 'Abbāsid period.

A far more substantial work is Aḥmad Amīn's *Ḍuḥā 'i-islām* (The Forenoon of Islam) [3 vol., Cairo, 1938]. The author is a prominent Egyptian linguist, historian and folklorist, and in three parts of his book expounds, in the usual idealist light, the very diverse phenomena of social, cultural and religious life in the Baghdad Caliphate until the end of the ninth century, the whole being based on numerous Arabic sources without any influence from European scientific literature. Fairly varied material (but without source references) is contained in a work by Aḥmad Farīd al-Rifā'i *'Aṣr al-Ma'mūn* (The Epoch of Ma'mūn, Cairo, 1928); the author, as an inspector in the Ministry of the Interior, refrains from any analysis of the rather abundant data he has assembled, and quotes rather from the original. Certain phenomena (such as the religious policies of Ma'mūn) are simply left unmentioned, apparently too touchy to discuss.

Two Arabic-language histories deserve especial mention for the authors' attempt at serious sociological analysis of historical events. The first of these by Bandali Jūzi (The Arabic form of Panteleimon Zhuze, late professor at the Azerbaidzhan State University in Baku) is *Min ta'rīkh al-ḥarakat al-fikriya al-islām* (From the History of Currents of Ideas in Islam) [Jerusalem, 1928]; the second by an Arab Marxist politician, Amīl Tūmā, is *Al-*

'arab w-al-taṭawwūr al-ta'rīkhi fi al-sharq al-awsaṭ (The Arabs and Historical Evolution in the Middle East, Haifa, 1962).

Research by Soviet Arabic medievalists has been published in general works such as B. N. Zakhoder's *Istoriya vostochnogo srednevekov'ya (Khalifat i Blizhnii Vostok)* (History of the Oriental Middle Ages—The Caliphate and the Near East, Moscow, 1944); the *Vsemirnaya istoriya* (Universal History [collective authorship], t. III, Moscow, 1957), *Istoriya stran zarubezhnogo Vostoka v srednie veka* (History of the Countries of the non-Soviet Orient during the Middle Ages [id.], Moscow, 1957) and a number of articles in various Soviet encyclopaedias.

Only Yakubovskii has dealt specially with certain problems of the history of the Baghdad Caliphate. This outstanding scientist has also written a substantial chapter on "Iran under the Rule of the Arab Caliphate" in *Istoriya Irana s drevneishikh vremen do kontsa XVIII veka* (History of Iran from the Earliest Times to the End of the XVIIIth Century), published by Leningrad University in 1958.

THE 'ABBĀSIDS

The vast empire ruled by the Caliphs of the 'Abbāsid dynasty is usually referred to as the Baghdad Caliphate, after the name of its capital. This city, officially named *Madīnat al-Salām* ("The City of Peace"), was founded in 762 by the second 'Abbāsid Caliph, Manṣūr, on the site of a small town known locally as *sūq Baghdād,* "the market of Baghdad."

In the early days of the Arab conquests, an inhabitant of Ḥīra had reported to the Arab war leader Muthannā that a very active market was held annually in the little township of Baghdad, to which rich merchants from Ctesiphon brought much money and precious merchandise. The troops of Muthannā therefore streamed toward Baghdad and, butchering some of the merchants and putting the others to flight, claimed a rich booty. Muthannā ordered his warriors to take only "the yellow and the white" (gold and silver) and the most valuable merchandise, as much as each warrior could carry away.

The Caliphs of the new dynasty originated from 'Abbās, uncle of the prophet Mohammed. Thus like the offspring of 'Alī ibn-Abi-Ṭālib, they belonged to "the house of Allah's apostle," to whose representatives agents of the anti-Umayyad rebellion in Khurāsān and central Asia had induced their followers to swear allegiance. Abū-l-'Abbās, the founder of the 'Abbāsid dynasty, was in hiding in Kūfa until the end of 749, fearing the reprisals of the Caliph Marwān II; only when it was quite clear that Marwān's cause was lost did he appear in the main mosque at Kūfa in the capacity of supreme ruler, promising a generous reward to the citizens of Kūfa for their fidelity and threatening severe punishment to all opponents. He declared that he was taking the regal title of al-Saffāḥ, "the generous," a word usually applied in ancient Arabic poetry to a man of outstanding hospitality who would "slaughter" many sheep to feast his guests. Formerly, this nickname was held to mean "he who sheds blood" (in reference to the many members of the Umayya clan butchered in the reign of Abu-l-'Abbās), but today this is considered incorrect.

After the oath of allegiance by the people of Kūfa, Abu-l-'Abbās went to the town of Anbār, near which he founded a Caliphal residence and called it al-Hāshimiyya after the clan of Hāshim of which his forefather 'Abbās was a member. The new city attracted from far and near all the Caliph's relatives, all the old and new partisans of the clan of 'Abbās who now sought positions in the entourage and at the court of the Caliph and appointments in the army and the administration.

Nearly all members of the Umayya clan (more than eighty) were slaughtered, although they had proclaimed their readiness to submit to the new Caliph. Only the infants escaped, together with a few adults who found refuge in Andalusia. Here, in Spain, the Umayyad *amir* 'Abd-al-Raḥmān seized power; he had managed to flee his estate in Irak when assassins had been sent to murder him, and after many wanderings in North Africa became ruler in Cordova, in 756, with the support of Kalbite tribes.

Reprisals were carried out not only against live Umayyads but even against the corpses of dead Caliphs of the fallen dynasty. Only that of the Caliph Hishām proved to be well-preserved, so it was taken out of the tomb, lashed, crucified and burned, and the ashes thrown to the wind.

Several uprisings, initiated in Syria by Umayyad war leaders, were easily crushed. The population of Damascus, after rebelling against the last Umayyad Caliph, also rose against the first 'Abbāsid viceroy, 'Abdallāh ibn-'Ali, and defeated his army.

Caliph Abu-l-'Abbās (749–754), who died when he was not much over thirty (perhaps from smallpox), had designated as his successor his brother Abū-Ja'far, who took the regal name of al-Manṣūr ("the Victorious"). The Caliph Manṣūr (754–775) was the organizer of the 'Abbāsid Caliphate and the founder of its capital Baghdad, the "round city," surrounded by a double circle of strong walls.

This Caliph was the son of a Berber slave girl, and became a Machiavellian-type ruler, ordering the treacherous murder of Abū-Muslim, whose popularity and influence he perceived as a threat to the Caliphal autocracy. During his long reign, the political role of Iranian feudals increased. Members of the Iranian feudality—namely the family of the Barmakids—provided the *wazīrs* [vizirs, or prime ministers] and therefore headed the administration of the Caliphate.

Uprisings of the working masses in protest against feudal exploitation were merely local in character and were easily crushed by the mercenary army of the Caliphate, which had replaced the former levies of Arab tribes from the previous dynasty. With these local but frequent rebellions, the political situation became quite complex, the more so with the growth of the bureaucratic apparatus and of court intrigues. The same conditions prevailed under the Caliph Mahdi (775–785), the son and successor of Manṣūr, and still more markedly under the later 'Abbāsids. Rivalry between groups of courtiers resulted in the murder of the Caliph Hādi (785–786), son of Mahdi, and in the accession of another son of Mahdi, Hārūn.

The Caliph Hārūn al-Rashīd (786–809) has been immoderately and quite undeservedly glorified both in the Orient and in the Occident. His fame as a kind, just and wise Caliph is due to the charming tales collected in the so-called "Arabian Nights," which became known in French translation in eighteenth-century Europe and in which Hārūn is portrayed as an attractive personality, quite at variance with historical reality. He was in fact a cruel and crafty despot, quite deservedly hated by his subjects so much that he was even afraid to live in Baghdad, his capital, because of the open demonstrations of dissatisfaction with his rule, preferring to dwell near Anbār, in his castle, far from any hostile city crowds. On his occasional visits to Baghdad to collect arrears of taxes, however, the citizenry suffered beatings and imprisonment. It is hardly surprising that when Hārūn was in Ḥīra the inhabitants of nearby Kūfa proved to be "bad neighbors" who attacked their own lord. Hārūn also spent much time on campaigns so that he could be present at the crushing of his subjects' revolts.

With characteristic perfidy and in order to consolidate his autocracy, Hārūn al-Rashīd removed from power and ordered the execution of the Barmakids, whose influence and riches he envied. The unexpected and unjustified atrocities committed against these representatives of the Iranian feudal aristocracy caused great discontent among Iranian and non-Iranian feudals, who had been the supporters of the Barmakids. This discontent posed a serious threat to Hārūn's position, which was only saved by his previous year's appointment of his elder son Ma'mūn, born of an Iranian concubine, as his permanent viceroy in the eastern provinces, which gave relative autonomy to Iran, thus offering additional possibilities of exploiting the working masses to the local feudals and the upper classes in the cities.

In the days of the Caliph Amīn (809–813), son and successor of Hārūn, a struggle developed which soon turned into civil war: Ma'mūn levied an army in Iran which besieged and took Baghdad, Amīn was killed while fleeing the capital, and his brother became Caliph.

The Caliph Ma'mūn (813–833) has achieved fame for his cultural achievements. He promoted the development of science and literature in the Arabic language, and encouraged a wide interest in translations (started under Manṣūr), so that many outstanding works of classical Greek and Hellenistic science and philosophy now became accessible to Arabic-reading scholars. At the same time, the trend to assimilate certain achievements of Iranian and Indian civilization continued. In the reign of Ma'mūn a "House of Wisdom" was founded in Baghdad, endowed with a rich collection of manuscripts, and an observatory was built in the vicinity of the capital. The healthy influence of this cultural development reached even the teaching of Islam; with the direct participation of this enlightened Caliph, Moslem dogmatics came under the impact of classical philosophy and a "mu'tazilite" [to some extent "rationalistic"] doctrine developed, which was proclaimed as the official ideology and marked the beginning of the *kalām* or Moslem theology.

In the memory of later generations, the merits of Ma'mūn in the field of culture counterbalanced those reprisals which he took against the numerous uprisings during his rule. The most stubborn and bitter rebellion was that of the Khurramis, led by Bābak. This mighty revolt started in 815/816 and lasted for over twenty years; it spread through the mountainous districts of Azerbaijan, Armenia and northwestern Iran, and, despite the deployment of all the forces of the Caliphate, could not be crushed in the reign of Ma'mūn. Meanwhile, in 829–832, there was an uprising in Egypt, and, forced to visit this country, the Caliph directed the cruel repression of the rebels.

Under the successors of Ma'mūn, an increasingly important role was played in the politics of the Caliphate by the Caliph's Turkish bodyguard, recruited from among Turkish prisoners captured in the course of the nearly uninterrupted border warfare with the steppe tribes beyond the Jaiḥūn (Amu-Darya) and the Saiḥūn (Syr-Darya). These prisoners were enslaved and sold on the slave markets of central Asia and Iran; some of them finally found themselves in the barracks of the Caliphal army in Baghdad and provided an ever-ready means by which the Caliph could keep down the insubordinate and easily inflamed population of his capital. The advantage in using the Turks was their complete lack of connection with the Baghdadis and their indifference to the latter's interests; they thus formed a reliable defense of the Caliph against his subjects.*

The Turks had been a considerable body of troops as early

* [For a more comprehensive analysis of the introduction of the Turkish guard, see D. Ayalon, *"The Military Reforms of Caliph al-Mu'tasim,"* Proceedings of the XXVI Congress of Orientalists, New Delhi, 1964.]

as the days of Ma'mūn, whose successor, Mu'taṣim (833–842), frightened by the ceaseless uprisings of the Baghdad population, left his capital and made his residence at Sāmarra on the Tigris. Near this little town he built a palace as well as barracks for his Turkish guard; in this new Caliphal residence Bābak [the leader of the Khurrami rebels] was executed in 838, captured by treachery after long and bitter mountain warfare in which the Caliph's troops had finally succeeded in suppressing the rebel resistance. This Caliphal refuge became known as *Surra Man Ra'a* ("Pleased is he who sees it").

Now they had escaped their Baghdadi subjects, however, the Caliphs of Sāmarra soon became wholly dependent on their Turkish guards, whose discipline was rapidly declining: the higher officers began to intervene in the succession to the throne, putting forward their own candidates, and the Turkish chieftains, who wanted power and money, were soon using their undisciplined soldiery to dethrone one Caliph and raise another if the latter was likely to prove more generous in his gifts to these "pretorians."

The Caliph Wāthiq (842–847), son of Mu'taṣim and of his Greek concubine, attempted to follow the wide development of cultural activity established under Ma'mūn. He was a freethinker, a "mu'tazilite," but after his death two Turkish war leaders raised to the throne his brother Mutawakkil, (847–861), the son of a Khwārizmian* slave girl, who, seeking support outside his bodyguard, favored an orthodox policy. Mu'tazilites and other opponents of Moslem orthodoxy were persecuted, and decrees were issued placing Christians and Jews (*dhimmis* ["tributaries"] and "people of the Book") in a position of inequality to Moslem "Sunnites" [followers of the *sunna,* the orthodox tradition]. Counting now on the sympathy of the orthodox population of Irak and of the Sunnite clergy, the Caliph Mutawakkil attempted to escape the dominance of the Turkish guard, for this purpose selecting a new residence, which he called Ja'fariya. But the flight from Sāmarra did not save the Caliph: the two chieftains of the guard, with the connivance of his elder son, killed him,

* [Khwārizm or Chorasmia was the land of the lower Amu-Darya.]

and the son became Caliph under the name of Muntaṣir. The reign of Muntaṣir lasted only six months (861–862); it is possible that he was poisoned.

The Caliph Musta'īn (862–866), grandson of Mu'taṣim and son of a Slav concubine, was simply a cipher manipulated by Turkish commanders, rivalry between whom resulted in the flight of two of them to Baghdad, taking with them the shadowy Caliph in the hope of using him as a religious-political tool. They were consequently besieged in Baghdad by the army of their adversaries, who demanded the abdication of the Caliph in favor of their own candidate. Musta'īn, having duly complied, was to go into exile in the "holy cities" in Arabia, but was put to death *en route* by the orders of his successor. The head of the murdered man was sent to the new Caliph and the corpse left on the spot until it was buried by some compassionate local people.

Thus raised to the throne by a group of Turkish commanders, the Caliph Mu'tazz (866–869), son of Mutawakkil, tried to free himself from this intolerable guardianship by using the Berber soldiers of his bodyguard, but his courtiers, who were terrified of the Turks, thought such an attempt foolish, and it failed completely. The Turkish guards broke into the palace, deposed the Caliph and imprisoned him; he died in prison six days later, probably at the hands of the same guards. This Caliph had lived in such fear of one of his war leaders that he would not be parted from his weapons at any time: he kept his sword and spear ready while taking his meals, and slept with them in his bed.

The new Caliph, Muhtadi, son of Wāthiq and of a Greek slave girl, reigned only eleven months (869–870). He tried to be a pious and just ruler, abstaining from wine and festivities and sometimes himself dealing with the judicial affairs of his subjects. But the by now unattainable need to control the troublesome Turkish guard cost him his life, for he was murdered one night by his drunken guardsmen as he slept in his chambers. It is in Muhtadi's reign that the uprising of the Zanj broke out in southern Irak (see below).

The next Caliph, Mu'tamid (870–892), the son of Mutawakkil and of an Arab slave girl, was a dull and dissolute man, interested only in pleasures of the flesh. He lasted an exceptionally long time on the Caliphal throne, but only because of the tolerance shown by his brother Muwaffaq, a gifted and active warrior who was the *de facto* ruler. The army, raised to a high combat value under his command, protected Baghdad (which had meanwhile again become the Caliphal residence) from the threat posed by the Iranian war leader Ya'qūb ibn-Laith as well as from the Zanj rebels. But Muwaffaq fell gravely ill during his campaign to Azerbaidzhan, and died in Baghdad in the summer of 891, soon after a tremendous uprising of the capital's workers. The populace looted the richer houses and set free the inmates of the prisons.

Mu'taḍid, son of Muwaffaq and of his Greek slave girl, took the place of his inept uncle Mu'tamid, who died from overeating or had perhaps been poisoned. The Caliph Mu'taḍid (892–902) acquired notoriety as a miser and a sadist, but spared no means to glorify his reign by the construction of beautiful buildings. He was a fairly active ruler and died on a campaign against Byzantium, also probably from poisoning.

THE TERRITORY OF THE BAGHDAD CALIPHATE

During the first century and a half of their rule, the 'Abbāsids proved unable to retain all the territories that had belonged to the Caliphate under the previous dynasty. Firstly, Arab Andalusia *(al-Andalus)*, the conquered part of the Iberian Peninsula, was not included in the Baghdad Caliphate, for this rich and civilized country was ruled by the Cordova Umayyads, a dynasty founded by *amīr* 'Abd-al-Raḥmān I. In the late eighth century, the Caliphate lost the "Extreme West" *(al-Maghrib al-Aqṣā)*, present-day Morocco, to the Shī'ite *imām* Idrīs, founder of the independent Idrīsid dynasty (788–985), who seized power in 788. In the year 800, the 'Abbāsid viceroy of the Maghrib (North Africa), Ibrāhīm ibn-Aghlab, also proclaimed his independence and founded the local dynasty of the Aghlabids (800–909).

Thus, by the ninth century, when the Baghdad Caliphate was finally forming into a feudal empire, it could well have been a new embodiment of the Iranian kingdom under the later Sassanids; indeed, the conquests of Khusro II had added Syria,

Palestine and Egypt to the kingdom, and Baghdad, the political center of the ʻAbbāsids, arose not far from the old Sassanid capital, Ctesiphon. In the Baghdad Caliphate, the preponderant economic role belonged to Irak, in close connection with western Iran and with Transcaucasia and central Asia.

Unlike the Umayyads, the ʻAbbāsids were not aggressive in their foreign policy; the battle fought in 751 between Arab troops and a Chinese army on the Talas River in central Asia, in which the Chinese were defeated, was fought, as it were, by inertia from the preceding period. Warfare with the Turkish tribes on the central Asian steppe frontiers was mainly defensive, and the Arabo-Byzantine wars which went on in northern Syria, Anatolia and Mesopotamia resulted in no large-scale conquests.

ECONOMIC CONDITIONS IN THE BAGHDAD CALIPHATE

In the first century of ʻAbbāsid rule (the latter half of the eighth and the first half of the ninth centuries), production, exchange and culture developed considerably within the Baghdad Caliphate, but this development, especially cultural progress, important as it was, was only relative. The level of production was no doubt higher and the exchanges more active than under the Umayyads, but these achievements were modest compared with those of the Near and Middle East countries in the tenth and eleventh centuries. To quote Bartol'd: "The Caliphate, before its dismemberment, was still on the whole a barbarian empire; the works of civilization which were later to make famous Baghdad, Iṣfahān and the other principal cities of the Moslem world were only starting under the early ʻAbbāsids"[18]

AGRICULTURE

The main branch of production was agriculture, based on artificial irrigation. Irrigational agriculture had reached its highest level in Irak, especially in the south, the Sawād, where grain crops gave high yields, gardening was developed and palm trees produced particularly succulent and sweet dates. Cotton and sugar beet were successfully grown in Irak and in the adjacent regions of Iran. On low ground, where the floodwaters of the two mighty rivers of Mesopotamia remained for the longest period of time, rice was grown on a large scale. Besides Irak and southwestern Iran, Egypt was also a country with well-developed irrigational agriculture, especially in the fertile Delta. Here, in addition to grain crops, much flax was grown. In comparison with these lands, which played a leading role in the economy of the Baghdad Caliphate, Syria—having lost her former privileged position—was of secondary, though still considerable, importance.

In most Oriental countries (including those of the Caliphate), agriculture is only feasible under irrigation. The Arabs have expressed this in their saying: "Where the water ends, the land ends." Land which is not regularly irrigated is infertile and economically valueless for the agriculturalist, no matter how much labor is expended on tilling it. The farmer could not rely on "water from the sky," rainfall, for in some Oriental countries the short rains fall very seldom (no rain may fall for several years), while in others there may be thunderstorms which erode the topsoil more than they irrigate it. Therefore, a rather complex and advanced system of artificial irrigation, supervised by the central governmental authorities, had been developed since antiquity in the slave-holding states of the Near and Middle East. In principle, this system was preserved in the Baghdad Caliphate. Of course over the many thousands of years of its existence it had been destroyed more than once by nomadic invasions and destructive wars resulting in the downfall of dynasties and empires, but the untiring energy of the working masses had always restored irrigation, essential as it was for agriculture.

At the time of the 'Abbāsid rise to power, the irrigation system of Irak was in a state of decay caused by the major socio-political disturbances and nearly uninterrupted uprisings and wars of the Umayyad period. The 'Abbāsids, from the days of the Caliph Manṣūr, had social as well as economic reasons for attending to agricultural development, for this would raise the standard of living of the population (in particular of the peasants) and thus end the discontent which had been chronic under the Umayyads. The 'Abbāsid authorities directed the efforts of farmers first of all towards reconstruction and improvement of the irrigational system. This was a relatively easy task, since most of the cultivated land was state property and the farmers who tilled it were directly dependent on the administration. Reconstruction works included cleaning abandoned canals which had become silted or filled with sand and digging new ones. The enlarged irrigational network immediately resulted in an expansion of cropping area and higher crop yields.

The 'Abbāsid rulers concentrated particularly on agriculture in Irak, which provided more than 30% of the receipts of the state treasury. We may quote here the founders of Marxism on the three departments which Oriental governments used to maintain: "Governments in the Orient always possessed only three departments: finances (the plundering of their country), war (the plundering of both their own country and of foreign lands), and public works (care of increased production)."[19]

Under the Umayyads, the running of the third department was feeble and erratic, but under the 'Abbāsids it began to function as actively as the first one. The positive results of agricultural development, however, were very often restricted and sometimes nullified by the activities of the finance department, which carried out its systematic plunder of the working population.

Agriculture in Irak was troubled not only by insufficient water reaching the fields but also by the destructive effect of floodwaters in the annual floods (the torrential waters of the Tigris were particularly dangerous). To prevent such disasters, which eroded the topsoil and killed both humans and cattle, the banks of the rivers had to be strengthened and levees and protective dykes constructed along the fields; the inhabitants of riverine townships put much effort into this work. Only in the southern part of the Sawād, in the district of the Shaṭṭ al-'Arab [the united stream of the Tigris and Euphrates] were local agriculturalists aided naturally by the two mighty rivers together. Here, when the Persian Gulf was at high tide, the seawater entered the channel of the Shaṭṭ al-'Arab and impeded its flow so that the sweet water level of the river would rise rapidly, overflow the banks and inundate the riverine gardens, vineyards and palm groves. This daily inundation not only irrigated the land but also fertilized it by leaving a thin layer of silt.

Farming and irrigational techniques remained on a low level, matters of routine, as is typical of the early-feudal stage of production. The most complex technical achievement was a large irrigation wheel, the "noria." This carried clay or leather buckets around the periphery which dipped into the river or derivation channel and poured the water into a trough leading to the irrigation ditches. The wheel rotated on an axis which was usually supported by two uprights, and was set in motion by a pair of buffalos or camels. Invented in antiquity, this apparatus was used in Irak and Syria and considered one of the technical "wonders" of those days. An easier machine to construct, and therefore far more common among peasants, was the "shadoof," a bucket attached to a [counterpoised] sweep, with which the water was drawn by hand and poured onto the field. In Egypt, the "shadoof" had been in use since the days of the Pharaohs, while the Archimedean screw had been introduced in the Hellenistic epoch.

Agricultural implements were even more primitive. The hoe, spade, pitchfork and sickle were used everywhere, in the very same shapes they had acquired several thousand years earlier, at least as early as the Sumerians and the builders of the Egyptian pyramids. The plow had also not changed since antiquity, being a primitive wooden plow without moldboard or [metal] share, for soil and climatic conditions obviated the need to plow with deep or sliced furrows and it was quite enough to loosen the soil.

The idea of easing the lot of the farmer by improving agricultural implements occurred to no-one. Such complete stagnation in farming techniques was due very largely to the widespread use of slave labor in agriculture and irrigation under the Umayyads. Under the 'Abbāsids, the importance of slaves in production began to decrease, but their exploitation was retained in those fields that required the hardest labor—irrigating virgin land, draining swamps and cleaning salt flats—and also in salt production and mining for metals. The main cause of technological stagnation in agriculture, however, was most probably the lack of interest of the farmers themselves in any increase in production, as all additional produce, and often part of his subsistence amount, was in any case taken from the peasant in the form of land tax.

Most of the land was considered state property, and, as such, ground rent was collected as land tax, meaning in fact a combined tax and rent to be paid to the officers of the fiscal administration. Collection of taxes was often subject to various abuses committed by these officers, who were frequently grafters and blackmailers exploiting the ignorance and defenselessness of the peasantry. The official calendar was lunar, from the *hijra,* but it was customary to collect the land tax according to the solar calendar, which corresponded to the seasons; using the discrepancy between the official and solar calendars, the publicans sometimes managed to collect dues twice a year.

The ʻAbbāsid government went on increasing taxes until they reached a state of alarm at the reaction of the working people. Under Manṣūr, the people on lands owing the *kharāj* (mainly state-owned lands) were made to pay the combined tax and rent either according to acreage in both money and natural produce, or as a proportion of the crop in produce alone. Moreover, in some lands the dues were still collected in accordance with contracts established in the days of the conquest. Other lands, known as *mulk,* which were the hereditary property of the farmers, paid dues of a "tenth" *(ʻushr).* There was also a third category of land which was free from taxation, comprising the holdings of the Caliph and members of the ruling family and of certain high dignitaries, and also the *waqf* lands, the real estate (including land) belonging to mosques and other Moslem religious institutions, the income from which was at the disposal of the clergy.

To increase the receipts from taxation of *kharāj* lands, the successors of Manṣūr replaced the dues in nature (part of the crop) by dues in money, assessed according to the area under crops. This innovation, enforced with particular zeal under Hārūn al-Rashīd, laid an additional burden on the tax-payers. For the treasury and the ruling class, however, it had the advantage of ensuring a fixed sum of tax yields. Collection of dues in nature in a poor harvest year or in a case of crop failure (disastrous of course for the peasants themselves) meant lower incomes for both the farmers and the treasury, whereas taxation according to cultivated area placed the whole burden on the shoulders of the peasants, who had to pay the set tax whatever the crop yield, even if the crop had failed due to floods or to locusts. Moreover, payment in cash meant that the farmers were now dependent on the fluctuation of market prices.

As the state owned water as well as land, the taxation rate also depended on the source of irrigation of cultivated fields. The highest rates (no less than half the crop) were paid by farmers who irrigated their land directly from the state-owned irrigation network; the rates were lower (down to one quarter of the crop) if the farmers themselves had dug the canals which conducted the water from the state network to their own fields.

Abū-Yūsuf [author of *Kitāb al-kharāj*] advised the Caliph that taxes should be collected relentlessly; not one non-Moslem should be exempt from taxation: "He must not show leniency to a single one among them by exempting him from part of his dues." Nor should tax collectors make agreements with representatives of non-Moslem communities as to the amount of tribute they should pay without first checking the numbers of the tributary population, for there were apparently many cases when collectors (after receiving a bribe from the headman of some village) reduced the total sum to be paid, thus causing a loss to the treasury. Other sources also reveal that bribes were the most effective and most widespread means of evading tribute payments.

Abū-Yūsuf was decidedly opposed to taxing the needy, the sick and the aged, or to torturing defaulters. (We can conclude that such practices, though illegal, were common everywhere.) The jurist from Baghdad was also against the practice of beating *dhimmis* to make them pay poll tax. He states that they should not be laid in the sun or submitted to other forms of torture, but "they should be treated kindly, and imprisoned until such time as they have paid their dues." He advises the Caliph to order that the *dhimmis* "should not be dealt with unjustly, nor mishandled, nor overburdened; nor should anything be taken from their property, over and above their rightly dues."[20]

Such humane advice, given to a feudal despot by one of the outstanding ideologists of the ruling class, aimed chiefly at forestalling the uprisings that were to shake the Baghdad Caliphate. The policy of increasing exploitation caused widespread dissatisfaction among the peasant masses, expressed in rebellions of increasing gravity, especially under the rule of Hārūn al-Rashīd. A decree was therefore issued in 820, under Ma'mūn (sometimes described as "the law of Ma'mūn"), which set the maximum tax at two-thirds of the crop.

Besides crop farming, sedentary animal husbandry [as opposed to nomadic shepherding] was of considerable economic importance. Stock was kept not only for dairy and meat but also for raising draught animals used in agriculture and to some extent in irrigation. Hides were also required for the well-developed artisanal production. The widespread nomadic grazing included extensive camel herding, as the camel provided the chief means of transportation: commerce by land between states, regions and cities was conducted by camel caravans, which transported goods over enormous distances.

ARTISANAL PRODUCTION IN THE CITIES

The second major differentiation in the social division of labor—that of the crafts from agriculture—had occurred among Arabs even prior to the rise of Islam. In the conquered lands, it had taken place in antiquity, in the days of the slave-holding regime. The numerous and diversified craftsmen of the Baghdad Caliphate dwelt mainly in the cities, but there were also villages which lived not by tillage but by artisanal pursuits, mainly textiles or leatherwork.

In the latter half of the eighth and during the ninth centuries, with the development of irrigational agriculture, the lands of the Caliphate saw a concomitant expansion of artisanal production. Spinning and weaving were the most common crafts. The craftsmen produced excellent fabrics from flax, cotton, wool and silk; high-grade flax materials (cloth and linen) were produced in lower Egypt and were famous for their quality, finding buyers far beyond the Egyptian boundaries. Sericulture was well-developed in Syria, and the experienced local craftsmen produced elegant silk fabrics and artistic brocades. In nearly all the countries of the Caliphate fine and durable broadcloth was made, sometimes artistically dyed by specialized dyers, who used natural dyes obtained from leaves, bark and roots of various plants.

Another important craft was leatherwork, with advanced methods of tanning. Manufacture of clothing and footwear was closely connected with the textile and leather crafts. The produce of hard-working and experienced craftsmen, who reached an artistic level in their work, was destined firstly to satisfy the heavy demands of the ruling class, starting with the Caliph himself, as well as the rich townsmen and higher clergy. The working masses, whose tastes were perforce limited by lack of money, contented themselves with cheap and mostly crude products of cotton, flax and wool. Nor could the mass consumer afford the boots and slippers of excellent colored morocco, adorned with silken, golden and silver threads, but had to be satisfied with crude leather sandals, which protected his feet from the burning contact of stone and sand in the sun. Many rural inhabitants were content with homespun and locally made footwear, although textile and leather goods were so abundant and varied in the city bazaars that foreign visitors marvelled at them.

Also in high demand was the work of harness- and saddle-makers, who manufactured harnesses for camels and horses as well as various saddles for horses, camels, mules and asses. Saddles for noble, rich riders were embroidered with many-colored silks or adorned with metal plates studded with pearls and semi-precious stones.

Metalwork, especially the manufacture of weapons and vessels, achieved high standards and was widely practiced. The excellent armorers provided the armament (swords, spears, shields, mail, armor and helmets) of the Caliphal forces; swords of Damascus steel, produced by masters who held the secret of a special method of tempering, were particularly famous. Metalware (mainly copper plates, bowls and pitchers) was used for service in the homes of prosperous townspeople, where Syrian glassware was also popular.

Villagers and the poorer city people used earthenware and wooden utensils, but in the palaces of the Caliph and of his dignitaries and in the houses of the rich, food and drink was served in gold and silver vessels, often artistically finished. The artistic crafts (including jewellery) were indeed quite developed, as they had to satisfy the tastes and vanity of the powerful and rich.

Many economic factors favored the expansion of artisanal production: the abundance of raw material obtained from the extensive nomadic grazing regions (hides and wool), the competent cultivation of industrial crops, the well-tried methods of mining. Ships and boats, as well as camel caravans, brought silver bars from Iran, mainly from the mines in the mountains of Hindu Kush, gold from the Maghrib, especially from Nubia and the Sudan, copper from the vicinity of Iṣfahān and iron from Iran, central Asia and Sicily by sea, river and land to Baghdad and the other major centers. Moreover, Africa provided precious wood and ivory, from which the artist-craftsmen produced luxury items to adorn the homes and enhance the elegance of members of the ruling class.

Crafts connected with food manufacturing also flourished, especially the production of sweets and pastry made of flour and fruit with honey and cane sugar. There was also a great demand for cosmetics and medicinal products.

Free producers were predominant in the arts and crafts, but slave labor was also still used, as slave craftsmen were thoroughly exploited in shops belonging to the state, to feudals or to merchants. The free artisans usually worked in their own shops in the city bazaars, and made use of the labor and gifts of their sons or other relatives, sometimes also employing their slaves to help them. These shops were grouped in separate streets or alleys in the bazaar, according to crafts. Handicrafts were not necessarily separated from trade: the craftsman might sell his ware in his shop to customers. We have no information on any organization of craftsmen in the period under consideration; unions of artisans similar to the guilds of western Europe arose much later in the Caliphate.

The cities of the Caliphate were not solely military-administrative strongholds, but were also very important economic and cultural centers for each particular land or region. According to the definition of Arabic-writing medieval geographers, a "city" was a township possessing a mosque, a governor's palace, a bath, a school, a *khān* [caravanserai], a hospital and a *maidān* [central plaza]. In the big cities there were tens, even hundreds, of such buildings and institutions.

The feudal estates in the lands of the Caliphate, contrary to the sequence of events in western Europe during the early Middle Ages, never acquired any economic or political preponderance over the cities. Moreover, the feudals of the Baghdad Caliphate dwelt not on their estates but in the cities, whose economic role was particularly enhanced by the growth of money exchanges in a framework of well-developed crafts and commerce.

The largest city of the Caliphate was the capital, Baghdad. Its founder, the Caliph Manṣūr, had given it the official name of *Madīnat as-salām,* but the people called it *Madīnat al-Manṣūr* ("the City of Manṣūr"). The building started in 762 on the right bank of the Tigris, to the north of the big canal of Sarat which connected this river with the Euphrates, and Manṣūr had laborers driven there not only from Mesopotamia [the Jazīra] and Irak but also from Syria and Iran, so that, according to traditional Arabic data, there were 100,000 there. By the second year after the foundation, in 763, the state treasury and governmental departments *(dīwāns)* were moved from Kūfa to Baghdad. The building of the "city of Manṣūr" was completed in 766. It was a "round city," with a double circle of fortified mud-brick walls, to which a third, external wall was later added with a moat which was always kept full of water.

In the central part of the city, surrounded by the "inner wall," towered the Caliph's palace, which came to be known as "the Golden Gate" or "the Green Dome," for a huge dome faced with turquoise-colored tiles rose over the audience chamber. A mosque was built nearby, and farther away were the government buildings, the barracks of the Caliph's bodyguard and the palatial homes of the Caliph's family and of state dignitaries. The prison was farthest from the palace. Four gates (the Baṣra, Khurāsān, Syrian and Kūfa gates) led from the central part of the city to that part between the "inner" and the "main" walls, where Manṣūr had ordered the inhabitants of former townships close to the new capital to be settled in the various quarters. Artisans and merchants from other cities also settled here, attracted by the Caliph's promise to grant the capital's population certain privileges in regard to customs and taxes.

The Caliph apparently cheated the people of his capital, however: from the very beginning they showed such discontent and anger with Manṣūr that he could not even trust his "inner wall" completely, and was afraid to ride out of the central city. Thus, only a few years after the founding of Baghdad, Manṣūr ordered the dissatisfied craftsmen and small traders to be resettled outside the walls altogether, in the suburb of Karkh, with the special injunction that the market of the resettled butchers be far away from the city gates, for he was sure that butchers are inclined to make trouble with such sharp implements at hand.

Baghdad grew fast as it acquired exceptional importance in the economic life of the vast Caliphate of the 'Abbāsids. As early as the ninth century it became one of the major international centers of production and commerce. The enlarged city also spread over a considerable area on the left bank of the Tigris, where numerous craftsmen had settled and lively bazaars had opened; the right- and left-bank quarters were connected by means of a pontoon bridge. Baghdad also acquired a leading role as the cultural center of the Caliphate, attracting and retaining the best intellectual forces in the world of Arabic-language culture, especially from the days of the Caliph Ma'mūn onwards.

On the other hand, Baghdad also had a vast population of paupers; many homeless and hungry people roamed particularly the major bazaars, the mosque areas and the vicinity of the river harbor, perhaps the liveliest place in the entire city. This Baghdad *Lumpenproletariat* found some sustenance by occasional small jobs, insistent and obnoxious begging, and stealing and sometimes worse crimes. The most abject prostitution was rife among this populace.

Another active and lively city was Baṣra, the southern maritime outlet of the Caliphate.

COMMERCE

The position of the Baghdad Caliphate at the crossroads of commerce between the Far East and India on the one hand and Europe on the other determined its outstanding international significance. Still more important for the economy of the Caliphate were the commercial relations between different countries of the extensive empire, now situated between two oceans (the Indian and the Atlantic) and washed by four seas (Mediterranean, Black and Red seas and the Persian Gulf). Supporting this lively trade was a developed artisanal and metal production.

The principal cities were important terminals of caravan and sea trade. Merchants and buyers were attracted by the populous bazaars, while the depots were full of merchandise, produced both locally and abroad: Egyptian flaxen fabrics could be procured in city markets not only in Africa but also in Asia and even in Europe; Syrian silks and glassware, weapons and metal vessels were in demand everywhere; western Iran provided rugs and artistic embroideries; Khūzistān [southwestern Iran] exported sugar, and here, as well as in the Kūfa district, cotton was grown. Copper was mined in Iran, central Asia, Armenia, Ifrīqiya (Tunisia) and Andalusia; northern and western Iran were rich in tin and lead, and mercury was mined near Iṣṭakhr; southwestern Iran and northern Irak (Mesopotamia) were known for their abundance of mineral oil and bitumen, and southern Iran provided valuable goods such as opium and indigo.

Trade caravans from North Africa and Egypt penetrated into the region of Lake Chad and often reached the Equator. Arab caravan-traders were quite familiar with the routes and tracks across deserts, steppes and forests to the south of the Sahara, attracted by high and easy profits, to be procured by trading with the people of West Africa, where they exchanged salt against gold and acquired great numbers of slaves at a low price. In Timbuktu and Gao they bought ivory as well as gold, and out of "black" Africa exported ostrich feathers and skins of wild beasts, of which there were plenty in the forests and savannas.

Maritime commerce expanded greatly in both the Indian Ocean and the Mediterranean Sea, and merchantmen went on distant voyages into the Indian Ocean. As early as the fifth century, Hīra and Ubulla (in Irak) had been visited by ships from the Red Sea, India and China. In the Caliphate, Baṣra now became one of the major ports of international maritime trade, with which only the harbor of Sukhar in 'Omān could complete. (Musqāt was later to inherit its role.) Sīrāf in Karmān, on the Iranian coast of the Persian Gulf, was also a very active harbor.

Until the eighth century, the initiative of trade relations across the Indian Ocean had belonged to the Chinese, who were more enterprising than either Arab or Iranian merchants. Chinese merchantmen came to anchor in Sīrāf with crews of as many as 400–500 sailors. These big ships were well armed against pirates, being supplied with flame-throwers which spurted flaming oil. By the early eighth century, however, the seafarers from Baṣra were already superior to the Chinese and Indians in the arts of navigation and shipbuilding. Under Ḥajjāj, Baṣra ships were being built with metal nails, whereas earlier shipwrights had used only wooden fastenings and ropes.

The men of Baṣra thoroughly explored all the islands of the Persian Gulf and familiarized themselves with the natural harbors, and then, going out into the ocean, established trading posts on the islands of Socotra and Zanzibar and on the coast of East Africa. From Africa the Baṣra ships carried black slaves, ivory, precious wood, gold dust and precious stones, and having established contact with the merchants of Ceylon, began to export ivory and precious stones from the ports of this island too. On the western coast of India (Malabar) there were several trading centers where thousands of Moslem merchants, subjects of the 'Abbāsid Caliph, lived, building mosques and having their own *qādī*. India exported spices and textiles, including the finest silks, to the Caliphate, and trading posts of merchants from the Caliphate were also established on the southeastern, Coromandel coast of India. Here several tens of thousands of horses were imported each year from Sīrāf.

The tales of Sindbād the Sailor in the "Arabian Nights" echo the commercial activity of merchants from the Caliphate in the South Seas; Sindbād presumably reached as far as the town of Kala in the Malacca Peninsula, from which gold and tin were exported. Moslem traders obtained a particularly vast amount of precious goods from Sumatra, namely gold, spices, incense, medicinal plants and camphor. From northern Borneo they exported pearls, and from the Philippine Islands gold and ivory [sic]; these islands were probably the mysterious Far Eastern land of Wak-Wak, of which a tale was told of a tree growing on that island on which the fruit was live women.[21] It was at one time incorrectly identified as Japan, while another hypothesis stated that it was an island off China.

By the middle of the eighth century, the Arab and Iranian traders knew the way to China. At first they used to sail on Chinese junks returning from Baṣra to China, but soon Moslem foreigners peopled several quarters of Canton (Kan-fu) [Kwangchow], where mosques had been built and *qādis* judged their coreligionists according to the *sharī'a* [Moslem canon law]. In 758, the native people of Canton rebelled against the Chinese Emperor's authority. To quell the rebellion, the Son of Heaven sent out Iranian mercenaries who were in his service: the subjects of the 'Abbāsid Caliph living in this big city looted and burnt the native quarters in connivance with the Iranians, loaded their loot on ships, and made off toward the harbors of the Caliphate. Some time later, however, the port of Canton was again inhabited by many Arab traders, who had their own *qādī*. Many of them, with their goods, found their way into inland China. Moslem merchants in the Caliphate imported porcelain ware, artistic fabrics and silk from China.

Maritime commerce between the Caliphate and China did not mean an end to the caravan trade along the northern "silk route," which had been in use since antiquity: Chinese merchandise was transported via Samarkand, Bukhāra, Rayy and Hamadhān to Baghdad, whence one route branched off toward the west, leading to Trebizond (on the Black Sea), where the Oriental goods were loaded on Byzantine merchantmen, and to the Syrian harbors on the Mediterranean, and another route led toward the southwest, into Arabia and Africa via Kūfa, Medina, Mecca and the ports of the Red Sea or via the Suez Isthmus. The same merchandise was transported on the "silk route," namely porcelain and textiles, including silk, from China to the lands of the Caliphate.

The chronicles of the T'ang dynasty (618–907) preserve the names of some 'Abbāsid Caliphs, much altered in their Chinese rendering, but the question of whether an exchange of official embassies occurred between the Caliphs and the Sons of Heaven remains unanswered. Arabic-language sources give no indication of any arrival of Chinese ambassadors in Baghdad or Sāmarra. Perhaps certain merchants arriving in China from the Caliphate posed as official envoys of the Caliph in order to obtain customs privileges and prevent their goods being looted by local authorities.

The trade relations of the Caliphate with India, Indonesia and China left considerable traces in Arabic literature. In the ninth century, when sea routes toward distant and formerly unknown lands became familiar to Arab and Persian merchants, a great many tales were told which Krachkovskii has described as "geographical fairy tales." They contain authentic information on foreign countries and peoples intermixed with unlimited fancy, and found a ready audience in Baṣra, Sīrāf and Baghdad.[22]

The tales of "Sulaimān the Merchant" refer to the mid-ninth century, but were put into literary form in the following century. This merchant-adventurer journeyed several times to India and thence, via the Malacca Strait, to China. "He gives a vivid description of coasts, islands, various harbors and cities with their inhabitants, products and trade goods."[23] Some twenty years later, Sulaimān's tales were completed by those of Ibn-Wahb, another merchant-adventurer who sojourned in Khumdān (or Singanfu). Soon after his stay in this capital of T'ang China, the colony of Arab merchants in Canton was destroyed in the course of a widespread peasant uprising in 878. Thereafter, traders from the Caliphate did not penetrate eastward beyond Malacca, and relations between the Arab Orient and China were resumed only in the thirteenth century. However, these merchants did develop trade relations with the land of the Khmer (Cambodia), whence they imported silver.

Navigation to China had been so secure that even some inhabitants of central Asia preferred to journey to that remote country by the southern, maritime route. Thus, a merchant from Samarkand went there via Irak, taking ship with his rich merchandise from Baṣra to Malacca, whence he proceeded to China on a Chinese ship.[24]

Commerce between the Caliphate and Byzantium was rendered more difficult now by the rather frequent Arabo-Byzantine wars, but trade exchanges did not cease between these two major powers and the "ships of the *Rūm*" [the "Romans"] continued to dock in the harbor of Trebizond, the northern commercial gate of the Caliphate, for Byzantium needed Oriental goods, which it was able to obtain only from Moslem merchants.

Arab commercial shipping dominated the Mediterranean, where Egypt played as important a role as Irak in the commerce of the Indian Ocean. Through the Nile valley, trade relations were maintained with the Maghrib, with Andalusia and with western Europe. But whereas trade between Andalusia and the Maghrib on the one hand, and Egypt on the other, and through Egypt with the Asian territories of the Caliphate, were quite permanent, commerce with western Europe was rather sporadic. The Belgian historian Henri Pirenne conceives of the Arab conquests and the formation of the Caliphate as disturbing those economic connections that had existed since antiquity between the Orient and western Europe, so that these two extensive areas had become isolated.[25] Pirenne's theory is quite convincing, though it met with some scepticism from European medievalists.* His main conclusions, based on abundant and interesting factual data, deserve serious attention. In particular, there is no doubt that the maritime trade of the Syrians with the Frankish kingdom of the Merovingians in the fifth and sixth centuries was quite regular and fairly active, and that it ceased almost entirely after the establishment of Arab domination in Syria; nor did it develop in the days of the Carolingians, the royal dynasty which began in 751, almost simultaneously with the 'Abbāsid rise to power.

A question directly related to that of the "Franco-Moslem" trade relations is the problem of diplomatic relations between the 'Abbāsid Caliphs and Frankish rulers. West European bourgeois historians had accepted the view (following a tradition dating from the Catholic Middle Ages) that such "Franco-Moslem" diplomatic contacts were established under Pippin the Short (751–768), a contemporary of the Caliph Manṣūr, and widely developed under Charlemagne (768–814), a contemporary of

* [This theory was criticized by eminent orientalists as well. See D.C. Dennet, "Pirenne and Muḥammad," Speculum XXIII (1948), pp. 165–190; Cahen, "Quelques problèmes concernant l'expansion économique musulmane au haut moyen age," L'Occidente e l'Islam nell'Alto Medioevo, Vol. I, Spoleto, 1965, pp. 391–432.]

Hārūn al-Rashīd. This notion most probably arose at the time of the Crusades and was quite definitely clerical in inspiration, for according to this concept, Charlemagne was a Christian king whose rights as protector of the "Holy Places" in Palestine had been recognized by the Moslem Caliph.

Bartol'd, in his research on "Charlemagne and Hārūn al-Rashīd,"[26] has proved the total fallacy of such tendentious views. He stresses the complete silence of Arabic-writing authors concerning any kind of relations between the 'Abbāsid Caliph and the Emperor Charlemagne; indeed, nothing was known in the Caliphate of this emperor. In the same period, Eginhard and other Frankish chroniclers give no indication at all of any knowledge of the Caliphate, let alone the names of any Caliphs.

Some west European Christians made their way to Palestine as pilgrims, visiting Jerusalem and other holy places in that country. Caring for the welfare of such pilgrims, Charlemagne established friendly relations with the Patriarch of Jerusalem through eastern and western monks who travelled from time to time to both the Empire of Charlemagne and to Palestine.

In addition to such contacts through pilgrimage in the "Holy Land," western Europe and the Orient were connected through commerce, which was almost entirely in the hands of Jewish merchants. Their activity was also known to Arabic-writing geographers; they imported eunuchs, male and female slaves, furs of beaver and ermine, and swords to Oriental lands, usually shipping their merchandise by the Mediterranean Sea via Egypt to the Red Sea, and further on to India and China. From the Orient they imported into Europe highly valued goods such as musk, aloe, spices and camphor. The consumers of such rare items were the relatives of Charlemagne and his court nobility, and these merchants were therefore honored and treated with confidence at Charlemagne's court. The Frankish Emperor entrusted to them certain tasks of intelligence and diplomacy. A mission of this kind was given, for example, to the merchant Isaac, who at the very end of the eighth century journeyed to the Orient and stayed there for several years; he returned through Tunisia and Sicily to Italy, bringing back with him an elephant and other gifts, allegedly sent by Hārūn al-Rashīd; he presented himself as the

Caliph's envoy. In the eyes of the Europeans, the elephant (nicknamed Abū-l-'Abbās) seemed far more important than the self-appointed envoy. The beast, quite unheard-of in Europe, attracted crowds of onlookers everywhere; it traversed Italy, made the difficult crossing over the Alps, and in 802 appeared in Aachen, with its master, at the court of Charlemagne. The elephant was immortalized by a mention in the Frankish chronicle, and in 810 died suddenly, of unknown causes.

The gifts which were supposed to have been sent by the Caliph to the Emperor (a water clock with figured ornaments, a silk tent, and so on), since they never existed, were not and could not have been preserved. The well-known art specialist Ya.I. Smirnov has written [concerning them] that there is no documentary proof of any relations between Charlemagne and Hārūn al-Rashīd.[27] The outstanding Byzantinist Vasil'ev opposed Bartol'd's conclusions,[28] accusing him, quite groundlessly, of "hypercriticism," and defending the traditional opinion inspired by Christian pietism. Bartol'd replied in another article "On the Question of Franco-Moslem Relations,"[29] and the result of this debate in learned reviews may be considered as proving Bartol'd's thesis of the legendary nature of any diplomatic connections between the 'Abbāsids and the Carolingians.

Commerce [of the Orient] with eastern Europe had not yet developed by the ninth century, but ways were already known through the Caspian Sea and the Lower Volga into the *Khaganate** of the Khazars. Contacts had also been made with Kievan Russia. In the Khazar city of Itil (on the Volga), high-grade fur skins could be bought but at that time Siberian furs were sold as far afield as Tibet. From the Kiev Slavs and from the Russians [Scandinavian adventurers in what was to become Russia] amber could be obtained, brought from the shores of the Baltic along the trade route "from the land of the Varangians [Scandinavians] to that of the Greeks." White slaves were driven from eastern Europe to the Caliphate, and honey and wax were imported, the latter being used for candles.

* [*Khayan,* or its contracted form *Khan,* means "ruler king" in the Turkic languages. At that time, the Khazar Khagate already professed Judaism.]

By its structure and official ideology, the Baghdad Caliphate of the eighth and ninth centuries may be defined as a feudal theocratic despotism. According to the norms of Sunnite public law, the authority and functions of supreme *imām* and supreme *amīr* were united in the person of the 'Abbāsid Caliph; in other words, he was invested with supreme power, both spiritual and temporal. As the head of the Moslem community, the successor and lieutenant to the apostle of Allah or even the representative of Allah on earth, the Caliph was considered the paramount owner of all land and water in the state. He was an autocratic ruler, the only limit to his autocracy being the sword of his own bodyguard (in the case of the successors of Ma'mūn).

During the first hundred years of the 'Abbāsid dynasty, Caliphal autocracy was indeed a political reality. The élite of the ruling class, the immediate entourage of the Caliph, strove to carry out a centralizing policy: provincial viceroys and military commanders were appointed by the Caliph and obeyed only his orders; tribute, taxes and other dues from the population reached Baghdad and were paid into the state treasury; viceroys and other officials who appropriated any revenues from taxation were considered as acting illegally and were therefore punishable.

The Arab aristocracy had forfeited their peculiar privileges and were forced to share power and profits with Iranian feudal lords, who provided the highest state dignitaries, the *wazīrs*. There was no such function and dignity under the Umayyads, for it was created by Manṣūr, on the model of the governmental organization of the Sassanids. For half a century, this highest post in the government was held by the Barmakids, who represented the Iranian feudal aristocracy and were big landowners from the vicinity of Balkh [on the frontiers of Iran and central Asia], descendants of Buddhist priests in that city.

The chief *wazīr* was considered as the right hand and the most authoritative counselor of the Caliph. As such, he headed the administrative-fiscal apparatus, the army and the department of state accounting. His activity was limited by nothing but the arbitrary will of the Caliph himself. As the keeper of the Caliph's seal he disposed of full powers: decrees and other state documents were not signed by the Caliph but sealed with his seal, and the *wazīr* used this seal on documents without the need for prior permission from the ruler, being obliged only to report to the Caliph on each case of such use of the seal. Thus, through the Barmakids, the Iranian feudals were actually in control of the Arab Caliph.

Hārūn al-Rashīd, as we have seen, perfidiously deprived the Barmakids of their power and their lives. A quite different, fanciful version of these events was given in literary form, where it was believed that the fall of the Barmakids was caused by a love affair between the sister of Hārūn, 'Abbāsa, and the *wazir* Ja'far ibn-Yaḥya the Barmakid. It was said that this enlightened princess, already thrice married and widowed, often took part in the entertaining evening talks and festivities of the Caliph and his *wazīr*. To avoid offending the *sharī'a,* which prohibits the presence of a woman in male society unless she is related to them by marriage or close kinship, the Caliph ordered a marriage ceremony, in name only, to be performed between his sister and his *wazīr,* but on learning that the marriage had actually been consummated, he flew into a rage and had Ja'far executed, also murdering the other Barmakids in the bargain. The inauthenticity of this version has already been shown by Ibn-Khaldūn,[30] who cites it as an example of the gullibility of historians.

The policy of centralization of military administration was often counteracted by provincial rulers and commanders, the success of any of whom would depend upon the numbers of troops in his pay and his connections with local feudals and rich townsmen. The main pursuit of each was personal enrichment. As they sometimes required vast sums to make good expenses incurred in bribing high dignitaries in the capital to obtain their profitable posts, the viceroys often arbitrarily increased taxes and tribute, appropriated a good proportion of the receipts from taxation, or seized land and other real estate likely to yield profits. On the other hand, the Caliphs and the heads of central institutions, wanting to protect their own incomes, tried to curb the arbitrary actions and acquisitiveness of the provincial rulers, resorting to armed force against them if necessary. But whenever circumstances became difficult and dangerous after rebellions had broken out, menacing the very existence of the powers that be, the central authorities willingly presented the viceroys with all the resources of their provinces to crush the rebels. Indeed, wherever popular movements were directed against Arab rule in non-Arab countries, the Caliphs found themselves powerless and forced to retreat. Thus they had to accept the formation of independent and semi-independent states in North Africa, central Asia, Afghanistan and Iran.*

The central government had one department which could obtain information on the activities of provincial rulers and thus check on them, the *barīd.* The word is of Latin (or perhaps Persian) derivation, and was originally, under the Caliph Mu'āwiya, the term for a mounted messenger carrying governmental correspondence. Under 'Abd-al-Malik, *barīd* came to mean the "postal service," which ensured written communications between the Caliph and his viceroys or military commanders in the provinces and developed in the reign of the Caliph Manṣūr into one of the principal governmental departments *(diwans)*. The director *(ṣāḥib al-barīd)* became a very important and influential office holder in Baghdad. He had under his orders the employees of the numerous "postal stations" dispersed throughout the vast territory of the Caliphate in cities and on highways laid out as early as Achemenid and Sassanid or Roman and Byzantine times. In each station messengers and their mounts were always on the alert; depending on the geographical environment, the mounts used were horses, camels or asses *(īshāk)*. The duties of the *barīd* employees were not merely to forward official correspondence, but also to collect and convey to Baghdad first-hand and precise information on the state of agriculture and irrigation, the mood of the local population, the activity of the provincial administration and the amount of coined gold and silver money in the local mint (if there was one). The written reports arrived regularly in Baghdad, at the central office of the *ṣāḥib al-barīd.* The information digested, the *ṣāḥib al-barīd* reported daily to the *wazīr* on the state of the empire. If events warranted it, the *ṣāḥib al-barīd*

* ["Independent and semi-independent states" were formed, however, in such regions as Egypt, northern Syria and the Jazira.]

could ask for audience not just with the *wazīr* but directly with the Caliph.

In fact, the *barīd* was a department of control and detection, making use of numerous spies and informers, male and female, both in the Caliphate and abroad. The budget of this department amounted to 159,000 dinars.

The archives of the *dīwān al-barīd* ("Department of Posts"), with their detailed itineraries, provided reliable data which were used in economic geographies of the type known as *al-masālik w-al-mamālik* ("Routes and States").

RELATIONS BETWEEN THE CALIPHATE AND BYZANTIUM

When the 'Abbāsids came to power in the Caliphate, the Isaurian dynasty was reigning in Byzantium (717–802), and was to do so throughout the reigns of the first five 'Abbāsid Caliphs. Its founder, Leo III, the Isaurian (717–741), had been an outstanding statesman and general of Syrian origin who could speak Arabic and had a precise knowledge of affairs in the Umayyad Caliphate. A few months after he assumed power, the Arab troops occupying important strategic positions in Asia Minor crossed the Hellespont (the Dardanelles) and with the support of a huge fleet besieged Constantinople, but failed under the walls of the Byzantine capital, when the war shifted again to Asia Minor. Toward the end of Leo III's reign, the Arab army suffered defeat at Akroina (present-day Kara-Hissar) and retreated into eastern Anatolia, where, until the start of the ninth century, warfare consisted merely of border clashes and raids.[31]

Throughout the ninth century, the Arabs were very active militarily both on the land frontier with Byzantium and in the vast arena of the Mediterranean. In the frontier region of the Caliphate on the Arabo-Byzantine border, where they were based, they called *'Awāṣim,* meaning "defensive" (cities) from the Arabic verb *'aṣama,* "to impede, protect, defend." The main center of this region was Antioch (Anṭākiya). The 'Awāṣim also included the cities of Balis on the Euphrates, Manbij and Samosata [Sumaysāt]. A line of fortresses was built along the very border to defend these cities and the entire region against unexpected incursions by the enemy, the most important of which was the town of Tarsus, near the Cilician Gates leading into Byzantine territory. This line of border fortresses became known as *thughūr,* "the front teeth," and was countered by a line of fortresses built by the Byzantines. Nearly every year (in spring and summer, sometimes also in winter), the Arabs launched raids into Byzantine territory, which, though they resulted in no territorial acquisition, caused much economic damage to the frontier population.

Arabo-Byzantine relations in the time of the Caliph Ma'mūn and his immediate successors were marked by a tendency to use the internal complications and difficulties of the enemy state to further one's own aims in foreign policy. At this time the Amorian dynasty was in power in Byzantium (820–867). Under its first Emperor, Michael II the Stammerer (820–829), a mighty popular rebellion broke out, which had started in Asia Minor under the leadership of Thomas the Slav, a pretender to the title of Emperor. Attempting to make use of Thomas, the Caliph Ma'mūn gave permission for him to be crowned in Arab-held Antioch in return for promises of territorial concessions in Asia Minor. The uprising, in which various nationalities and different social classes participated, spread throughout Asia Minor. The Byzantine fleet in the Aegean sided with the rebels and enabled them to cross into Thrace and Macedonia and besiege Constantinople, but the army of Michael II, supported by the Bulgar nobility, succeeded in beating back the numerous rebel forces. In 823 Thomas was captured and executed: Ma'mūn's gamble had failed.

Meanwhile, the rulers of Byzantium managed to make rather more successful use of the powerful movement of the Khurramis, led by Bābak, which lasted from 815/816 to 837 (see below). The friendly relations and military cooperation of Byzantium with the Khurramis in their war against the Caliphate were the main reason for the four campaigns which Ma'mūn led into Byzantine Asia Minor in 830, 831, 832 and 833.[32] Having at last quelled the Khurrami rebellion and executed Bābak, the Caliphal army again invaded Asia Minor in 838, and after a prolonged siege took the well-fortified city of Amorium. The success seemed so important that the Caliph Mu'taṣim started planning a campaign against Constantinople, but the plans were not to be fulfilled.

In the Mediterranean, Byzantium suffered defeats and territorial losses in the struggle with the Arabs, losing Crete in 825, which was of great strategic and commercial importance to the Byzantines. This fertile island, with its many cities and villages, was seized by emigrants from Cordova, who had been driven out of Andalusia in 814 after rebelling against the Umayyad *amīr*, Hakam I. These people from the Cordova suburbs, some 15,000 plus women and children, sailed to the Orient and disembarked in Egypt. Four years later, in 818/819, profiting by a revolt of the Egyptian viceroy against the Caliph Ma'mūn, they seized Alexandria, where they remained in power until the rebels were crushed by 'Abdallāh ibn-Ṭāhir in 825, who then became the new ruler of Egypt and suggested that the Andalusians should leave the Nile valley. Therefore they embarked again and sailed toward Crete, which they took without opposition, as the whole of the Byzantine army and fleet were engaged elsewhere against the followers of Thomas the Slav. Like earlier Arab invaders they built a military camp surrounded by a trench *(khandaq)*, hence the name of the city, Candia. Crete was thus now a lair of Moslem pirates, who attacked the islands and coasts of the Aegean Sea; attempts by the Byzantines to reconquer Crete remained unsuccessful for many years, until 961.

The Arabs from North Africa also gained considerable success in the western Mediterranean. The large and well-equipped Arab navy was superior to the Byzantine fleet here and contributed substantially to the success of Arab arms.

The conquest of Sicily by the Arabs followed upon the revolt of the Byzantine general [and local governor] Euphemius, who had proclaimed himself Emperor. Not all the cities and regions of Sicily accepted his rule, however, so he turned for military help to Ziyādat-Allāh I of the Aghlabid dynasty, ruler of Ifrīqiya. The troops sent by Ziyādat-Allāh landed in Sicily and began their conquest of the island. Euphemius having been killed meanwhile by supporters of the Byzantine Emperor, the Aghlabid troops occupied Palermo, Messina and most of the other cities on the island, establishing the dominion of the North African

Arabs there and leaving only Syracuse under Byzantine administration until the fall of the Amorian dynasty.[33]

From Sicily the Arabs crossed into Italy and captured Taranto, which belonged to the Lombard Duke of Benevento, going on to take some points in Byzantine Calabria and Apulia, including the important fortified harbor-town of Bari. They defeated a Venetian fleet which sailed into the Gulf of Taranto, and later also beat and repulsed an army under the command of the [Carolingian] Emperor Louis II.

The ports of Sicily became convenient bases for Arab pirate ships, which launched audacious raids on the coasts of Italy and southern France and on the islands of the western Mediterranean. These pirates took rich booty on land and sea, including captives who were sold on the slave markets of North Africa. In 840, Arab pirate ships entered the mouth of the Tiber and threatened Rome, whose population was siezed with indescribable panic.

POPULAR MOVEMENTS

Popular movements, expressing social contradictions and class struggle, formed the mainspring of the history of the Baghdad Caliphate. Peasants as well as the urban plebe participated en masse in these movements, and sometimes also the slaves, who were still fairly numerous. Certain groups within the dominant class of feudals, dissatisfied with the rule of the 'Abbāsids and struggling with them for power, sometimes joined (or at least made use of) such movements for a time.

The main cause of these movements— which became violent rebellions against the feudals and their 'Abbāsid rulers— was the oppression and exploitation of the workers. The hard lot of the popular masses was becoming intolerable under the illegal extortions and exactions at the hands of the Caliphal administration.

In Syria, which had lost its privileged position in the Caliphate under the later Umayyads, there remained many who were faithful to the overthrown dynasty, and who at times could persuade a considerable proportion of Syrians that the re-establishment of the Umayyads (whom they pictured in an idealized way) would free the land from ‘Abbāsid oppression, arbitrariness and looting. Rebellions aimed at restoring the Umayyads thus flared up in Syria until the beginning of the tenth century. The rebels, fighting under the Umayyad "white banner," placed their fond hopes in the advent of a "Sufyānid" (an offspring of Abū-Sufyān) who would deliver them from all evil. Such pro-Umayyad political messianism became so widespread among Syrians that even the ‘Abbāsid propaganda was forced to come to terms with it, the ‘Abbāsid agents representing this "Sufyānid" as an evil instigator and perverter of Moslems, the forerunner of a reign of darkness and atheism.

After the extermination of the Umayya clan by ‘Abdallāh ibn-‘Ali, uncle of the Caliph Abū-l-‘Abbās, an uprising was instigated in the Ḥaurān and at Qinnasrīn (Syria) by two Umayyad war leaders, one of whom acted in the name of some mysterious "Sufyānid." At the same time, the people of Damascus rebelled and defeated the army of the ‘Abbāsid viceroy, and in 754, learning that Abū-l-‘Abbās had died, they rose again and swore allegiance to one of the surviving Umayyad *amīrs*. Some Syrians, on the other hand, had joined the army of ‘Abdallāh ibn-‘Ali, who had started fighting for the Caliphal throne against his nephew Manṣūr, but this army was defeated in Mesopotamia by the troops of the famous Abū-Muslim.

The Syrian attitude toward Manṣūr is well characterized by the following anecdote. This Caliph once declared his satisfaction that the plague had ceased to devastate Syria during his reign; but a certain Syrian replied: "Allah is far too merciful to unite against us both the plague and yourself!"[34]

The increasing fiscal exploitation of the people, accompanied by the abuses practiced by the fiscal agents, caused an uprising in Lebanon in 759–760. The rebellious mountain farmers came down into the Biqā‘ valley, were joined there by local villagers, and moved toward Baalbek. Pushed back by superior numbers of Caliphal troops, the farmers retreated into their native mountains. Punitive detachments were sent after them and cruel reprisals were carried out: many Lebanese were expelled from their villages and resettled in the plains of Syria.

At the start of the reign of Hārūn al-Rashīd, a terrible epidemic of the plague depopulated many villages in Palestine. The survivors fled in panic; the situation of these peasants was so desperate that the Caliph even announced that those who would return to their deserted villages and again till the abandoned fields would be exempt from taxation.

The tension and troubles in Syria were made worse by armed clashes between the local Kalbite and Qaisite tribesmen, who continued to pursue their endless feuds under the ʻAbbāsids.

Soon after the death of Hārūn, while his sons Amīn and Ma'mūn were struggling bitterly for the throne, the Egyptian army rose in mutiny while "Sufyānids" again appeared in Syria. One of them, who was proclaimed Caliph in Damascus in 811, was supported by the Kalbites and another by their foes the Qaisites. A bloody civil war began in Syria, disconnecting all communications between Egypt and Irak and breaking up the economic system of the Syrian population, which in turn resulted in severe famine throughout the country.

When Ma'mūn's reign started, the popular movements increased in scope and violence. The entire reign of this Caliph may be considered, as defined by Mednikov and Vasil'ev, a "time of troubles." Until the year 204 of the *hijra* (819/820 A.D.), Ma'mūn was fully absorbed by the task of quelling revolts and fighting off the various pretenders to the throne. Only in that year was he able to enter Baghdad, but before he could take possession of the Caliphal palace he had to distribute 2,400,000 gold dinars in gratuities in order to be received properly. Even after his admission into the capital he had to send out armies against rebels in various lands of the Caliphate. The very next year, 205 of the *hijra,* for instance, the uprising of the Zutt tribes began in southern Irak. These are usually identified as gypsies who, according to tradition, had migrated from India in the fifth century, in the days of the *shahin-shah* Bahram Gor (420–438). They gradually spread through the marshy districts between Baṣra and Wāsiṭ where they lived by raising cattle, fishing, and various trades. It is known that there were gifted musicians among them.

The rebel Zutt tribes successfully resisted the punitive columns sent out by the Caliph, and interrupted communications between Baghdad and Baṣra by attacking camel caravans and [fluvial] shipping. The uprising lasted for fifteen years, from 820 to 835, ending only when the Caliphal authorities promised a full amnesty, that is, respect of life and property of the rebels. The causes of the rebellion and its slogans are still not definitely known.

In the year 210 of the *hijra* (825/826 A.D.), Ma'mūn sent troops under the command of 'Abdallāh ibn-Ṭāhir to subdue the Syrian and Egyptian populations, but the reprisals ordered by 'Abdallāh and later by the heir to the throne, Mu'taṣim, were effective only for a short time. Hoping to achieve permanent results, Ma'mūn himself arrived in Syria in the year 216, and then proceeded to Egypt.

In Egypt, the rebellions of Arab troops continued, joined by the lowermost classes of the population, described by local historians as a "scum" of "vagrants." The situation became particularly tense in 216 (831/832) when an uprising of the Copts occurred; the Copts had been in repeated rebellion since the last quarter of the eighth century due to the burden of taxation, worsened by the predatory methods and violence of Caliphal viceroys and tax collectors.

Ma'mūn's army carried out cruel reprisals against the rebel Copts: on his orders, those that were taken alive were executed and their wives and children sold as slaves. The deserted Coptic villages were given to Moslem fellahs (peasants), and many churches were turned into mosques.

Under the two successors of Ma'mūn there was a widespread revolt of the peasants in Palestine, which broke out in 226–227 of the *hijra* (840–842 A.D.). This peasant rising began simultaneously with an uprising of the inhabitants of Damascus; its leader was Abū-Ḥarb, who hid his face behind a veil and purported to be a "Sufyānid," thus finding support among some noble Kalbites. Near Ramla, where his command post was located, many peasants gathered (according to the usual Arabic expression: "a hundred thousand"), but as soon as the spring farming time came, nearly all of them went back to their villages. Only 2,000 fighters were left under the banners of Abū-Ḥarb, and the Caliphal troops thus easily broke their resistance and captured the leader.

The anti-'Abbāsid movement in North Africa, with the participation of both the Arabs and the Berbers, resulted in the formation of two independent states under the rule of the Idrīsids [in Morocco] and the Rustamid dynasty [in Algeria].

Popular movements in Iran, central Asia and Transcaucasia were more complex than those in Syria and Egypt. The situation of the rural and urban working masses had not improved at all under the earlier ʿAbbāsids; in fact in many cases it had deteriorated. The feudals of these countries (especially the feudal aristocracy of big landowners) began to accept the religion of the conquerors, Islam, soon after the Arab invasions in order to preserve their estates and class privileges even under Arab rule. Within the Caliphate, the peasantry found itself under a twofold oppression from which it tried to escape by means of rebellion. Under the ʿAbbāsids, revolts were directed not merely against Arab domination but as much against the local feudal lords, who supported the Arab rule and exploited the popular masses in concert with the descendants of the conquerors. Thus, the movements of these masses aimed both at political liberation from foreign rule and at social emancipation from all forms of oppression and exploitation.

The anti-Umayyad uprising in central Asia and Iran had brought hope to the rebels for both these aims, but the ʿAbbāsid rise to power in fact made no diffierence to the hard lot of the working masses. They were thus bitterly disappointed and dissatisfied, and recommenced their protests.

As early as 755 a peasant uprising broke out in Iran, in the regions of Nishapur and Rayy, under the leadership of Sumbat the Magian, a Zoroastrian, at the murder of Abū-Muslim by order of the Caliph Manṣūr. Abū-Muslim had been the leader of the anti-Umayyad rebellion and was very popular among the peasant masses: his activity and his name were connected in their minds with hopes of social emancipation. A Caliphal army 10,000 strong defeated the rebel troops of Sumbat, dispersed them and in part annihilated them. Sumbat himself was killed in the retreat; the rebellion had lasted only seventy days.[35]

A much more important and more stubborn uprising was that of the so-called "white-robed men" in *Mā-warā'-n-nahr* in 776–783. Its leader and religious propagandist, Muqannaʿ ("the veiled one"), had been an opponent not only of the ʻAbbāsids but also of Abū-Muslim. Because of his anti-ʻAbbāsid propaganda, he had been arrested in Merv by order of the Caliph Manṣūr and imprisoned in Baghdad, but he escaped, returned to Merv and made his way into *Mā-warā'-n-nahr.*

Even prior to the arrival of Muqannaʻ in Transoxiana, the movement of the "white-robed" had involved a considerable part of the population in the valley of the Kashka Darya and the Zeravshan and later in the district of Bukhāra, though the rebels never seized this city itself. Yakubovskii, author of a paper on the rebellion of Muqannaʻ, describes the rebels as mainly farmers living in rural communes. The forfeit of their personal liberty had begun even before the establishment of Arab rule, but under the Arabs, who made them pay tribute and the *corvée,* their freedom was completely lost. Whole villages of them therefore joined the ranks of Muqannaʻ.[36]

On reaching *Mā-warā'-n-nahr,* Muqannaʻ ordered a strong fortress to be constructed in the Sanam Mountains which would be the center of the uprising. The considerable forces required to quell the uprising encountered a stubborn resistance; the Caliph Mahdi came personally to Nishapur to direct operations, removed some commanders for inaction or delay and appointed others, but the rebellion was checked only after seven years, and then solely because of the numerical and technical superiority of the Caliphal troops. The rebels defended their fortresses bravely, and finally, according to tradition, on the eve of the fall of his last stronghold Muqannaʻ took poison. The "white-robed" persisted in their fight for another few years, though not in any organized way, still awaiting "the second advent" of their leader.

The ideology of the mass movements against Arab rule and the feudal regime in Iran, central Asia and Transcaucasia was essentially Mazdakism or a doctrine derived from it: the teachings of these movements were characterized by a dualist conception of an eternal struggle between light and darkness, good and evil, with a forlorn hope for the triumph of the former over the latter. The working masses identified the existing regime of oppression and exploitation with darkness and evil, seeking light and goodness in a remote past. By idealizing this past, they imagined the free communal regime as a Golden Age of universal equality and abundance, and therefore sought to re-establish the communal rules of life, which in the days of their remote ancestors made for happiness without cruel feudal domination or the abuses and extortions of publicans. They considered the basic cause of all misfortunes and suffering to be feudal property, which they wished to replace by communal property.

The proponents of this ideology were known as Khurramis. The meaning of the term is still obscure, but it is perhaps derived from the Persian *khurram,* "clarity" or "light." Another acceptable derivation is from *khur, khwar,* "sun" or "fire."[37] The Khurramis were also known as *muḥammir,* "the Reds," or *surkh 'alam,* "the Red-Banner men." Red, the color of blood, symbolized their willingness to sacrifice themselves in the name of liberty. The aims and ideology of the Khurramis found their fullest expression in the movement of Bābak.

This uprising started in Azerbaijan and, due to the military successes of the rebels, spread over an immense territory, including Khurāsān, Jibāl ["the Mountains," that is, ancient Media], Armenia, Ṭabaristān, Jurjān, Dailam and the region of Hamadhān as far as Iṣfahān. The revolt began in 815 or 816 and lasted for more than twenty years, until 837. In the main it was a mass rising of the peasants, involving some 300,000 people in Azerbaijan alone. As the Khurammis' chief target was to overthrow Arab rule, and as they gained many brilliant successes in their struggle against the Caliphal armies, many members of the local ruling class were attracted to their side, not only from the lower and middle feudality but also from feudal aristocracy and even the Caliphal viceroys and regional governors. These were of course temporary and not very willing fellow-travellers of a movement which remained basically anti-feudal, but by making contact with Bābak, or at least refraining from opposing him, they sought to protect their lives and property and ultimately perhaps their class privileges. These motives of the fellow-travellers were to be a grave menace to the movement, as was apparent during the last stage of the uprising.

The scope of the movement, the numbers of its followers and their exalted fighting spirit may be gauged by their persistent successes in battle against the troops sent out by the Caliph Ma'mūn. In 820 they defeated the first Caliphal army which had marched against them; two other such armies were likewise defeated in 823/824 and in 828, the second of which was 30,000 strong. In 829/830 the Khurramis destroyed one more Caliphal army, even its commander being unable to escape.

The numerical strength of the Khurammis and their program of liberation from foreign rule, which they considered as the basic cause of social oppression, account for their great military success. Another important factor in the Khurrami victories was the organizational and military ability of Bābak himself. Like other leaders of Khurrami rebellions, he was of humble origin and in his youth had suffered deprivation and oppression. He had been employed as a camel driver in trade caravans, and in this capacity had travelled through many cities and villages, seeing the distress of the working people and sharing their hopes. Now the head of a movement which had spread over a huge territory, Bābak showed himself a very capable war leader, who knew how to direct the revolutionary energy of the masses in revolt. He also made a quite correct assessment of the international situation, especially of Arabo-Byzantine relations.

He started a correspondence with the Byzantine Emperor Theophilus (829–842), stating that he was prepared to join with him in operations against the Caliphate. At all events, on the eve of Ma'mūn's campaign into Byzantine territory in 830 some 14,000 Khurramis were transferred there. The Byzantine command distributed them in the "themes [military-administrative districts], and formed them into special units which became known as the "Persian turmae." The Byzantines even found wives for those soldiers of the "turmae" who wanted to marry.

One of the aims of the campaigns of the Caliph Ma'mūn against Byzantium in the last four years of his reign was possibly to prevent any union between Bābak's rebels and the Byzantine armies.

In the first years of the rule of Mu'taṣim (833–842), the war against the Khurrami rebels of Bābak took priority in Caliphal policy. According to some reports, Ma'mūn advised his successor in his will to entrust the leadership of this war to some energetic and ruthless commander, provided with all the necessary forces and means.

As early as 833, a Caliphal army was sent out against the Khurramis and defeated them, for the first time, near Hamadhān; in this battle and during its sequel, 60,000 Khurramis perished. Those that escaped annihilation retreated into Byzantine territory.[38] Until 837, there were no hostilities on the Arabo-Byzantine frontiers, as the main forces of Byzantium were then engaged in Sicily. These four years of *de facto* armistice in Asia Minor enabled the Caliphal command to use all its available troops (including those that had been withdrawn from the border region of 'Awāṣim) in the struggle against Bābak. The Caliph's armies were well-provided with weapons, equipment and victuals, and they also had siege-and-assault engines specially designed for mountain warfare.

In 835, the Caliph Mu'taṣim appointed as commander-in-chief of the armies operating against the Khurramis a Turk, Afshīn, who had distinguished himself as a specialist in repression under Ma'mūn when the revolt in Egypt was being quelled. The Caliph ordered higher pay for this commander: 10,000 dirhems a day for those days on which the Khurramis were engaged in battle, and only 5,000 dirhems when there was no fighting.[39] Under Afshīn's orders were two well-known war leaders, Ja'far al-Khayyāṭ and Itāḥ al-Ṭabbākh. When the Caliphal forces began their assault on the rebel troops, Bābak informed the Emperor Theophilus that the Caliph was directing all his men against the Khurramis, including his tailor and his cook, a pun on *khayyāṭ* meaning "tailor" in Arabic and on *tabbākh* meaning "cook." Certain information also states that Bābak posed as a Christian in his correspondence with Theophilus, promising to convert all his followers to Christianity.[40] This was not necessarily a mere diplomatic maneuver, for the ideology of the Khurramis indeed stood closer to Christianity than to Islam.

To create a diversion against the Caliphal armies, Bābak insistently requested that Theophilus start military operations, assuming quite correctly that this would induce the Caliph to withdraw some of his forces from the Khurrami front in order to throw back or delay the Byzantine offensive. In fact, the Byzantine command, profiting from the depletion of Arab troops in the border region, invaded the territory of the Caliphate. In 837 the Byzantine army, which included Khurramis who had previously retreated into Byzantine territory, went on a campaign to Zaperta (Zibarta), a fortress in Mesopotamia; Zaperta was taken and burned, the male population slaughtered and the women and children taken captive. The cities of Malaṭya and Samosata were also taken, their capture being accompanied by atrocities rather common in Byzantine warfare: many prisoners were blinded, others had their noses and ears cut off.

This inroad by Byzantine troops was merely a major raid, after which the Byzantines retreated into their own territory. The Caliphal armies had not been weakened and continued to press the Khurramis back into the mountain districts of Azerbaijan. The rebels were still a menacing force, however, and their leader Bābak still played a prominent political role: we know that Afshīn, the Caliph's commander-in-chief, began secret negotiations with Bābak and with the governor of Ṭabaristān, Māziyār, who was in correspondence with the Khurrami leader and approved of his actions, aimed at establishing a joint plan of operations against the Caliph. Afshīn proposed that the Caliph be deposed and that he establish his own rule in the Caliphate, giving his accomplices dominion over certain parts of the territory, but no agreement was concluded, probably because Bābak was unwilling to ally himself with a representative of the ruling class against which the Khurrami masses were fighting.

Besides the troops and siege engines used in combating the Khurramis, Afshīn made full use of his agents operating in the rear of the enemy. His spies and provocateurs kept him informed while at the same time remaining in touch with and working upon those feudals who had joined the Khurramis solely out of opportunism. The military successes of the Caliphal armies in 835–837 frightened these fellow-travellers, who were afraid of losing their lands and privileges or of being put to death by the Caliph's executioners. They began to renounce their alliance with Bābak, sometimes even attacking him from the rear.

In late 837, the army of Afshīn besieged the fortress of Badẖdẖ, the residence and headquarters of Bābak. When the fall of the fortress was imminent, Bābak left it through an underground passage, intending to make his way to Byzantium in order to continue fighting the Caliphate with the help of the Emperor Theophilus' troops; but he was treacherously seized by a local feudal lord in Armenia and delivered to Afshīn, who ordered his prisoner to be sent by elephant to the Caliph's residence in Sāmarra. When Afshīn himself arrived there in great triumph, Bābak was crucified and quartered as a state criminal.

Feudalistic Moslem historians, in expression of class hatred of those masses who struggled for freedom, spread calumny against Bābak and his followers. Fictions about the repulsive morals of the Khurramis were also repeated by bourgeois historians of the Arabs and of Islam. Thus, for instance, Clément Huart in his "History of the Arabs"—a quite typical product of western bourgeois historiography—makes the following statement: "Azerbaijan fell under the power of Bābak, head of the communist sect of the Khurramis, who believed in the reincarnation of the godhead in the person of their leader and who preached a community of property and of women."[41] Even in our own century, the Indo-Moslem scholar Ameer Ali shows hatred and scorn for Bābak: "Early in Ma'mūn's reign, whilst the empire was convulsed by internecine struggle and warfare, a brigand of the name of Bābak had made himself the master of a stronghold in one of the most inaccessible defiles of Mazanderan. He belonged to the Magian sect of Khurramis, who believed in metempsychosis (transmigration of the soul), and recognized none of the rules of morality enforced by Judaism, Christianity or Islam. From his mountain fortress he mercilessly harried the surrounding country, slaughtered the men and carried away the women, Christian and Moslem, into loathsome captivity."[42]

As we have already noted, the opponents of the Mazdakite movement made it an object of utter calumny; they persisted in this for a century, applying their efforts against the Khurramis too. The fighters against feudal exploitation were indeed in favor of a community of property in the free agricultural communal regime which they sought to restore, but they were not and could not be "Communists" in any scientific sense of the term. Bourgeois scholars, defining them in this way, use the word "Communism" not in its scientific meaning but merely to frighten their petty bourgeois readers. As to the ugly legend about a "community of women," this could have arisen as a reflection of the enlightened position of Khurrami womenfolk in the distorted Moslem mirror of the world. The peasant women (especially among the mountaineers) took a full part in productive work and even in Moslem countries enjoyed a relative independence entirely alien to the idle city women and especially to the wives and daughters of the feudals, the merchants and the clergy [sic]. It is known that Khurrami women wore neither the veil nor any restricting garments such as the *paranja,** and were not subject to any kind of seclusion, for all this would have been incompatible with their work at home and in the fields. These women sat at the same table (or rather, on the same rug) as their menfolk, and had the right to choose their husbands themselves (marriage thus being based on love); if necessary, they fought in battle, and some of them sat on councils of war. Such a position for women, with their share in work and in combat, seemed immoral and even perverse to those feudalistic ideologists who accepted the enslavement of the Moslem woman as a matter of course and it is on these grounds of intolerance and oppression of the female sex that the absurd notion arose of a "community of women" among the Khurramis.

THE UPRISING OF THE ZANJ

One of the most specific peculiarities of feudal society in the Baghdad Caliphate was slave-holding. Despite the development of a feudal mode of production and the corresponding relations, the slave regime persisted for a long time. Soviet historians of the Orient have not yet fully accounted for the use of slaves in the social production of the Caliphate. The present state of research on the employment of slaves in agriculture, irrigation and the trades can voice only the following considerations. Firstly, slave-holding was a common trait of early feudal society in both

* [Upper garment of city women in central Asia, from Arabic *faranjiyya* "Frankish dress".]

Byzantium and the Middle East. After the Arab conquests, the slave regime was not only retained but was greatly expanded, as the dominant Arab tribal aristocracy actually promoted slavery. Under the orthodox Caliphs and the Sufyānids, then, the numbers of slaves increased sharply and the development of feudal relations ceased temporarily in those countries conquered by the Arabs. Secondly, the slow decay of rural communes, which strenuously resisted their reduction to a state of serfdom, as well as the existence of the tax rent [the tax-like ground rent] and the absence of the *corvée,* meant that slaves had to be used in those spheres of social production that required most labor, especially artificial irrigation, mining and some crafts involving hard labor.

The demand for slaves in social production and the wide development of domestic slavery were met by a very active slave trade. Slave caravans and ships crammed with slaves reached the Baghdad Caliphate from the north and south. Particularly large numbers arrived from Zanzibar (Zanj in Arabic), which Arabic-language geography regarded as not just the island of Zanzibar but the entire coastline of East Africa. The island itself was renowned among slavers for its markets teeming with black slaves. Ships carried the slaves from the harbors of Zanzibar to the district of Shaṭṭ al-ʻArab [in southern Irak]; these African slaves were known in the Caliphate as the "Zanj."

In the neighborhood of Baṣra there were always a great many Zanj, brought by Arab and Persian slavers, waiting to be sold. In the ninth century, some of these slaves were selected for the Caliphal army, but most were taken to southern Irak or to Iranian Khūzistān, where they were mercilessly exploited on state lands and on private estates. They dug ditches, drained marshland overgrown with reeds, cleaned salt flats by removing the salt crust, procured saltpeter and extracted salt from seawater; they were also used on cotton and sugar cane plantations.

The Zanj lived in camps (from 500 to 5,000 per camp), and were forced to labor under the most difficult circumstances: they dwelt in dirty, stifling huts, haphazardly made of reeds and palm leaves; their daily ration was a few handfuls of flour and dates; they suffered and perished from marsh fever, from exhaustion and from the bestial treatment meted out by the slave drivers. Sometimes the slaves rose in rebellion only to fall victims to inhuman reprisals by the Caliphal authorities. The first such rebellion occurred in 694.

The most violent uprising of the Zanj, which lasted for 14 years, broke out in 869. We have fairly detailed information on it in the "Universal History" of Ṭabari, a contemporary; but a work written by one of the ideologists of the Zanj rebels, a companion of their leader, unfortunately has not survived. Some data on the uprising can also be found in the writings of Mas'ūdi.

The Zanj rebellion began in the vicinity of Baṣra. In the year 255 of the *hijra* (868/869 A.D.), writes Ṭabari "there appeared a man around whom there gathered the Zanj who were cleaning the salt flats."[43] This man was one 'Alī ibn-Muḥammad, who became the leader and ideologist of the black slaves in rebellion. Only confused and contradictory information exists on the early period of his activity: it seems that he started on his career in Ḥajar in eastern Arabia, where he proclaimed himself prophet and direct descendant of the Caliph 'Alī, but we do not know the exact contents of his preaching. Many of the inhabitants of this town joined him, but others opposed his rule and fighting broke out. At this he departed for Baḥrain, where the population acknowledged him as a prophet, though when he tried to collect tribute from them they chased him out. With some of his followers he started roaming through Ḥasa, shifting from one bedouin encampment to another and preaching certain new, hitherto unknown, verses of the Koran. He gained many additional adepts and with these set out on a campaign against the people of Baḥrain; here his "army" was defeated and soon dispersed. It was at this time, when he was in desperate straits, that 'Alī, as reported later by his followers, heard a mysterious voice out of a thundercloud enjoin him to proceed to Baṣra.[44]

In 868 he appeared in Baṣra, where civil war was then raging between two groups of townsmen. The attempt by 'Ali ibn-Muḥammad to control and lead one of these groups ended in failure; the governor of the city imprisoned those few citizens who had sided with him, and his wife, son, daughter and slave girl were also thrown in prison, though he himself escaped to Baghdad. Here he found followers among the capital's inhabitants, but after less than a year returned to Baṣra on learning that the governor had been replaced and the "instigators of the disorders" had freed those in prison. 'Alī ibn-Muhammad came back to Baṣra in the month of Ramaḍān 255 (August 869).[45]

Under the heading of this year, Ṭabari[46] relates the story of a *ghulām* (slave) of his conversation with the future leader of the Zanj. 'Alī, meeting this slave near Baṣra, asked him what was the ration of a slave in flour, soup and dates; he then suggested that the *ghulām* bring other slaves to him, and when 150 had come from one place and 500 from another, and still more from other places, he gave a speech. In this, the first appearance of 'Alī ibn-Muḥammad before the Zanj, he promised them "power and property" and swore that he would neither deceive nor abandon them. He commanded the masters of these slaves to be brought before him, as well as the slave drivers, and threatened them with death for their persecution of the slaves. The threat was in part carried out: each slave owner and slave driver was given 500 strokes with fresh palm branches. 'Alī also ordered them to divorce their wives who would otherwise tell tales of his whereabouts and the number of his followers; he probably kept these divorced women and found new husbands for them among his fellow rebels.

By the end of the first year of the uprising some 15,000 slaves had gathered around 'Alī ibn-Muḥammad in the vicinity of Baṣra. Addressing them, he stated that he wanted to improve their condition so that they themselves would be owners of slaves, property and houses.[47]

His ideology was syncretic; he was a Shī'ite who gave himself out as the "hidden *imām*," the direct descendant of 'Alī ibn-Abi-Ṭālib, or even as an incarnation of the deity, therefore veiling his face, but his behavior in the course of the rebellion was definitely that of a follower of the Khārijite doctrine in its extremist Azraqi form. Mas'ūdi in fact considers him an Azraqi, and to prove his affiliation to this intolerant sect points out the murder of women, infants and elderly people at his orders, as well as the Khārijite slogans and formulas which he used in his public appearances.[48]

The mass of the Zanj, of course, had neither the desire nor

the ability to assimilate the Khārijite teachings. Their mental development and cultural level was far below that of even the ignorant, illiterate peasants of Irak. Nor did they understand the Arabic discourses of their leader, who had to address them through translators; but these African slaves, brought from various lands of the "Dark Continent," spoke very many different tongues and dialects, and it was quite impossible to find translators for all of them. Thus for many of the Zanj their eloquent chieftain and preacher was like a dumb man, and they were deaf to his preachings.

Suffering the shame and cruelties of slavery, the Zanj hated people in general, and wanted to eat their fill after long years of hunger. This alone accounts for the slaughter and plunder with which the rebel slaves terrified all men of property.

They could not capture Baṣra, which was protected by high strong walls, and perhaps did not even aim to do so; they were not yet militarily organized, lacked weapons for hand-to-hand combat, and had no storming equipment whatsoever. Their situation was thus very difficult at first, but their leader proved energetic and a good organizer, forming them into units, appointing commanders and forbidding them to drink wine. In 256 (869/870), the Zanj took and sacked Ubulla, upon which 'Abbādān surrendered to them. In the same year, the uprising spread to Khūzistān, where it was welcomed and supported by the peasants and indigent townsfolk. In Ahwaz, the principal city of this region, a revolt had apparently broken out which enabled the Zanj to seize this important center easily and capture its governor. They defeated a Caliphal detachment sent out to quell the rebellion, whose survivors, together with their commander, fled and took refuge behind the strong walls of Baṣra.

The successes of the Zanj caused panic among the richer inhabitants of Baṣra. Many left the city in a hurry and fled northward. Meanwhile the Zanj defeated another detachment of the Caliph's army.[49]

In 257 of the *hijra* (870/871 A.D.), they gained several more victories over the Caliphal troops. The reasons for these repeated successes of the rebel slaves were not merely their extremely embittered fighting and their tactics of sudden night attacks on enemy camps; far more important, and quite unexpected for the Caliphal command, was that many troops of the Caliph, recruited from among the Zanj, sided with their rebel brethren, with whom they felt an ethnic and social solidarity. Such reinforcements vastly increased the combat capacity of the rebel slaves, for the deserters from the Caliphal army were well-trained and well-armed warriors. Thus, two years after the start of the uprising, the rebel bands had developed into a true army.

In autumn 871 the Zanj finally took Baṣra. Many inhabitants perished (according to Mas'ūdi, 300,000),[50] fires destroyed much of the city, and property was looted. But the Zanj did not use this major city as their military and political headquarters, as that would not fit their strategy. Continuing their operations against the Caliphal troops, they built fortified refuges on islands in the channels of the Shaṭṭ-al-'Arab and in various canals, choosing places densely overgrown with thickets of reed. These refuges were surrounded by earthen walls, protecting the dwellings and stores, so that, when unable or unwilling to face open combat, several detachments of the Zanj would sit it out in these strongholds amid the swamps and complicated networks of waterways, defying the Caliphal troops sent to dislodge them. Here too they brought the booty taken from the camps of the Caliph's army or from townships, or captured in attacks on trade caravans and commercial shipping. One of these refuges, the residence of 'Alī ibn-Muḥammad himself, developed into a big fortified town, Mukhtāra, to the southwest of Kūfa, and was finally to become the capital of the Zanj state.

Until the late seventies of the ninth century, the war between the Zanj and the Caliphate proceeded on the whole to the advantage of the rebels. The Caliph's soldiers were less steadfast than the Zanj troops, who were more often victors than vanquished. In 875 the Zanj acquired an unwilling ally in the person of the Iranian war leader Ya'qūb ibn-Laith al-Ṣaffār, who was in revolt against the 'Abbāsid Caliph, though his campaign against Baghdad ended in defeat. His lieutenant in Khūzistān took the field together with the Zanj, but their combined forces were beaten in 876 near Sūs, after which the Zanj and Ya'qūb al-Ṣaffār parted company and soon began hostilities against each other. ‘Alī ibn-Muḥammad was forced to evacuate Ahwaz, ceding it to al-Ṣaffār, in order to avoid the latter’s military threat.

In 265 (878/879), the Zanj captured Wāsiṭ and advanced northward in the direction of Baghdad. The next year, however, a Caliphal army commanded by Abū-l-‘Abbās (the future Caliph Mu‘taḍid), son of Muwaffaq, defeated the Zanj and entered Wāsiṭ, and in the same year Muwaffaq himself took command of the army operating against the Zanj. This army was supported by a large river fleet, including decked ships, barges and open boats which could penetrate through the channels and canals to the very strongholds of the rebels.

By that time, great changes had occurred among the Zanj, which were ultimately to bring about their defeat. These former slaves, freed from oppression and exploitation, by no means abolished slavery; as we have seen, ‘Alī ibn-Muḥammad had promised them, at the very start of the uprising, that they themselves would be rich slave owners. Indeed, as the rebellion spread over more and more territory, the number of slaves increased as captives and even part of the free population were enslaved. As reported by Mas‘ūdi, the Zanj auctioned Arab women of noble origin—‘Alids, Quraishites, and so on—on the markets. apparently supply exceeded demand to the point where a young girl would be sold for next to nothing: 2 or 3 dirhems. Every Zanj, Mas‘ūdi assures us, possessed 10, 20 or even 30 women who served him as despised concubines and performed dirty menial work.[51]

The peasants, the principal allies of the Zanj, remained under the burden of taxation in the areas overrun by the former slaves. Townsmen (especially the rich among them) suffered great losses from fire and looting, and many were slaughtered. Commerce declined within the area of Zanj rule, and traders and craftsmen suffered. Social support for the Zanj was thus quite unreliable; the rebels could depend only on their own military strength.

By the late seventies of the ninth century, the leadership of the Zanj had become a ruling group of big landowners and slave holders, in which capacity they exploited the peasants and urban workers, appropriating most of the booty and receipts of taxation to the detriment of the rank-and-file Zanj. With their unlimited power and vast wealth, this leadership saw Caliphal despotism as the ideal political regime. 'Alī ibn-Muḥammad actually proclaimed himself Caliph within the areas conquered by the Zanj, ordering prayers for him in the mosques as if he were a sovereign ruler and coining money in his own name. The formation of this "lesser Caliphate" manifested the deep social differentiation within the ranks of the Zanj: their alliance with the free working masses had come to an end, and sharp economic and political inequality now divided the Zanj themselves, their interests conflicting more and more. The rebels became disillusioned, hesitant, uncertain of the future, and the combat capacity of their troops decreased.

In 880 they again defeated a Caliphal detachment, but the troops and fleet commanded by Muwaffaq were slowly and cautiously advancing toward the south, methodically reconnoitering the territory held by the Zanj. Contrary to earlier Caliphal commanders, who used to slaughter all those rebels who fell into their hands, Muwaffaq followed a reasonable policy: he dealt mercifully with captive and unarmed Zanj and forbade his warriors to torture or kill them,[52] doubtless hoping to lessen their resistance by means of avoiding driving them to despair.

Meanwhile the Zanj went over to the defensive and scattered their armed forces among their fortified camps, which Muwaffaq now stormed one by one. His river fleet enabled him to approach any Zanj stronghold and subdue its defenders. The main center, Mukhtāra, the residence of 'Alī ibn-Muḥammad, withstood a three-year siege and repulsed several assaults by the Caliphal troops. Muwaffaq had to build a well-fortified camp in order to reduce the considerable losses inflicted upon his army by the daring night sorties of the besieged. He offered 'Alī ibn- Muḥammad a promise of pardon if he would capitulate and swear allegiance to the Caliph,[53] but, although further resistance seemed hopeless, the Zanj leader refused. As the food situation in the Mukhtāra garrison became more and more desperate with Muwaffaq's blockading forces cutting off all supplies, part of the besieged Zanj deserted the fortress and went over to the enemy camp, where they were well received. Finally, in 883, the exhausted garrison of Mukhtāra was unable to resist the last onslaught, and the fortress fell. The head of 'Alī ibn-Muḥammad was thrown at Muwaffaq's feet.

Once the uprising had been quelled, the Zanj suffered cruel reprisals; many were slaughtered, the others again reduced to slavery. Their faithful companions, the Azraqis, were also mercilessly persecuted. After the Zanj had captured Baṣra, the leading political role of the city had been played by Muhallibi, a companion of 'Alī ibn-Muḥammad. In his preachings and prayers, Muhallibi had invoked divine blessings upon the leader of the Zanj and upon the first two Caliphs, Abū-Bakr and 'Omar, while cursing the 'Abbāsids as despots and tyrants. Many of the people of Baṣra were followers of this enthusiastic Azraqi, and (even after the recapture of the city by the Caliphal troops) would not renounce their convictions, still gathering each Friday to pray and listen to the sermons. Many of them fled Baṣra to escape persecution at the hands of the Caliph's authorities, and the majority of those left in the city were killed or thrown into the river. A considerable number survived, however, hiding in inner courts and in wells, and emerging from their hiding places only at night to roam the deserted streets and kill dogs, cats and mice for food. Once these animals had been exterminated the Azraqis in hiding began to eat the corpses of their own dead.[54]

The main result of the Zanj uprising was the dying out of the slave regime; although it did not entirely disappear, slave labor still being used for a long time in artisanal production, exploitation of slaves in agriculture and artificial irrigation generally ceased. Furthermore, the slave trade from Africa was very much reduced as the demand was now limited almost solely to domestic slaves.

[1] I. Yu. Krachkovskii, *Arabskaya geograficheskaya literatura* (Arabic Geographical Literature), Izbrannye sochineniya (Selected Works), t. IV. Moscow-Leningrad, 1957.

[2] Cf. N.A. Mednikov, *Palestina ot zavoevaniya ee arabami do krestovykh pokhodov po arabskim istochnikam* (Palestine from its Conquest by the Arabs until the Crusades, according to Arabic sources), t. IV—"Pravoslavnyi Palestinskii sbornik," t. XVI, vyp. 2, p. 1307. St. Petersburg, 1897–1903.

[3] Abou Yousouf Ya'koub, *Le livre ce l'impôt foncier l'impôt (Kitâb al-kharâdj)*, traduit et annoté par E. Fagnan. Paris, 1921.

[4] N.A. Mednikov, *Palestina...*, t. IV, pp. 1308–1328; A.Yu. Yakubovskii, *Ob ispol'nykh arendakh v Irake v VIII v.* ("Share-Cropping in Irak in the VIIIth Century). – "Sovetskoe vostokovedenie" ["Soviet Orientalism"], IV, pp. 172–176. Moscow-Leningrad, 1947.

[5] *Le livre de l'impôt foncier de Yahya ibn Adam,* publié par Th. W. Juynboll; Leiden, 1896; English translation: *Taxation in Islam,* Vol. I, Yahyā ben Ādam's Kitāb al-kharaj, ed., translated and provided with an introduction and notes by A. Ben Shemesh. With a foreword by Prof. S.D. Goiten. Leiden, 1958.

[6] A. von Kremer, *Culturgeschichte des Orients under den Chalifen,* Bd. I–II. Wien, 1875–1877.

[7] Carra de Vaux, *Les penseurs ce l'Islam,* t. I–V. Paris, 1921–1926.

[8] R. Levy, *An Introduction to the Sociology of Islam.* Vol. 1–2, London, 1931–1933; second edition entitled *The Social Structure of Islam. Cambridge,* 1957.

[9] J. Zaydan, *Umayyads and Abbasids* (Gibb Memorial Series IV, 1907).

[10] *"Histoire générale des civilizations,"* publiée sous la direction de M. Grouzet, Vol. III, Paris, 1955. Reviewed (in Russian) in "Kratkie soobshcheniya Instituta vostokovedeniya" (Bull. of the Institute of Orientalism), XXXII, pp. 53–68. Moscow, 1958.

[11] B. Lewis, *The Arabs in History.* London, 1950.

[12] G. Wiet, *Grandeur de l'Islam de Mahomet à Francois Ier.* Paris, 1961.

[13] A. von Kremer, *Uber das Einnahmebudget des Abbasidenreiches,* Denkschr. d. Wien. Akad., ph. hist. Kl., XXXVI, 1888.

[14] D. Sourdel's, *Le vizirat abbaside de* 749 *à* 936, *t. I–II,* Institut Français de Damas, 1959–1960.

[15] Guy le Strange, *Baghdad During the Abbasid Caliphate from Contemporary Arabic and Persian Sources.* Oxford, 1900.

[16] R. Levy, *A Baghdad Chronicle.* Cambridge, 1929.

[17] *Handbuch der Islam-Literatur,* von Prof. G. Pfanmuller. Berlin-Leipzig, 1923; J. Sauvaget, *Introduction à l'histoire de l'Orient musulman.* Eléments de bibliographie. Edition réfondue et complétée par Cl. Cahen. Paris, 1961.

[18] V.V. Bartol'd, *Khalif i sultan* (The Caliph and the Sultan).—"Mir islama" (The World of Islam), t. I, No 2, pp. 214–215, 1912.

[19] Letter from Engels to Marx, 6 June 1853.

[20] Quoted from N.A. Mednikov, *Palestina...*, t. IV, pp. 1311–1314.

[21] I.Yu. Krachkovskii, *Arabskaya geograficheskaya literatura* (Arabic Geographical Literature), p. 281.

[22] *Ibidem,* p. 141.

[23] *Ibidem.*

[24] *Ibidem,* p. 144.

[25] H. Pirenne, *Mahomet et Charlemagne,* 2e, éd. Paris, 1937. [English version: *Mohammed and Charlemagne,* Norton and Co., 1939; Meridian Books, New York, 1957.]

[26] V.V. Bartol'd, *Karl Velikii i Kharun-ar-Rashid* (Charlemagne and Hārūn al-Rashīd).—"Khristianskii Vostok" ("The Christian Orient"), t. I. vyp. 1, pp. 69–94. 1912.

[27] *Ibidem,* pp. 76–77.

[28] A.A. Vasil'ev, *Karl Velikii i Kharun-ar-Rashid* (Charlemagne and Hārūn al-Rashīd). – "Vizantiiskii vremennik" ("Byzantine Review"), t. XX, vyp. 1, otd. 1, pp. 63 – 116. 1913.

[29] V.V. Bartol'd, *K voprosu o franko-musul'manskikh otnosheniyakh* (Franko-Muslim Relations).—"Khristianskii Vostok," t. 111, vyp. 3, pp. 263–296. St. Petersburg, 1914.

[30] Ibn-Khaldūn, Muqaddima, t. 1, pp. 18 – 24.

[31] A.A. Vasil'ev, *Lektsii po istorii Vizantii* (Lectures on the History of Byzantium), pp. 212 – 213. Petrograd, 1917.

[32] A.A. Vasil'ev, *Vizantiya i araby* (Byzantium and the Arabs). pp. 82–104.

[33] *Ibidem,* pp. 53 – 75; also A.A. Vasil'ev, *Lektsii po istorii Vizantii,* pp. 262 – 263.

[34] H. Lammens, *La Syrie, Précis historique,* Vol. I, p. 131. Beirut, 1921.

[35] A.Yu. Pigulevskaya, A.Yu. Yakubovskii, I.P. Petrushevskii, L.V. Stroeva, A.M. Belenitskii, *Istoriya Irana s drevneishikh vremen do kontsa XVIII veka* (History of Iran from Earliest Times to the End of the XVIIIth Century), p. 107. Leningrad, 1958.

[36] A.Yu. Yakubovskii, *Vosstanie Mukanny – dvizhenie lyudei v "belykh odezhdakh"* (The Rebellion of Muqanna'—the Movement of the "White-Robed Men").—"Sovetskoe vostokovedenie" (Soviet Orientalism), V, pp. 47–48. Leningrad, 1948.

[37] Cf. Z.M. Buniyatov, *Azerbaidzhan v VII–IX vekakh* (Azerbaidzhan in the VIIth–IXth Centuries), a thesis, p. 33. Baku, 1963.

[38] A.A. Vasil'ev, *Vizantiya i araby* (Byzantium and the Arabs), p. 104.

[39] Z.M. Buniyatov, *Azerbaidzhan v VII–IX vekakh* (Azerbaidzhan in the VIIth – IXth Centuries).

[40] A.A. Vasil'ev, *Vizantiya i araby,* p. 114.

[41] Cl. Huart, *Histoire des Arabes,* p. 300.

[42] Sayeed Ameer Ali, *A Short History of the Saracens,* pp. 271–272. London. 1924.

[43] Ṭabari, III, p. 1742.

[44] *Ibidem,* pp. 1743 – 1745.

[45] *Ibidem,* pp. 1746 – 1747.

[46] *Ibidem,* p. 1748.

[47] *Ibidem,* p. 1751.

[48] Maçoudi, *Les prairies d'or,* t. VIII, pp. 31 – 32.

[49] Ṭabari, III, pp. 1834 – 1838.

[50] Maçoudi, *Les prairies d'or,* t. VIII, p. 58.

[51] *Ibidem,* p. 60.

[52] Ṭabari, III, p. 1972.

[53] *Ibidem,* p. 1981.

[54] Maçoudi, *Les prairies d'or,* t. VIII, pp. 58 – 59.

INDEX OF ARABIC AND ORIENTAL TERMS (see NOTES page v)

INDEX OF PERSONAL NAMES (see NOTES page v)

INDEX OF GEOGRAPHICAL NAMES (see NOTES page v)